THE ONE-WAY STREET
OF INTEGRATION

THE ONE-WAY STREET OF INTEGRATION

Fair Housing and the Pursuit of Racial Justice in American Cities

Edward G. Goetz

CORNELL UNIVERSITY PRESS   **ITHACA AND LONDON**

First published 2018 by Cornell University Press
First paperback printing 2020

Library of Congress Cataloging-in-Publication Data

Names: Goetz, Edward G. (Edward Glenn), 1957– author.
Title: The one-way street of integration : fair housing and the pursuit of racial justice in American cities / Edward G. Goetz.
Description: Ithaca : Cornell University Press, 2018. | Includes bibliographical references and index.
Identifiers: LCCN 2017036243 (print) | LCCN 2017037755 (ebook) | ISBN 9781501716706 (pdf) | ISBN 9781501716690 (epub/mobi) | ISBN 9781501707599 (cloth)
Subjects: LCSH: Discrimination in housing—United States. | Low-income housing—United States. | Housing subsidies—United States. | Community development, Urban—United States. | Housing policy—United States. | United States—Race relations.
Classification: LCC HD7288.76.U5 (ebook) | LCC HD7288.76.U5 G64 2018 (print) | DDC 363.5/9900973—dc23
LC record available at https://lccn.loc.gov/2017036243

ISBN 978-1-5017-4847-9 (pbk.)

Contents

Preface

In 1966 Stokely Carmichael wrote in *The New York Review of Books* that integration "has been based on complete acceptance of the fact that in order to have a decent house or education, blacks must move into a white neighborhood or send their children to a white school. This reinforces, among both black and white, the idea that 'white' is automatically better and 'black' is by definition inferior." The solution, he argued, was real power for black people and black communities such that "Negroes become equal in a way that means something, and integration ceases to be a one-way street." This expression of the tension between integration on the one hand and community development on the other is as relevant today as it was in 1966. Indeed, given the current policy interest in residential mobility and moving people to "opportunity neighborhoods" as a way of addressing inequities, and given what I describe in this book as the aggressive spatial strategy of current fair housing advocacy, a renewed examination of the one-way street of integration is well warranted.

Many will no doubt see this book as a lamentable indulgence that has greater potential to foment tension than to explain or resolve it. Most of those people, however, are fair housing advocates who have mounted a systematic and far-reaching challenge to community development and affordable housing efforts. Community developers and affordable housing providers feel themselves subject to attack and thus are a bit more willing to see these issues broadly addressed.

I spent a couple of years working for community development corporations (CDCs) in San Francisco and Los Angeles, served for many years on the boards of directors of two of the most productive and successful CDCs in Minneapolis, and have conducted research on the housing and community efforts of nonprofit organizations. While I agree with fair housing advocates about the need for more affordable housing in white, suburban areas, I disagree strongly with the notion of some in that movement that CDCs are ineffectual in the neighborhoods in which they operate and that their efforts are harmful. This book is prompted by that perspective and also by the fact that I live in a metropolitan area where the debate between fair housing and community development is especially contentious.

I have been assisted by many in this endeavor, though none should be blamed for its shortcomings. Neeraj Mehta of the Center for Urban and Regional Affairs does the work of connecting community development efforts to larger questions of regional equity in the Twin Cities, and as such helps to establish the model for efforts to combat the problems of segregation and inequities of place without setting integration as the solution. He joins many in this work, among them Maura Brown, Owen Duckworth, Caty Royce, and Nelima Sitati-Munene. Their work is the inspiration for mine. I don't know who among these activists was the first to say, "Everyone deserves to live in an opportunity neighborhood," but this idea animates the current work, and you will see that I have borrowed the phrase for my conclusion. I am also indebted to the efforts of Jeff Matson, Kristen Murray, Andrew Tran, Tony Damiano, Ned Moore, Malik Holt-Shabazz, and Brittany Lewis at the Center for Urban and Regional Affairs at the University of Minnesota. Many in the housing and community development movement in the Twin Cities, including Alan Arthur, Jack Cann, Greg Finzell, Jim Roth, Deidre Schmidt, and Tim Thompson, have also influenced and encouraged my thinking on these issues. But these issues are salient across the nation, and the book has been spurred forward (knowingly or not) by many outside the Twin Cities, including Chris Walker of LISC, Catherine Bishop of the National Housing Law Project, Michael Bodaken of the National Housing Trust, and Sheila Crowley, formerly of the National Low Income Housing Coalition. David Imbroscio of the University of Louisville and Karen Chapple at the University of California, Berkeley, have helped make the manuscript better, as have the anonymous reviewers and my editor at Cornell University Press, Michael McGandy. I also benefited from the feedback of my favorite civil rights attorney, Sam Hall. Finally, my family, Susan, Hanne, Mary, and Greta, have taken a substantive interest in the book from the beginning and have made their contributions to its completion.

I would also like to acknowledge my cat Squirt for waking me up each morning at four thirty by sitting directly upon my head. This has made for some tense moments between us, but in the end it was always win-win—I got up to work on the book, and he got breakfast.

THE ONE-WAY STREET
OF INTEGRATION

ALTERNATIVE APPROACHES TO REGIONAL EQUITY AND RACIAL JUSTICE

There are two realities of American metropolitan areas that concern me in this book: first, patterns of racial discrimination and segregation in housing, and second, the critical lack of affordable housing for persons and families with very low incomes. These two problems have been the subject of much policy debate, political organizing, and collective action over the years. There are interest groups and professionals whose chief activities focus on one or the other. To a large extent, all these groups and professionals share values related to racial and class equity and the importance of housing in providing access to opportunity. On many issues they are allies. This book, however, is about those respects in which the values of these two movements diverge and in fact conflict. This book is about how the pursuit of fair housing can be at odds with the pursuit of affordable housing, and vice versa, and the conditions under which fair housing advocates and affordable housing advocates find themselves on polar opposite sides of issues related to housing, community development, and metropolitan equity.

In this book I address a number of questions central to the tension between fair housing advocates and affordable housing / community development activists. There are critical disagreements that shape the debate. At the core of these disputes are a constellation of issues related to the desirability and terms (for people of color) of integration, the means of achieving integration, and strategies for achieving political and economic justice for communities of color in the United States. Throughout the book I describe and analyze the conditions under which this debate surfaces. Much of the work of these two movements is complementary and compatible, but certain strategies pursued by each bring them into conflict with each other. Identifying when the tensions occur, and why, helps to illuminate the principal elements of the conflict and should provide a means of moving toward resolution or at least toward accommodation between these two movements. I also trace the history of these tensions since the mid-twentieth century, describing how the debate has manifested itself over time and with what outcomes. Finally, I examine the contemporary conditions that have produced a renewal and expansion of the fair housing / community development conflict since the 1990s. It is, in fact, the renewed intensity of this long-standing debate that makes the book relevant and necessary today. In addressing these issues, I argue that we need to move to a vision of urban and racial justice in the United States that does not hinge on the spatial rearrangement of people of color in the manner argued by fair housing integrationists.

The Issue

We can begin with a hypothetical situation. The community development sub-committee of the city council is in session. The room is full of spectators and those who wish to speak on the main topic of the meeting, the proposal by a local community development corporation (CDC) to convert an empty warehouse into twenty-four units of low-cost rental housing. The CDC is coming to the city to ask for a change in the zoning to accommodate the housing, and for a below-market interest-rate loan to renovate the building and convert it to housing.

As is typical in cases where affordable housing is proposed, some in the audi-ence oppose the project because they think it will create problems for the area. Nearby property owners are in attendance to tell the council members that they worry that their property values will decline as a result of the project and that their investments in their homes will be lost. Others are there to express con-cern about the potential for crime in the neighborhood to increase. They are not exactly worried about the new residents committing the crimes, they say, but they point to other parts of the city with lots of low-cost housing and higher crime rates. Others couch their opposition in terms of the lack of available parking or the unwanted increase in density that the project will produce for the neighbor-hood. Still others will profess concern for the lower-income families who will inhabit the units and argue that this neighborhood is not an appropriate one for raising children. These are classic NIMBY (not in my backyard) claims that plague affordable housing projects virtually everywhere. But compared to a hear-ing for a comparable project in the suburbs, or even in a more affluent or white part of the city, there are relatively few NIMBYists in the crowd. They are just a handful, and they are not particularly well organized, nor do they have any special "in" with any of the council members making the decision. Almost all in attendance know that if this project had been proposed for the middle-class neighborhood just a mile and a half north, or in any of the developing suburbs in the region, the room would be packed with vocal and well-resourced opponents to decry the project and foretell doom for the community should the project proceed. The lawyers among them might be investigating ways to sue to stop the project; others might have met ahead of time with the council members to make less-than-subtle threats about the councilors' political futures should the vote go in the wrong direction. But here in the city, in this particular neighborhood, not much of this happens. Instead, just a couple of homeowners and two business-people are waiting to make the NIMBY argument.

The CDC has, however, mobilized supporters of its own, and these constitute the second group of people in attendance. First, there are low-income residents of the neighborhood who might stand to benefit from the new housing built. They are ready to tell the council members about how difficult it is to find good, clean, and safe affordable housing in the city. The only units they can find are in poor shape, with plumbing leaks, cockroaches, and spotty heating. And even then, they have to pay close to half their monthly incomes to afford the places they find. In addition to the low-income residents, affordable housing advocates join in this argument, reminding the council members that a recent study showed that the region needs fifty-seven thousand more units of affordable housing to meet the existing demand. Most of that demand, they note, comes from low-income and very low-income households in the city. They remind the council members of the content of the city's comprehensive plan, which includes goals related to increasing the availability of affordable housing where appropriate. They may also point to the fact that the city is behind on its stated goal for developing such units, having funded only 127 units, compared to the annual goal of 350.

There are others from the neighborhood ready to tell the council members that they eagerly await the conversion of the warehouse. Since it has been abandoned, they will say, drug dealers have set up shop alongside it, and just last week two people were robbed right out in front. The empty warehouse has turned the adjacent street corner into a dangerous place, they will claim, and they want it cleaned up. The CDC, which has rehabilitated dozens of housing units in this neighborhood, has promised to repair the outside of the building, improve the lighting, and carefully manage the property. The residents who will speak in favor of the project trust the CDC; they have seen its work in the past, and they want the CDC to clean up this property just as it did when it bought and rehabilitated an old residential hotel three blocks away.

If these were the only two viewpoints represented at the committee meeting, it would be a fairly typical case. But there is a third group in the room that night.

Unlike the NIMBYists, this group is supportive of low-cost housing and readily sees the need for it. Unlike the CDC and its supporters, however, this third group opposes the current project. This third group points to the current demographic makeup of the neighborhood and reminds the council members that the neighborhood is predominantly African American and has a poverty rate that is more than twice the city rate. They will also note that eight of the city's last ten subsidized-housing developments have been placed within a two-mile radius of this proposed project. The project, they will say, will exacerbate patterns of racial segregation in the city because the likely residents of the housing will be people of color. Even were that not to be the case, the project will deepen the concentration of poverty that exists in the neighborhood because the twenty-four units being proposed will be subsidized and reserved for families with low incomes. There are other neighborhoods that are better suited for this type of housing, they will say, communities with better schools, with safer streets, and closer to job growth. This project should not be funded, nor should any others in this neighborhood until more affordable housing is built elsewhere, chiefly the suburbs. This third group identifies themselves as advocates of fair housing whose interests are in combating patterns of racial segregation and discrimination in housing, and who see the spatial concentration of subsidized housing as an important factor that produces and maintains patterns of inequality.

It is the conversation between the latter two groups, the advocates for affordable housing and community development on the one hand and advocates for fair housing on the other, that concerns me in this book. This is a conversation that pits two generally complementary and sympathetic movements against each other. The first group represents the ongoing effort to provide enough affordable, safe, and decent housing for low- and very low-income households ill-served by the private market. The second is focused on how opportunity and life chances are differentially distributed across metropolitan areas, and how patterns of racial segregation produce and perpetuate social, political, and economic inequalities. To the extent that fair housing advocates and affordable housing advocates generally occupy positions on the same end of the political spectrum, conflict between these two objectives are disagreements between allies, not adversaries.[1]

The practical conflict, furthermore, can be fairly summarized in a brief question: where should assisted housing for low- and very low-income households be placed? More specifically, what should our policy be about building, rehabilitating, or redeveloping assisted housing in core neighborhoods of our central cities (and increasingly in our inner-ring suburbs)? Should assisted housing be strictly limited in these areas on the principle of reducing concentrations of poverty or furthering integration objectives? Should we instead be focusing our policy efforts on building or in other ways creating more assisted housing opportunities in other neighborhoods, neighborhoods where the placement of assisted housing would integrate the community, racially and economically? Or do we continue to build or make available assisted housing in core neighborhoods because the need there remains overwhelming? Do we continue our efforts in core neighborhoods because doing so benefits those neighborhoods by bringing in new investment and benefits families by stabilizing their lives and improving economic self-sufficiency?

The easy and ultimately unacceptable answer, of course, is that we need to pursue both agendas—more affordable housing *and* greater integration. Some will say that the conflict between these two positions is overstated and that advocates of both can readily agree that the question is simply a matter of balance; that providing sufficient affordable housing to people in need and reducing patterns of segregation can and should be pursued simultaneously as long as there is a rough balance between the two. There are several reasons why such a response is insufficient, however. First and foremost, the federal government, along with state and local governments in the United States, has never devoted enough resources to affordable housing policy to adequately address needs. In an environment of scarcity, housing advocates are increasingly faced with a choice of where to put resources. If needs cannot be met everywhere, the question arises of where to focus. In this respect, the harmony between desegregation and affordable housing is, in reality, only a long-term alignment, a conviction that ultimately the pursuit of affordable housing cannot be undertaken without regard to effects on patterns of segregation, and in turn, that integration cannot be pursued at the expense of meeting affordable housing needs. Limited to such a "long-term" perspective, there is agreement between the two sides. Unfortunately, the conflict between these two positions manifests itself every time a community development corporation proposes an affordable housing development for a core neighborhood and fair housing advocates speak out against the project out of concern for its impact on segregation. The conflict manifests itself when local bodies produce comprehensive plans or housing policies that offer numerical goals for affordable housing in the core neighborhoods, and fair housing advocates speak in opposition, calling for a reduction in those numbers. The conflict manifests itself most prominently when fair housing attorneys sue to stop a project because of its presumed segregationist impact or to reorient state policy in ways to limit housing in the core parts of metropolitan areas. A variant of this form of opposition to affordable housing in core neighborhoods is the argument that as long as we continue to provide affordable housing there, communities on the periphery will be able to resist it. That is, without a conscious effort to direct resources to the periphery, the de facto pattern of geographic concentration will continue.

While each side in this debate supports many of the core objectives of the other, the question comes down to whether, in the pursuit of those objectives, the principle of integration should be given greatest priority. Though there may be agreement about long-term balance and the need to provide affordable housing options everywhere, the day-to-day challenges of affordable housing development produce repeated conflict between these two ideals.

Such short-term conflict, however, is not the only source of tension between these two positions. There is debate, for example, over the presumed effectiveness of each strategy to accomplish its stated goals. This is an argument that, ironically (or depressingly), each side makes against the other. Some in the fair housing movement question the effectiveness of community development efforts, noting the continued decline of central city neighborhoods despite decades of work by CDCs and others. Community developers point out the very limited gains achieved by integrationist policies and the entrenched political opposition to such policies that render such efforts ineffective.

There are philosophical disagreements between the two sides as well. While some extol the benefits of integration and diversity at all scales, and employ rationales to those ends based on social justice and democratic theory, others see legitimacy in a more multicultural society that allows for group identity and differentiation and acknowledges the pursuit of cultural, political, economic, and institutional strength within groups as a means of achieving racial justice.

Finally, even where there is no disagreement about integration as an end, there can be disagreement over the means to that end. The actual act of "mixing"—that is, the coercive nature of integration efforts that involve, for example, the demolition of affordable and subsidized housing in core neighborhoods and the forced relocation of low-income people of color, or the restriction of housing choices for people of color in order to maintain integrated living patterns—generates debate and conflict.

The main purpose of this book is to engage both the philosophical arguments at stake and the more practical elements of this dilemma and what they mean for housing policy. In the following pages I argue that this conflict is not merely an academic or theoretical question that might, under the right circumstances, produce difficult policy choices. Instead, this fundamental question has confronted policy makers, advocates, and members of the judicial branch with regularity since the advent of low-income housing policy in the United States. Recent developments in the way that fair housing activists conceive of their work have served, furthermore, to make this question more relevant now than it has ever been in the past.

The relevance of this issue is readily demonstrated by the fact that the leading national organization for affordable housing advocacy, the National Low Income Housing Coalition (NLIHC), and a group of nationally prominent fair housing advocates have both felt it necessary to issue recent statements pertaining to this question. In 2012 the NLIHC published *Affordable Housing Dilemma: The Preservation vs. Mobility Debate*, a thirty-six-page report on the debate over whether to preserve existing affordable housing or disperse subsidized households in an effort to desegregate and deconcentrate poverty.[2] The authors note that the best "solution" to this debate would be to expand the level of housing subsidies in the country to adequately address needs, allowing the pursuit of both objectives. They also acknowledge, however, that there are those "who fervently support each side of the debate."[3]

Similarly, in 2012, the Ford Foundation and the Open Society Foundation supported an effort to bring together fair housing advocates and housing and community development professionals to strike a balance "between addressing priority housing and redevelopment needs in low income communities while also providing access to housing opportunities in integrated communities."[4] A national meeting of dozens of actors in November 2012 managed to draft a set of principles related to the "intersection of community development and fair housing." The principles called for (1) "giving families a choice," by which they meant improving the quality of life in low-income neighborhoods while also making possible mobility to "high opportunity neighborhoods"; (2) "balancing housing investment priorities"; and (3) incentivizing affordable housing in high opportunity areas.[5] While the effort alone reflects the level of importance that those on both sides of the debate give to the issue, the principles articulated provide little guidance for short-term decision making about affordable housing strategies in an environment of scarcity.[6]

Racial Policy Alliances and the Fair Housing Question

It is important to acknowledge that there is more shared between the two camps than separates them. Most notable is a baseline agreement on the core arguments of each side—namely, that there is a critical lack of affordable housing in the country, and that our metropolitan areas suffer from dangerous and debilitating levels of spatial and racial inequality. The lack of adequate affordable housing is a burden borne by the most economically disadvantaged, and the welfare of these groups is the core concern of the fair housing and the affordable housing / community development movements. Both sides agree there is a racial disproportionality to housing needs—that people of color, especially African Americans, suffer from various forms of housing deprivation at rates far greater than whites, including adverse neighborhood conditions that unfairly limit life chances.[7]

This point is critical because, of course, race is at the center of the policy conflict explored in this book. That there is a conflict between fair housing and community development on the role and importance of racial integration through housing policy does not mean that there is disagreement as to the importance of racial equity in the nation's housing system. In Desmond King and Rogers Smith's book, *Still a House Divided: Race and Politics in Obama's America*, the authors argue that racial politics in the United States are dominated by two "racial policy alliances"—one arguing for a "color-blind" approach and the other advocating a "race-conscious" strategy.[8] A policy alliance, according to the authors, is a "coalition of participants in social movements, civic organizations, political parties, and government officials."[9] The color-blind policy alliance supports the goals of nondiscrimination but also seeks foremost to preserve individual property rights and to protect the character of traditional communities and the rights of communities to define themselves to a considerable extent. The essence of a color-blind approach to policy is to treat people "as individuals without reference to their racial identities" and to assume that effective nondiscrimination provides benefits to all.[10] For these reasons the color-blind approach is often called a "universalist" approach because its preferred policies apply to all groups rather than to a single group.

The race-conscious alliance also supports nondiscrimination efforts but is attuned to the legacy of discrimination in the country and the systematic and structural disadvantages that racial inequalities and discrimination have created for racial minority groups. Thus, race-conscious policy attempts to redress those inequalities proactively. The race-conscious alliance opposes color-blindness as a policy approach, arguing that it is ineffective in addressing the costs of segregation and discrimination and ignores differences of power and access already in place as the result of segregation and discrimination.[11] As King and Smith argue, the two racial policy alliances in the United States align themselves (and have since the 1970s) with the two major political parties. The color-blind approach has been adopted by Republicans, while the Democratic Party is more aligned with the race-conscious alliance.

King and Smith further note that sometimes divisions occur within these alliances. Specifically, they note that racial policy alliances "display significant internal diversity in regard to motivations, tactics, and ultimate goals."[12] The tension addressed in this book—that between affordable housing advocates and fair housing advocates—is best understood as just such a division, a split within the race-conscious policy alliance. The disagreement between these two camps is not about whether our policy should be race conscious (that is, focused explicitly to redress inequities across racial lines), but rather about strategy and on the relative importance of one goal in particular—that of integration.

The Geography of Fair Housing Advocacy

At this stage it is useful to make a distinction between the spatial elements of fair housing advocacy and its other aspects. Fair housing advocacy can be distinguished by whether spatial goals related to racial settlement patterns are involved. Many suggest that the Fair Housing Act of 1968 contains two core objectives: the elimination of discrimination (or what we can call the "equal access" objective), and the furthering of integration.[13] The core principle of equal access in housing has no inherent spatial dimension. That is, discrimination against "protected classes" (groups identified in Title VIII as entitled to protection by the law) is to be contested wherever it occurs and whatever the particulars.[14] At its foundation, the principle of equal access serves the objective of providing members of protected classes with greater choice in housing—it is a concern about equal process that could have any spatial outcome. Much contemporary fair housing advocacy addresses discrimination in a nonspatial manner by, for example, targeting predatory lending, foreclosure practices, and landlord abuses without regard for how these acts contributed to any particular spatial distribution of protected class members.

The second core principle expressed by fair housing advocates, however, is explicitly spatial—a commitment to racially integrated residential patterns. Thus it is possible to identify a set of strategies pursued by the fair housing movement aimed at achieving or maintaining a particular spatial arrangement of households—that is, creating integrated living patterns. Whereas the strategies related to equal access (the elimination of discrimination) are chiefly aimed at private-sector actors (for example, ending "steering" or "blockbusting" or differential treatment of real estate customers based on their race), the strategies related to spatial outcomes have been aimed more typically at public agencies, requiring either changes in public decisions (e.g., where to site new subsidized housing), new initiatives on the part of public bodies (e.g., integration maintenance programs, or housing dispersal programs), or the elimination of exclusionary land-use and development regulations that serve as barriers to low-cost housing production.

There are instances, of course, where the content of discrimination is spatial, as for example when minority home-seekers are steered away from predominantly white communities. In these instances, the pursuit of remedies for discrimination is indistinguishable from the pursuit of desegregation objectives. But the distinction between the purposefully spatial goals of desegregation and the nonspatial goals of antidiscrimination is valid and useful for several reasons. First, spatial discrimination is common only for some of the protected classes in Title VIII (groups defined by race, color, and national origin). There are other protected classes named in Title VIII (groups defined by disability status, religion, sex, and familial status) for whom antidiscrimination efforts are less commonly about enforced spatial segregation. For these groups the two goals (nondiscrimination and desegregation) are more conceptually distinct and distinct in practice. Not only are these goals frequently distinct; there are instances in which the pursuit of integration affects protected-class households *in the absence of any discriminatory acts against those households*. So-called integration maintenance programs, for example, have limited the entry of minority households into predominantly white neighborhoods where they had such access, in order to avoid a complete racial turnover in those neighborhoods.[15] Here, the pursuit of spatial goals in fact *introduced constraints upon members of certain protected classes* in the absence of any prior, specific discriminatory act against them.

As we proceed with the argument it will become clear that the distinction between the spatial and nonspatial objectives of the fair housing movement has two additional implications important for housing policy. First, one can think of the integration objective of fair housing as being outcome focused, while equal access is focused on process concerns.[16] An outcome focus—that is, a desire to create a particular spatial arrangement of households—necessitates a much more activist role for the government in housing markets, and justifies the substitution of choices sanctioned by the state for individual mobility choices.[17] Second, and perhaps more important, these two approaches can be distinguished by how they treat the issues of choice and burden. The equal-access goals of fair housing can be understood as efforts to increase the housing choices available to members of the protected classes *regardless of what those choices may be*, by eliminating illegal, non-market-based restrictions on their participation in the housing market. The integrationist focus puts no such premium on choice, and in fact accepts intentional restrictions of choice for protected class members in the service of specific spatial outcomes.[18] These restrictions of choice, through the restricted access to integrated neighborhoods mandated by integration maintenance programs, or the forced relocation of dispersal and deconcentration initiatives, place the burden of achieving integrationist policy objectives squarely on the back of minority groups. It is through the manipulation of *their* mobility patterns that the integrationists hope to achieve their preferred settlement patterns. Indeed, the limits of white tolerance in the area of residential integration (i.e., white settlement preferences) are typically used as the parameters within which minority settlement patterns are managed.[19]

The Stations of Fair Housing Spatial Advocacy

It is my argument that the distinction between the equal access and integration objectives has become more pronounced as the spatial strategies of the fair housing movement have evolved over time. In fact, it is possible to identify three stations of fair housing spatial strategy that represent an ever more aggressive approach to achieving integration goals: (1) opening up exclusionary communities; (2) preventing further segregation; and (3) dismantling existing communities of color. Each of these strategies is an extension of the movement's reach—that is, the progression is an accumulation of strategies, not the replacement of earlier methods with new ones.[20] The second and third stations, in particular, are the ones that produce tension between fair housing and community development. To repeat, there is no conflict between fair housing and community development advocates in the pursuit of nondiscrimination—that is, equal access. The debate between the two positions arises only in relation to the spatial strategies of fair housing.

Opening Up Exclusionary Communities

In its early stages, the fair housing movement was known alternatively as the "open housing movement," to denote its concern for openness in the housing market and access to all communities regardless of race/ethnicity. During these early years of the 1940s to the 1960s, this manifest itself most frequently in calls to open up the suburbs to nonwhite families, reflecting the dominant spatial dynamic of white flight from the core, and exclusionary suburban development.

Policy initiatives in this station have been of four types: (1) expansion of various housing subsidy programs to increase low-cost housing production in the suburbs; (2) the elimination of land-use regulations that have the effect of excluding lower-income housing in suburban communities; (3) the elimination of private deed restrictions and covenants aimed at excluding people of color and other groups from certain communities; and (4) voluntary "mobility" programs that provide portable housing voucher subsidies to families to move from areas of segregation or poverty concentration to neighborhoods that are characterized by neither. Fair share regional housing approaches establish concrete goals for affordable housing development for all communities within a region in an effort to enhance the spread of affordable housing options, diversify communities that currently are not diverse, and ultimately to enhance the housing options of very low-income people and people of color.[21] In some locations, higher levels of government have been given review powers over local land-use decision making when those decisions have prevented affordable housing developments from going forward.[22] Some jurisdictions have used "inclusionary housing" programs that require or incentivize private developers to build a number (or percentage) of affordable units in exchange for approving a market-rate housing development proposal.[23]

On these issues and about these policies there is general agreement between fair housing and community development advocates. Indeed, members of both camps would point to the need for greater efforts to build affordable housing in those communities where it does not yet exist in large numbers. Yet even this agreement is strained by the issue of insufficient resources and the opportunity costs of pursuing affordable housing in one area versus the other.

Preventing Further Segregation

Fair housing advocacy, however, quickly expanded beyond "open housing" to incorporate efforts to mitigate the development or perpetuation of racially defined housing submarkets (i.e., "ghettos").[24] Programs of this sort, which mark the second station, have come in three varieties: (1) the elimination of discriminatory private-sector actions within the housing market, such as steering, which have the effect of creating and maintaining neighborhood color lines intact; (2) "impaction" rules that limit the production of subsidized housing in neighborhoods that are already considered impacted in terms of concentrations of people of color; and (3) "integration maintenance" programs that manage and limit the entry of minority families into communities in order to establish and maintain prescribed integration levels. The first of these strategies simply has the effect of increasing choices for low-income families of color and thus, like the integration programs of the first station, does not produce significant conflict with the affordable housing or community development movements. Reduction of private discrimination that has specific spatial content (e.g., steering) is similar to the elimination of exclusionary zoning; both are ways of opening up housing submarkets previously closed to disadvantaged groups, and they emerged as strategies in the early stages of the "open housing" movement.[25]

Impaction rules and integration maintenance programs, however, although they share the characteristic of attempting to forestall further segregation, are fundamentally different in that *they place the burden for integrating on members of the protected class.* These policy approaches work by limiting housing choices for members of the protected class so as to avoid concentrations or resegregation. Because of this, impaction and integration maintenance programs were the first that brought the fair housing movement into conflict with affordable housing / community development advocates. Impaction rules limit the amount of subsidized housing in areas of high need, leaving families who might have benefited from subsidized housing without it. It is arguable even that impaction rules limit the overall amount of assisted housing because of the great resistance to subsidized housing by residents who already live in the areas that integrationists find acceptable. Impaction programs were first considered in the 1960s. The decision in *Shannon v. HUD* (1970), for example, was an early demonstration of the intent of the fair housing movement to prevent further ghettoization by restricting the placement of subsidized housing in core neighborhoods, and of the court's interpretation of the Fair Housing Act as authorizing such action.[26] More recently the objective of preventing further segregation has surfaced in criticisms of the Low Income Housing Tax Credit (LIHTC) program as being too spatially concentrated. Community development advocates chafe under these restrictions, which they claim limit their ability to effectively address the housing needs that exist in core neighborhoods.

In a similar fashion, so-called integration maintenance programs worked by limiting the access of disadvantaged groups to communities or to housing developments in order to maintain a degree of racial diversity deemed appropriate by program designers. The access of disadvantaged groups was limited to prevent the racial turnover of these neighborhoods and resegregation of disadvantaged families.

Dismantling Existing Communities of Color

The third station of fair housing's spatial strategy is the dissolution of existing communities in the name of desegregation. As such, it is the most interventionist of the three stations. This strategy is most prominent in a series of desegregation lawsuits pursued by fair housing attorneys in the 1980s and early 1990s, and also arises with respect to demolition and redevelopment of public housing through the federal HOPE VI program and other forms of subsidized housing through the Choice Neighborhoods Initiative. While many of the residents of these public housing developments welcome the chance to move, the universal nature of the approach (usually involving demolition of housing and displacement of all residents) virtually ensures the displacement of many who do not. Some residents, typically very low-income African Americans, not only object to their forced displacement, but actively protest it.[27] To the extent that these efforts involve the involuntary displacement of lower-income families and relocation to other neighborhoods, this strategy also generates opposition from affordable housing advocates.

Approach

Throughout portions of this book I will present criticisms of integration efforts, dispersal programs, mixed-income housing schemes, poverty deconcentration efforts, and at times the very principle of integration. It is striking to me how frequently I, and others with similar views, find it necessary to stress that our position is not tacit acceptance of spatial inequalities, nor an ignorance (willful or otherwise) of the negative conditions attending enforced racial segregation. Virtually every piece of writing that I have reviewed for this work that criticizes integrationist efforts includes what I have come to see as this obligatory caveat. That we do this, myself included, reflects two important realities about the current discussion related to spatial inequalities in urban areas. First, the proposition that integration or social mixing is the natural solution to the ills of racial segregation and poverty concentration is so deeply ingrained in the political discourse of our time as to be frequently taken as a given. Those of us critical of integration initiatives must therefore note that our criticism does not entail an acceptance of spatial inequalities.

The second reason why critics must make explicit their condemnation of the harms of segregation is that in many venues integrationists reinforce the simplified notion that to be critical of integration is to accept the inequities of segregation. This choice that integrationists present, that one either commits to the integrationist ideal or surrenders in the fight on segregation, is, of course, a false one. Community development and affordable housing development are tainted by this false choice and in fact are at times implicated by fair housing activists as complicit in the continued inequalities that mark our urban areas.

This book presents a challenge to the fair housing critique of community development. To make this case it is necessary first to understand the integrationist argument and its criticisms of community development and affordable housing practices. The strength of the fair housing perspective comes from its emphasis on the evils of enforced segregation and the ways that urban exclusionism creates and perpetuates racial inequalities in the United States. The regional inequities that result from enforced segregation and the public and private disinvestment that ensues in communities of color are targets of both fair housing and community development. Thus, the counterargument to the integrationists evolves initially as a response to the weaknesses of the policy approaches embedded within the fair housing integrationist case, and to the fallacies of the fair housing critique of community development. The full counterargument requires an affirmation of the positive value of community development efforts, including the benefits to individuals and to communities of safe and decent affordable housing, and the importance of economic and political self-reliance, self-determination, and power for all groups. The community development argument asserts a set of values different from those embedded in the integrationist strategy. Community development demands political and economic development in ways that integrationist strategies do not. Integrationist strategies accommodate majority dominance in ways that community development does not.

A recapitulation of how the integration versus community development conflict has played out over the several decades since the 1940s provides a number of opportunities to see these values in debate. Specifically, the roots of community development in the black empowerment and community-control movements of the 1950s and 1960s help to highlight the critical distinctions between an integrationist view of urban and racial equity and the community development view. The subsequent era, lasting from the early 1970s through the 1990s, also provides important lessons on the limits of the integrationist approach. Finally, realities of metropolitan development patterns in the twenty-first century and current policy debates over urban sustainability provide new light for the consideration of these competing models of regional equity and racial justice. What emerges from this analysis is not only the insufficiency of the integrationist approach, but a clear call for a community development approach that is race-conscious and focused on issues of urban and regional political economy, an approach in which housing, critical in its own right, is also enlisted as part of a larger movement for racial and place equity.

There is an important imbalance in contemporary scholarship related to U.S. housing policy. Fair housing scholars have produced a large body of work asserting the need for and benefits of pursuing integration. They have also presented a coherent legal justification for fair housing integration efforts in a range of scholarly venues. Furthermore, they have presented a strong vision of racial justice that focuses on geography. The achievement of residential integration is central to this vision of racial justice and urban equity. The literature on community development / affordable housing, on the other hand, is more diffuse and has not evolved in a fashion parallel to the fair housing work. More precisely, this literature tends to focus on program outcomes and analyses of implementation, and not on more fundamental justifications for community development in the first place.[28] Most important in this respect, there is nothing in the literature that specifically provides a comprehensive response to the critiques of community development by fair housing advocates or an alternative to the integrationist argument.

This work is an attempt to at least partially correct that imbalance. The argument in this book highlights the legitimacy of place-based, neighborhood-scale initiatives in housing and community development in response to the challenges to such policy presented by fair housing critics. The argument is based on a vision of urban and racial equity that does not hinge on the imperative of integration or the mobility strategies of integrationists and regionalists, and is intended to present a view of racial justice, rooted in historical experience, that acknowledges the value of relatively homogeneous neighborhoods of people of color and the importance of self-determination for all communities.

THE INTEGRATION IMPERATIVE

The fair housing position on the siting of affordable housing is based on the empirical observation that most publicly assisted housing is located in central cities, in higher-poverty neighborhoods, and in neighborhoods dominated by people of color. This is not an item of contention. Analyses since the 1980s have demonstrated and reaffirmed this phenomenon.[1] This concentration of assisted units is the result of two "impulses," according to Tulane University law professor Stacey Seicshnaydre. The first of these is the desire to meet low-cost housing needs by building as many units as possible, wherever possible. The second is NIMBYism, the repeated and consistent resistance to affordable housing that is most prominent in more affluent and white communities. The result of these two dynamics is that most assisted housing follows a "path of least resistance" and ends up in disadvantaged neighborhoods.[2]

Once there, concentrations of assisted housing contribute to further concentrations of poverty and reinforce patterns of racial segregation.[3] There is also, according to some, a durability to neighborhood poverty, meaning that once a neighborhood becomes identified as poor or racially segregated, change that would modify those basic characteristics is unlikely.[4] Neighborhood hierarchies can be fairly stable over time. Neighborhoods that rank relatively high in incidence of poverty and racial segregation, for example, tend to remain that way over time, according to this argument. In fact, once poverty and racial segregation are established in a neighborhood, according to sociologists Robert Sampson and Jeffrey Morenoff, "further change is likely to be in the direction of its becoming increasingly poor and black."[5] Finally, there is evidence that the disadvantages of neighborhood are inherited, and that families that remain in lower-income or segregated neighborhoods pass on the disadvantages of place from one generation to the next.[6]

Given these dynamics, the decision on the part of a needy family to live in subsidized housing often carries with it acceptance of certain neighborhood conditions. Since the 1970s, principals within the fair housing movement have considered publicly assisted housing "to be unfair if those who occupy it or seek to occupy it are thereby forced to live within certain designated areas, prescribed by race and/or income."[7] As a result, publicly assisted housing is, according to the fair housing argument, a means of reinforcing racial inequalities. The residents of subsidized housing, disproportionately people of color, are consigned to neighborhoods in which crime is higher, public services inferior, and the environment more threatening.

To continue affordable housing programs in the manner that they have been operated in the past, according to Chicago civil rights attorney Alex Polikoff, is to "knuckle under, to accept the posture of the political establishment as a fact of life, [and] to permit all or nearly all subsidized housing and assisted housing to go into minority neighborhoods."[8] Fair housing advocates assert that "the great need for low-income housing cannot continue to be used as a justification for the inequity and segregation that results from these programs."[9] Unless integration is an explicit goal of housing assistance programs, and unless those programs are operated consciously and purposefully in a manner to achieve integration, they reinforce and intensify racial segregation and poverty concentration.[10] Integration thus occupies a privileged place in the objectives of the contemporary fair housing movement.

Race or Class?

It should be clear already that there is significant fusion of race and class in the integrationist argument. This is so for three reasons: (1) there is great overlap between race and poverty in the United States; (2) some forms of racial discrimination operate through class-based mechanisms; and (3) policies that focus on poverty are less unpopular in the United States than are race-based initiatives. Two central concerns of the fair housing movement, the location of subsidized housing and exclusionary zoning, can serve as useful illustrations. Eligibility for subsidized housing is, of course, determined largely by income and certainly not by race. Fair housing arguments concerning subsidized housing, therefore, are based on the fact that people of color disproportionately reside in subsidized housing. Concerns about exclusionary zoning are also based on the race/

income correlation, since the offending land-use regulations typically do not reference race per se but rather make it difficult to build lower-cost housing—the type of housing more frequently needed by people of color because of their lower incomes.[11] To address the full range of discriminatory and segregationist factors influencing people of color in American housing markets, therefore, one is forced to talk also about class and income-based restrictions. Finally, it should also be noted that although significant progress has been made in liberalizing racial attitudes in the United States, a large gap persists between public opinion support for abstract notions of racial equity and support for specific public policies to achieve greater equity.[12] The more integrationists can talk about poverty rather than race, the more likely they are to see their ideas enshrined in public policy. The prime example of this is the Moving to Opportunity (MTO) program, which was specifically designed with this political constraint in mind.[13] Though modeled on the racial segregation remedy in the *Gautreaux* case, MTO became a program of poverty deconcentration with no official objectives related to race.

The fusion of race and class concerns has led to common cause between fair housing activists and advocates of regionalism or regional equity.[14] Regionalists rarely refer explicitly to race, confining themselves, in the main, to issue of class-based place inequities. But the two movements (fair housing and regionalism) share a common vocabulary about access to opportunity and a common solution set centered on the dispersal of subsidized housing throughout metropolitan areas and the creation of mixed-income housing developments.[15] Thus, the fair housing / community development divide is similar to what former Albuquerque mayor David Rusk terms "the Inside Game v. the Outside Game."[16] There is further commonality between the fair housing argument and the "mobility" agenda that has dominated housing policy in the United States since the 1990s. Common across all these policy threads is a skepticism of community development (i.e., "the inside game") as an approach to addressing urban spatial inequities.

Segregation Injures

The case for integration begins with the identification of the personal and societal-level costs of segregation. Life in a racially defined ghetto carries with it a wide range of disadvantages that are insidious, extensive, and enduring. One set of hazards relates to personal safety and health; residents of segregated communities of color are statistically more likely to be victims of crime, be exposed to environmental dangers, and have less access to health care than others.[17] The life expectancy of blacks is lower than that of whites, and neighborhood mortality rates are higher where blacks make up a larger percentage of the population.[18] Racial segregation has also been tied to health disparities in children.[19]

Ghetto neighborhoods also suffer from fewer and inferior public services, including schools.[20] The poor quality of schools results in an inferior education for children living in segregated neighborhoods and contributes to higher dropout rates. Thus, children growing up in racially segregated and low-income neighborhoods emerge with significantly lower levels of human capital than do their counterparts in more advantaged neighborhoods. This produces inequalities of opportunity that reinforce themselves over the course of a lifetime and are reflected in disparities in labor force participation, income, and wealth.

The economic life of high-poverty, racially segregated neighborhoods is underdeveloped. The relative lack of private-sector investment reduces local retail and commercial options available to residents and can produce "food deserts" in which fresh and healthful food choices are unavailable in large areas within central cities.[21] The lack of nutritional grocery options in turn contributes to health problems for residents. Grocery stores that do locate within these neighborhoods often charge higher prices than stores located elsewhere. The lack of economic activity also manifests itself in a dearth of local employment opportunities for residents. To the extent that these ghettos tend to be located in central city neighborhoods that are far from areas of new job growth in the suburbs, a spatial mismatch between low-income job seekers and job opportunities further fuels the level of economic marginality characterizing these neighborhoods.[22] "Address discrimination" can add another layer of disadvantage when people are denied employment opportunities because of where they live.

Residents of racially segregated neighborhoods, occupying below-standard housing, are more likely to be disadvantaged in the housing market, more likely to be victimized by predatory lending, and when they own property, more likely to see much lower rates of real estate value and lower rates of appreciation in that value than do residents of other neighborhoods. Oliver and Shapiro, for example, report that from 1967 to 1988, white homeowners saw an average increase in home value of $53,000, compared to only $31,100 over that same period for black homeowners.[23] More recent analysis indicates that this gap has endured over time.[24] The gap, what David Rusk calls the "segregation tax," adversely affects the ability of black families to accumulate wealth and thus limits upward mobility and perpetuates socioeconomic disparities between whites and blacks.[25]

Finally, some have argued that the high crime and poverty of segregated neighborhoods inhibits the formation of the type of bridging social capital that can enhance upward mobility, primarily through access to job information from social networks.[26] Here the argument stresses the homogeneity (and therefore the redundancy) of social networks in segregated and high-poverty neighborhoods. When one's family and acquaintances are similarly situated in the labor market, the information one receives about job opportunities is limited.[27]

The individual and cumulative effects of these disadvantages produce and reproduce stark inequalities between people of color and whites in America.[28] Many of the dynamics mentioned here have lasting implications, as individuals have more difficulty in growing the human capital necessary for economic success, or accumulating the financial capital for greater economic security. Thus, current forms of disadvantage contribute to lasting differences between groups in a self-reinforcing manner.[29] Sociologist Lawrence Bobo calls residential segregation the "structural linchpin of American racial inequality."[30] Patrick Sharkey argues that the differential experiences of blacks and whites in their neighborhoods have stifled progress toward racial equality despite the elimination of formal and rigid forms of racial discrimination that characterized American life prior to the civil rights movement of the 1960s.[31]

The legacy effect of segregation is one of several features that make it a critical target of fair housing advocacy. By conditioning life chances in the ways described above, racial segregation in the United States perpetuates and accentuates inequalities even in the absence of active discrimination. It is also seen by some in the movement as causing current conditions of disadvantage. Florence Roisman, for example, asserts that segregation is more than merely the setting for adverse neighborhood conditions, but in fact is the cause of problems such as crime, drug abuse, and violence.[32] Finally, fair housing advocates point out that the adverse effects of segregation can be separated from the effects of discrimination even when discrimination is implicated in causing segregation in the first place. As Elizabeth Anderson notes, segregation allows the dominant group to "hoard opportunities without having to actively discriminate." That "segregation propagates many material inequalities on its own," beyond whatever damages discrimination may cause, establishes it as a separate target of fair housing advocacy.[33]

Segregation Is a Legacy of Public Policy

Not only is segregation a demonstrable problem in the ways briefly summarized above, but it is an avoidable result of illegal private acts of discrimination and ill-designed public policy. While some argue that segregation can and does result from purely market processes—that is, through the differential purchasing power of whites and blacks, which sorts them into neighborhoods that are also segregated by housing value—there is plenty of evidence that even blacks with higher income (and therefore greater purchasing power in the market) are highly segregated.[34] Others argue that some degree of segregation is the result of personal preferences and taste, such as through the desire to live with others who share cultural identities.[35] Nevertheless, there are two other causes of segregation that justify a vigorous public effort to eliminate it. First, discrimination in housing markets has a long and sordid history in the United States and has been used to create and maintain patterns of segregation.[36] Second, previous public actions at virtually all levels of government have contributed significantly to patterns of racial segregation.[37]

For much of our history, residential discrimination has been overt, and for decades it enjoyed explicit state approval and was defended by state actions. Important among these was the indifference of the state to tactics of racially motivated violence and intimidation as a means of discriminating and segregating in the housing market. Historian Stephen Grant Meyer documented decades' worth of episodes of mob violence and intimidation, firebombings, and race riots, and violence perpetrated by white residents intent on maintaining the lines of racial segregation in American cities.[38] Early twentieth-century racial zoning laws explicitly limited housing opportunities for blacks in some neighborhoods that were designated to remain predominantly white.[39] Suburban communities have rigged their zoning policies to reduce or eliminate the opportunities available for building low-cost housing, thereby limiting entry for lower-income people of color.[40] The federal government, especially, has been complicit in the creation of segregation and the facilitation of white flight out of racially changing central city neighborhoods. The Federal Housing Administration (FHA) mortgage insurance program, for example, recommended racially restrictive deeds in order to maintain segregation (and therefore, according to the agency, protect the property values of the houses it was insuring). Private deed restrictions were for many years a widespread and legally approved means of enforcing residential segregation by limiting ownership and residence of properties by race. This practice, like racial zoning, was eventually deemed unconstitutional by the Supreme Court.

The FHA restricted most of its initial activities to white suburban areas, providing a highly affordable housing option for whites fleeing the central cities. At the same time, the FHA severely limited its activities in mixed neighborhoods and in neighborhoods dominated by people of color. This starved these areas of needed capital and hastened their physical decline.[41] Federal urban renewal and public housing programs were also operated in ways that explicitly reinforced segregation.[42] This complicity in creating the current urban landscape serves then as a justification for calls for public policies aimed at producing more equitable and integrated outcomes. These discriminatory public policies have also had the effect of facilitating and supporting home ownership and wealth creation for whites while simultaneously constraining wealth creation among blacks.[43]

In a number of ways discrimination in housing is lucrative for the professionals who engage in it. A population that is systematically denied sufficient choice in the housing market can be made to pay more when that choice is slightly expanded. Thus, blacks typically pay a premium over what whites pay for comparable housing.[44] There is money to be made, too, in the rapid neighborhood turnover that can be generated by the introduction of black families to a street that had been white only. So-called blockbusting was often orchestrated by real estate agents who use the tactic to generate home sales and the resulting commissions.[45] Discrimination in housing has become less overt over time, as real estate practitioners shifted from outright and explicit discrimination to more subtle differential treatment of people based on skin color. Such studies as are done on the phenomenon of housing discrimination indicate that it remains pervasive.[46]

Segregation Persists

The evidence on racial segregation indicates that the United States has a severe problem. As measured by the most common indicator, the index of dissimilarity, rates of racial segregation are higher in the United States than in any other developed country. This index measures segregation on a scale of 0 to 100, and can be interpreted as being the percentage of minority residents who would have to move in order to create a condition of perfect integration (defined as a metropolitan area in which each neighborhood has the same racial breakdown). In some metropolitan areas of the country, chiefly older industrial cities of the Midwest and Northeast, the index is greater than 80. In 2010, thirty-nine of the largest metropolitan areas in the country (with populations over 500,000) have segregation levels that are regarded by experts as high (i.e., 60 or higher on the index).[47] An indicator of hyper-segregation that takes into account multiple measures and dimensions of segregation suggests that twenty-nine metropolitan areas in the United States were hyper-segregated (highly segregated on four or more of the five indices used) in 2000.[48]

Segregation, as measured by these indices, peaked during the 1960s and 1970s. The decline since then has been uneven. In some metropolitan areas, including Dallas, Phoenix, Los Angeles, and other, predominantly western and southwestern metro areas, the decline since 1980 has been significant (more than 10-point reductions). But in metropolitan areas of the Midwest and Northeast, regions that have higher percentages of African Americans, the reduction has been much less.[49] Segregation remains a central fact of life in most American metropolitan areas. Segregation in schools is another phenomenon that is showing very little sign of abating. In fact, during the 1990s, the level of student segregation in public schools actually worsened, although this was followed by modest improvements in the following decade.[50] The lack of significant progress on school desegregation, including the political failures of busing, and the judicial system's reluctance to require metropolitan-wide remedies for school segregation, has put more pressure on residential integration as a solution.

Concentrations of poverty are also seen as a sizable problem and, unlike racial segregation, a problem that continues to grow over time. American Community Survey data covering 2010–2014 show that there is more concentrated poverty in American cities now than at any other time over the past sixty years.[51] The more than forty-one hundred high-poverty census tracts in the United States and 13.7 million people living in concentrated poverty are more than double the figures from 2000.[52]

Through this much of the argument there is little that separates fair housing and community development activists. The severe and persistent urban inequalities that follow color lines and neighborhood boundaries are in little dispute. That American urban areas reflect a highly biased distribution of life chances and experiences is not an item of contention. Even the role of public policies in producing and abetting these inequalities is largely agreed on. The two movements split, however, on approaches moving forward, with the fair housing movement anchored firmly in strategies of integration.

Integration as the Necessary Solution

At the risk of oversimplifying, it is generally felt that there are two ways of addressing the spatial inequalities associated with residential segregation. The first is to focus on spatial mobility—that is, to desegregate. The strategy here is to facilitate and manage the movement of people in such a way as to achieve greater racial diversity across communities, to replace segregation with integration. The second strategy is to attempt to improve the conditions that exist within segregated communities, more specifically within minority-dominated neighborhoods. This has, in the past, been characterized as a choice between "dispersal" strategies on the one hand and "enrichment" strategies on the other. The contemporary fair housing movement emphatically pursues the dispersal/integration solution.

Integration as Source of Benefits

Integration is considered by fair housing advocates to be the best means of addressing the problems of segregation. The benefits of opening up racially exclusive communities have been a central element in fair housing for decades. To some degree the expected benefits of integration are simply the logical negation of segregation and its costs. Thus, if segregation limits access to areas of job growth, integration will increase that access.[53] Insofar as suburban areas have been the areas of greatest job growth over the past forty years, then making housing options available in suburban areas for lower-income people of color will put them within reach of employment opportunities.

Similarly, integration is seen as a means of improving the educational experience of children compared to what is available to them in segregated neighborhoods. The school benefits of racial integration have long been touted and are rooted in the extreme inequalities of education that characterized the "separate and unequal" era prior to *Brown v. Board of Education*. More equitable educational experiences for children across race and class categories, it is argued, would help to reduce intergenerational inequalities, as the sons and daughters of black and low-income families receive the same quality education as those of the middle class and white suburban families.

Integration, it is argued, will eliminate Rusk's "segregation tax" and provide minority homeowners access to the more rapid property appreciation that whites have enjoyed for decades. Integration will allow families to escape the high crime and dangerous environmental hazards that burden the segregated ghetto. And so on. For the costs of segregation identified earlier, for the social dysfunctions and public-service neglect associated with the ghetto, integration provides a solution.

Integration would also redistribute the costs of poverty so that central cities are not overly burdened with the social and service costs associated with poverty.[54] Currently, the segregation of disadvantaged and poor families in core areas of metropolitan areas ensures that a small number of local governments are burdened with the responsibility of providing antipoverty services. Given the extreme fragmentation of local governments in the United States, most do not have to deal with large numbers of poor households. This creates inequities of public finance and taxation that could also be evened out with a more integrated settlement pattern within regions.

It has even been argued that open housing laws, by facilitating the suburbanization of the black population, lead to increased employment and residential growth in central cities as those neighborhoods lose the stigma associated with racial segregation and concentrated poverty.[55]

In addition, integration is argued to provide other instrumental benefits such as supporting "regional and global competitiveness" and "smart growth and environmental values."[56] In the case of the former the argument rests on the idea that large socioeconomic and racial disparities within regions are harmful to overall growth and therefore to the competitiveness of a region.

The overall empirical basis for these claims is mixed. Whether movement of people of color to predominantly white communities produces greater access to jobs, for example, has received mixed support, whereas the benefits to children of color being educated in the same schools as white children have been more consistently demonstrated in the research literature. A number of studies of mobility and dispersal programs have dominated American housing policy since the early 1990s. In particular, advocates point to evidence from the Gautreaux mobility program in Chicago and to the Moving to Opportunity program that operated in five U.S. cities. Fair housers point to findings that people reported lower levels of fear of crime after moving out of high-poverty, segregated housing, and evidence from Gautreaux and MTO showing that adolescent girls reported health benefits from moving.

For some time, integration advocates focused on the Gautreaux study, finding those results to be more reassuring about the impacts of integrationist moves. The MTO program, on the other hand, a program that enjoyed a superior research design and thus could be said to provide more reliable data on the actual impact of desegregative moves by lower-income households of color, produced what most people regarded as disappointing results. In fact, the early results of the MTO studies were so disappointing to the advocates of dispersal that a great deal of further analysis was done to explain why the program had not produced the expected outcomes. Some argued for a more relaxed application of the experimental design that was more likely to show program benefits.[57] The most recent analysis of the program tracing the labor market outcomes of young adults who were children at the time of their MTO relocation has demonstrated benefits for some.[58]

Of course, whether the benefits of integration, such as they are, occur because of inherent qualities of integration rather than the privileged economic and political power of whites is another question. If integration works only because it spatially rearranges households in such a way that people of color get to experience a portion of the privilege that white communities routinely experience, then integration does little to address the fundamental reasons behind racial injustice. If integration can somehow alter existing power dynamics in American society, then it can be considered a more robust solution to urban and racial inequalities.

Integration as a Democratic Project

The argument for integration as a way to address fundamental inequities in power is based on claims about the ways in which it harmonizes with democracy and inclusive social relations among diverse groups. The best-known version of this argument is Gordon Allport's "contact theory," which postulates that under certain conditions, which include equal status and common goals, greater contact among members of different groups will reduce prejudice and improve intergroup relations.[59] The fair housing argument is that residential integration is an appropriate application of the thesis.[60]

The 1968 Report of the Kerner Commission on Civil Disturbances evinced a similar faith in integration. While acknowledging that both enrichment strategies and integration efforts could deal with the unequal conditions that minority households were forced to face in segregated neighborhoods, the commission concluded that integration was "the only course which explicitly seeks to *achieve a single nation*" (emphasis added).[61] In this sentiment and in its other statements, the commission was arguing that separate is inherently unequal and thus integration is a prerequisite for the egalitarian social and political relationships that are the foundation of American political beliefs. One finds reference to this phrase, "separate is inherently unequal," in a great deal of fair housing argumentation, and it carries a power and authority that derive from the political and historical discourse surrounding the discredited "separate but equal" doctrine embodied in *Plessy v. Ferguson*.[62]

Perhaps the most extensive recent articulation of a political theory of integration is Elizabeth Anderson's *The Imperative of Integration*, published in 2010. In this work, Anderson argues that the "democratic ideal holds that justice requires equality in social relations," that is, that political equality is not possible without social equality, and that neither is possible in conditions of segregation.[63]

Integration is also, according to Anderson, an inherent part of democratic processes. Negotiation and deliberation among groups that are part of democratic processes are facilitated by integration; indeed, she argues, they *require* integration.[64] Systematic inequalities along socioeconomic lines (though not limited to racial and ethnic divisions), on the other hand, are better served by conditions of segregation. Segregation, according to Anderson, allows dominant elites to be insular in their decision making and thus unaccountable and irresponsible. Residential segregation that "pack[s] blacks into majority-minority districts makes the remaining districts overwhelmingly white, insular, and free to promote racially polarizing policies."[65] This view of minority power in a representative system runs counter to, and explicitly challenges, the oft-expressed views of many minority political leaders in and out of government that minority districts are essential to building political power.[66] Anderson's view is the opposite, that integration, even if it means minority status in all electoral districts for communities of color, is the only condition under which political elites will have an accurate understanding of minority problems and issues and is the only condition under which political elites will be equally responsive to minority issues.[67]

Integration as a Realistic Outcome

For integration to produce benefits it must be accomplished at a sufficient scale. Fair housing advocates assert there is evidence that it is possible to engineer integration through public policy and judicial rulings. Important court rulings in *Gautreaux v. CHA*, *Gautreaux v. HUD*, the *Mount Laurel* cases, and a range of public housing desegregation lawsuits (all of which are described in more detail in chapter 4) have demonstrated the ability and willingness of the courts to impose integrationist initiatives upon jurisdictions that have been shown to be obstructive, exclusionary, or discriminatory in their application of assisted housing programs. These initiatives, according to fair housing advocates, have resulted in the resettlement of significant numbers of families of color into integrated settings.

The success of legislated programs is somewhat more limited. Here, fair housing advocates point more to the fact that we know how to shape policy in a way that will disperse subsidized housing residents. The federal Moving to Opportunity program provides housing choice vouchers to families who volunteer to move to low-poverty neighborhoods. Fair share housing programs that exist in New Jersey or have existed briefly in other areas are referenced as ways of rearranging the spatial distribution of subsidized housing.[68]

Community Development as a Failure

In addition to the merits of integration, the integrationist argument incorporates a critique of the alternative approach—referred to as "enrichment" or "community development." Enrichment strategies have been criticized for decades, derisively termed "gilding the ghetto" by those who argue that such methods will never alter the basic dynamics of disadvantage associated with concentrations of racial minorities. The implication of this term is that it is not possible to change the underlying nature of the ghetto as an area of systematic disadvantage; rather it is only possible to make cosmetic and superficial improvements.

Gary Orfield, for example, contends that enrichment does not work because efforts have been too limited in the past. The root problem, according to Orfield, is that there is not enough political support for large-scale improvements in predominantly black communities, that such efforts are based on "white goodwill" or the extent of support within the white communities for race-based efforts at community improvement. Instead, he argues, whites have spent most of the last sixty years trying to put as much distance between themselves and such communities as they possibly can. Orfield argues that efforts at improving ghetto conditions will always be too limited to make a true difference in living conditions.[69]

Elizabeth Anderson maintains that enrichment is workable only if the deprivation experienced by the community is solely material. She argues that segregation creates disadvantages in social and cultural capital as well, and enrichment strategies that do not alter the basic conditions of spatial segregation will not be able to address those disadvantages.[70] Others also argue more simply that community development impacts are limited.[71]

In this critique of community development, the fair housing advocates are joined by "new regionalists" who likewise see the "inside game" strategies of community development as insufficient and poorly equipped to meet the challenges of turning around segregated and poor communities in urban cores. Pastor et al., for example, see the actions of CDCs as "the equivalent of swimming against a raging stream" of policies and regional dynamics that combine to channel investment outward, away from core neighborhoods.[72] Rusk calls community development efforts the equivalent of "helping people go up a down escalator."[73] An important part of their assessment is that such community development activities do not connect with regional groups in order to ensure that whatever development does take place in core areas is connected to regional growth opportunities. Thus, Pastor et al. criticize community development that does not have a regional vision or link to regional partners. Similarly, Rusk says an "inside game" is doomed to failure without an aggressive "outside game" (initiatives aimed at creating greater regional equity) to match it.[74] The concern is that community developers are too parochial and too focused on the neighborhood scale to generate the type of change that will alter the larger patterns of spatial inequality that essentially produce and reinforce neighborhood disadvantage. A recent study of community-based organizations, for example, shows that high levels of racial and ethnic segregation produce conditions in which community organizations "become very territorial, highly protective of their own 'turf.'"[75]

The critique of community development connects with Sampson's argument about the hierarchical calcification of communities within a region. Sampson's research on Chicago showed that the hierarchy of places within that region has been fairly rigid and that movement of communities up and down the hierarchy is rare and limited.[76] Communities follow certain paths that lock them into positions relative to others in the same region. Thus, community revitalization efforts are largely incapable of changing those trajectories or path dependencies. In this way, communities within urban regions can become long-term "poverty traps" that operate to reproduce poverty and disadvantage. In such circumstances, community development will fail, and integrationist strategies are necessary.

Yet the fair housing critique of community development goes deeper than a mere allegation of ineffectiveness. According to some, community development is actually detrimental to fair housing objectives because it continues to place services and resources used by lower-income people of color in core neighborhoods and thus perpetuates and exacerbates patterns of segregation.[77] This argument, in fact, positions community development and affordable housing as part of the problem that integration efforts need to address. Community development is a problem to the extent that it works to anchor low-income people of color in declining communities. It is a problem to the extent that it perpetuates segregation and racial isolation.

An Unassailable Position?

The fair housing case, briefly sketched out here, is compelling in two aspects. The first is in the description of the harms of segregated living in American cities. These conditions have produced and reproduced patterns of severe inequality and injustice along racial lines. It is also demonstrably true that American public policy was complicit in the development of segregated residential patterns, either proactively through renewal programs that consciously disrupted communities of color, or passively through the malign neglect of the state in the face of aggressive white racism in building the walls of American urban segregation. This particular pillar of the integrationist argument, however, is one that is largely shared by those active in community development. The harms of segregation and concentrations of poverty are readily seen in the differential neighborhood conditions that prevail in mostly white communities as compared to communities of color. The improvement of those conditions is the very subject of community development activity.

A second compelling aspect of the integration arguments is the assertion that the harms of segregation demand a policy response that fundamentally alters the dynamics of segregation and in turn eliminates the structural disadvantages of life in an enforced ghetto. Whether integration is the only settlement pattern consistent with democratic governance and a well-operating political system is a question that community development activists cannot ignore. Community developers must be able to articulate either how integration falls short in altering political dynamics and structural disadvantages, or they must articulate an alternative approach to addressing racial justice and regional equity that simultaneously avoids the weaknesses of integrationism. In the next chapter, as part of a comprehensive case for community development, I argue that it is possible to do both.

AFFIRMATIVELY FURTHERING COMMUNITY DEVELOPMENT

The idea of community development embodies a set of strategies for the achievement of regional and racial equity in America's urban areas unlike those pursued by fair housing advocates. This is so even as it is also true that the movement takes as its challenge confronting the same patterns of spatial inequality condemned by fair housing activists. Constructing the case for community development as a means of addressing these inequalities requires no critique of residential integration in and of itself. Indeed, the community development position does not incorporate a critique of residential integration per se. Integrated neighborhoods that emerge and persist as a result of families of all races and ethnicities realizing their housing choices demand no judgment one way or the other. Residential integration *as a manipulated outcome and as a means of achieving urban and racial justice* does, however demand a justification.

The difficulty of the fair housing integration argument is not so much its ends as its means.[1] That is, the key problem is not so much *integration* as it is the *integrating*, especially when such efforts burden disadvantaged groups.[2] The pursuit of residential integration, as a rule, either assumes or subordinates the residential preferences of people of color. Integration, it is understood, will not work without white acquiescence, and thus the terms of integration must be those that whites accept. Such a bind requires that the interests of communities of color be subsidiary to those of whites during the process of integrating. In addition, as a result of existing inequities of power, integration almost exclusively involves managing the settlement decisions of people of color and certainly not those of whites. The resistance of whites to residential integration is one of the glaring truths of American urban development, and it has repeatedly frustrated attempts at scaling up programs of integration. Programs of residential integration that have been able to last over time simply do not show much in the way of progress on the first objective, the spatial rearrangement of people, let alone progress on the end goal of racial justice.

The case for community development, of course, must address these same criticisms. Has it produced the benefits that it has promised? What, in fact, can be expected from community development, especially in the way of racial and urban equity? The assessment of community development to date has tended to concentrate on lower-scale phenomena such as whether affordable housing and other development activities produce benefits for people and for communities. The record here is better than the integrationists allow. Research has demonstrated very specific positive outcomes resulting from affordable housing and community development activity. Beyond these, though, the larger equity goals of the movement originate in conceptions of community that acknowledge the legitimacy and in fact importance of social group distinction. The strategies for achieving these larger equity goals within the community development framework should thus focus on the redistribution of political and economic power across the urban landscape rather than the redistribution of people of color.

The Limits of the Integration Argument

The central element of the community development response is that integrationist objectives should not be given a privileged position in housing policy, concerns about the problems of segregation and racial inequality notwithstanding.

Integration Is Only One Goal

Fair housing and equal opportunity as defined by the integrationists do not constitute the entirety of the HUD mission, nor do they address the totality of housing needs in the country. HUD's obligations in no small measure include the provision of an adequate supply of affordable housing to meet the needs of *all* citizens. The most obvious measures of the agency's performance in this area are figures on the number of homeless persons nationwide and the number of households lacking decent, safe, and affordable housing. These numbers suggest that we have some distance to go in meeting national objectives. Millions of families in the United States and more than half of all renters lack affordable housing.

For very low-income families the shortage of affordable housing is most acute; in 2013, for every one hundred very low-income households only thirty-four units were available and affordable.[3] An annual income of $42,240 is needed to afford the average two-bedroom apartment at the fair market rent (FMR) in the United States in 2012.[4] This translates to an hourly wage of $20.30, or $5 more per hour than the average renter household makes. For those making the minimum wage, of course, the discrepancy between earnings and what the National Low Income Housing Coalition calls the "housing wage" is even greater.[5] There is not a single state in the country in which a person making the minimum wage can afford the average two-bedroom apartment at the fair market rent. For most low-income families, the typical FMR is well beyond their ability to pay; the typical very low-income household is able to afford a rent that is roughly $500 less per month than the national average FMR.

The acute lack of affordable housing in the United States, worse in some metropolitan areas than others, is by itself a fair housing issue. This is because there is a racial disproportionality to housing need in the United States. People of color account for more than half of the households experiencing what HUD calls "worst case housing needs" in 2013, a pattern that has been the case since HUD began to track this information.[6] The tremendous disproportionality of housing need is the result of long-standing patterns of discrimination in housing and employment. Addressing the significant racial gap in housing conditions that have resulted from discrimination ought to be a high priority of the fair housing movement.[7]

Much of the need for affordable housing is located in core neighborhoods that suffered significant disinvestment and decline during the postwar years of rapid suburbanization. These neighborhoods, disproportionately occupied by people of color, will require significant investment to improve housing and neighborhood conditions.[8] A narrow construction of fair housing, one that focuses on integration, ignores the racial justice dimension of housing need and generates opposition to subsidized housing in disadvantaged neighborhoods. Wilen and Stasell argue that those focusing on integration "have cast aside the more important goal of improving housing conditions for members of previously oppressed groups, thus actually harming the intended beneficiaries of civil rights legislation."[9] By not conceiving of fair housing in this broader sense, fair housing advocates have defined their goal narrowly, and pursued that goal to very little benefit of very low-income households.[10] The focus on integration sacrifices the objective of meeting housing needs to the spatial goals of dispersal and mix. Putting integration into a privileged position vis-à-vis the development of adequate affordable housing puts black communities in the position of having to wait for white communities to integrate before receiving the housing assistance they need. Given the fair housing concerns for resegregation, it is questionable whether black or near-black communities would ever be green-lighted for affordable housing investments by fair housing advocates.

Faulty Means

More than forty years ago legal scholar John Calmore pointed out that "truly bad things are happening in the name of integration."[11] At that time he was focusing his attention on the effect of "impaction rules" that have been applied to HUD programs since *Shannon v. HUD* in 1970.[12] Impaction rules require that HUD housing subsidies be limited in poor neighborhoods that are racially segregated, on the grounds that those subsidies will reinforce patterns of racial and economic segregation. The implicit judgment embodied in impaction rules is that the housing needs of those who wish to integrate should be given priority over those who do not. However, for some like Calmore, self-imposed limits on housing subsidies in neighborhoods with poor housing conditions and a large number of disadvantaged families in need are "unconscionable and counterproductive" in that they limit the amount of safe, decent, and affordable housing for the poor in the central city.[13] "The emphasis on dispersal tactics to achieve racial and economic integration," argued Calmore, "is too often curtailing the provision of housing opportunities and community enrichment for those most in need."[14]

In fact, the voluntary curtailment of housing investment in core neighborhoods is a type of voluntary, public-sector redlining. During the 1970s a national neighborhood movement emerged in the United States to advocate for the core neighborhoods of American cities. The chief concern of the movement was the systematic disinvestment in neighborhoods by the private sector. Lending institutions in particular were accused of draining communities of their wealth by taking deposits of residents while refusing to make loans in the neighborhood. Similarly, lending institutions were accused of directing their lending products toward predominantly white neighborhoods. Insurance companies were also criticized for imposing high rates in central neighborhoods. This general pattern of discriminatory and harmful business practices was opposed by neighborhood activists and local officials.

Public policies now exist to make banks and insurance companies more accountable to central city neighborhoods. In addition, public investment in core neighborhoods is seen as one way of countering the ill effects of these private-sector actions. By making low-cost loans available to property owners and residents in core neighborhoods, local, state, and federal governments have attempted to maintain a critical flow of capital into these areas.

Central city neighborhoods require an enhanced level of public-sector investment. As a rule, the building stock is older and therefore in greater need of maintenance and upgrading. In disadvantaged neighborhoods the level of physical deterioration and the effects of aging are even greater because owners and residents are less able to afford maintenance and upgrading. Community development corporations are the primary agents of maintenance and renewal in these neighborhoods. We know that community development investments in subsidized housing in core neighborhoods improve the housing stock, increase property values, reduce problems of crime, and contribute to economic development and the economic security of residents.

The restriction of CDC activities and the limiting of investments in subsidized housing in core neighborhoods, in the name of fair housing or in the name of deconcentrating poverty, would cut off or dramatically reduce the flow of public funds to central neighborhoods and ensure the further decline of these communities. When the private sector does this it is called redlining and it is opposed because of its obvious negative effects. The effects would be no better if the public sector pursued such a strategy. The restriction of community development activities, and subsidized housing efforts especially, in central neighborhoods is a form of redlining, this time imposed by public policy rather than by private-sector investors.

Interests of Low-Income Minorities

It is not at all clear that low-income people of color hold integration in as high regard as do fair housing advocates.[15] Such a proposition might seem preposterous in light of the civil rights activism of the 1960s in which hundreds of thousands of people of color marched and protested in order to integrate neighborhoods, public facilities, commercial establishments, and government offices. Yet the extent to which the civil rights movement was about equal rights versus a particular spatial arrangement of integration is debatable. Indeed, disillusionment with the integrationist strategies and objectives of mainstream civil rights leaders during the 1950s and '60s is starkly reflected in the strong black nationalist movement of the same era. Black nationalism and black power proposed a different vision of racial justice, one that focused on renewing black neighborhoods from within and building a base of power and community that was not dependent on integration. The black power countermovement called for community pride and improvements internally, rather than spatial integration into the larger white community. The neighborhood-based community development movement that emerged during the 1960s, furthermore, promised new means of achieving community improvements while retaining control of important economic and cultural assets. At the end of the civil rights era, there was less rather than more certainty about whether racial justice is better obtained through integration or through community action.

There remains strong empirical evidence for support of residential integration among blacks. Various studies of residential preferences, for example, seem to indicate that for many African Americans, a neighborhood mix of about 50/50 black and white is the ideal.[16] The meaning of this particular finding is contestable, however. When segregated living conditions carry with them extreme material disadvantage, support for integration on the one hand and support for better living conditions on the other are difficult to disentangle. The context and frame of reference for such a hypothetical choice is an American urban environment shaped by discrimination in which predominantly black neighborhoods suffer many disadvantages relative to white neighborhoods. Thus, it is hard to say that "ideal" preferences expressed in survey responses indicate a desire for integration per se, when it is quite possible that they reflect a desire for the better public services and physical environment that go with a substantial white population.[17]

Integration or Good Housing?

Integration, even if a goal, may not be the primary objective of many African Americans. Instead, it is possible that "the more fundamental concern among black Americans has been freedom from impediments to the fulfillment of their human potential."[18] It is similarly important to consider whether deconcentration is really desired by low-income African Americans, and whether such deconcentration is desired more than good housing in their existing neighborhoods.[19] Furthermore, Leigh and McGee suggest that integration is pursued not *for itself* but for the benefits it provides, such as good housing, good public services, and quality education. In this, the integrationists may not disagree and would simply add that the pursuit of these neighborhood benefits *requires* integration. But this is a contested point, and there is evidence that while lower-income people of color are obviously aware of the disadvantages they face in their current neighborhoods, their preferred solution is the upgrading of their existing communities rather than relocation to predominantly white neighborhoods.[20] The community development movement, furthermore, is the means by which lower-income communities attempt to improve conditions. Even prior to the emergence of the neighborhood-based community development movement, there was acceptance of public housing in communities of color.[21] The unrest in many urban ghettos during the 1960s was not a response to too much assisted housing being built in those areas; it was driven by discontent over existing living conditions and specifically the poor conditions that characterized much of the private-sector housing in African American neighborhoods.[22] The National Urban League position throughout the 1970s and 1980s was that "the overriding issue . . . is better, more affordable housing for minorities, not housing integration."[23] The League opposed policies of dispersal and deconcentration for that reason.

Questions about the degree of support for integration existed even as the integrationist movement was strong. As early as 1963, the newsletter of the fair housing movement's national organization (the National Committee against Discrimination in Housing, or NCDH) summarized a study "that found that when choosing a home, most African-Americans looked first for good quality housing and neighborhood amenities. 'Integration as such,' the study concluded, 'was a secondary consideration.'"[24]

Integrationists acknowledge the reluctance to move on the part of people of color, and admit that support for integration may not be what it was a generation ago, but they give this phenomenon a different interpretation. They often attribute the lagging support for integration to "integration exhaustion" brought on by the bitter resistance frequently encountered by those willing to be pathbreakers.[25] Certainly it is true that black families who have led the way by moving into predominantly white neighborhoods have generally suffered greatly as a result. The sordid American history of firebombings, rock throwing, and mob intimidation that unfolded throughout the twentieth century in city after city is terrible testament to what Orlando Patterson called the "ordeal of integration."[26] It is quite likely that much of the reluctance to integrate expressed by people of color is simply fear of the hostility they are likely to face should they move into predominantly white neighborhoods.[27] Similarly, racial prejudice and discrimination in the workplace can make the black neighborhood a refuge of sorts, a place where blacks don't "have to deal with white people anymore."[28]

The integration fatigue observation is important because it describes interracial experiences that are in direct contrast to what the contact theory suggests (and depends on). Contact theory hypothesizes improved relationships over time as contact increases; integration fatigue, to the extent that it exists, reflects interracial relationships that remain highly problematic for people of color.[29] In fact, on closer scrutiny, the contact theory rationale for integration is suspect even on its own terms. As philosopher Tommie Shelby notes, the assumption that contact will reduce white racism over time implies a period of interaction when whites will continue to act on their implicit and explicit biases. Black residents are to simply endure this period of time until the hoped-for racial accord occurs. Shelby rightly questions whether blacks must play this role in the moral reform of whites.[30]

It seems likely that at least part of the ambivalence toward integration within communities of color may be related to the nature of specific integration policies themselves. These initiatives, including judicial rulings and court-generated programs, often discount the expressed preferences of elements within disadvantaged groups in order to impose a particular solution. Integration mandates that impose particular remedies can restrict the liberty and choice of lower-income African Americans just as rigid segregationist practices did.[31]

The operating assumption of integration efforts seems to be that "absent discrimination all nonwhites would opt for integration."[32] So fundamental is this assumption, that the "target" population, people of color, is sometimes not even involved in the creation and shaping of integrationist initiatives. One of the most famous and far-reaching housing integration cases of the past fifty years is the *Gautreaux* case in Chicago. The lead attorney for the plaintiffs was Alexander Polikoff. In his memoir of the case, *Waiting for* Gautreaux, there is a remarkable section where Polikoff wonders if the five lawyers on the case ("five white guys," he notes) "should have consulted with the black community" about the nature of rulings made by the judge in the case. "In the end . . . we did not consult either our clients or surrogates for them," he writes. "*Gautreaux* remains a case in which neither the black class members nor others in the black community have had a meaningful role in litigation decisions."[33] What makes this so remarkable is that *Gautreaux* makes very specific proscriptions about acceptable levels of black residency within communities in the Chicago area and strictly limits the production of subsidized housing within areas based on the size of the black population. The court-approved levels of racial mix are also used to direct the movement of black families around the metropolitan area using housing choice vouchers. Moreover, *Gautreaux* has served as the model for expanding ideas of mobility programs across the country.[34] This massively important case was decided without so much as consultation with the black community about the remedies being established, and upon it we have based national housing policy related to the "improvement" of housing conditions for lower-income people of color.

Even within the fair housing movement itself there seems to have been a preoccupation with the attitudes of the dominant white majority. The fair housing movement's central organization, NCDH, focused on white racial attitudes and rarely explicitly scrutinized opinions of blacks. The NCDH newsletter, *Trends*, reported on seven national opinion polls between 1956 and 1966; all but one were polls of white attitudes. It was perhaps assumed by the early fair housing movement activists that the neighborhood preferences of people of color for integration were so obvious as to not require study.

The Feasibility of Integration Initiatives

The few integration initiatives that operate tend not to produce discernible benefits. First, long-standing and enduring white and suburban resistance to integration and deconcentration of poverty is a problem these programs have never overcome. Desegregation efforts have faced fierce opposition from whites since their advent in the 1960s.[35] When the battlegrounds of integration shifted from city neighborhoods to suburban areas, resistance to integration and the lack of political will to overcome or overrule that resistance persisted.[36] And years after that, sociologists have documented the resistance of whites to programs of racial integration and housing desegregation.[37] As suburbs diversify, whites continue to flee, moving ever farther away.[38]

Even though fewer white express racial prejudices in survey environments, there is often a gap between the portion of the white population that believes in overall equity across races and the population that expresses support for particular integration programs.[39] As Sniderman and Carmines argue, "large numbers of white Americans remain opposed to a wide array of public policies, from social welfare through affirmative action, aimed at finally achieving racial equality."[40] Some attribute this gap to "race fatigue," the notion that whites are impatient with the continuing demands for race-based policy, instead thinking that formal sanctions for discrimination that are embodied in various laws dating to the civil rights era have eliminated problems of racial inequality before the law. Such persons are much more likely at this point to support so-called color-blind laws that establish universal standards for conduct and treatment. In the housing policy arena, for example, only tentative steps have been taken on integration programs, and these have proven to be highly vulnerable politically.

The pattern of extreme political vulnerability has been depressingly similar from one era to the next. In Richard Nixon's first term, his HUD secretary, George Romney, pushed hard for integrative housing policies, trying to extend the reach of HUD-assisted housing into the suburbs. White resistance stopped him cold, and Nixon quickly reassured his suburban constituents that integration would not be a policy goal of his administration. In 1993, the federal government again tried a tentative step toward integrating subsidized households into higher-opportunity areas with the Moving to Opportunity (MTO) program. Again, suburban resistance shut down the effort, this time forcing nominally liberal congressional Democrats to quickly pull the plug on the program, sending the direct message that Congress will not support moving low-income blacks into suburban communities.[41] The sudden decapitation of the MTO program, coming as it did from liberal supporters in Congress, was a forceful reminder of the very limited and shallow base of support that housing integration policy enjoys in the United States. Liberal commitment to integration is, in fact, paper thin.[42]

The one integration-inspired program enacted by Congress that has endured over time and has been of consequence is the federal HOPE VI program and the related demolition and conversion of public housing developments across the country. This initiative has resulted in the movement of hundreds of thousands of very low-income families, mostly African American, out of their previous communities. In Chicago, the nation's largest effort at dismantling public housing has actually produced a noticeable decline in the African American population living in the central city.[43] There are several features of this effort that explain its exceptional status. First, it is self-consciously a "color-blind" program in the sense that nowhere in the materials explaining or justifying the initiative is race considered. The guiding concern of public housing redevelopment is the concentration of poverty. Of course, the MTO program was similarly color-blind in that policy makers specifically avoided the issue of race when justifying and creating the program. The target neighborhoods and the designated destination neighborhoods in MTO were defined by poverty level, not race. But the movement of low-income people of color into low-poverty areas meant de facto movement into predominantly white neighborhoods, and this fact policy makers could not hide. This brings us to the second important characteristic of public housing demolition that distinguishes it from MTO: public housing demolition did not mandate integration—by race or poverty status. The families displaced through redevelopment were not obliged to make integrative moves. Although it was *hoped* that such deconcentration and dispersal would take place, it was not mandated. In those cities where demolition of public housing might have been tied to real dispersal and integration, white communities reacted quickly. In New Orleans, for example, as the city moved to demolish thousands of units of public housing, the nearby predominantly white parishes took quick action "to counteract these deconcentration measures."[44] As a result, the record there and nationally shows that the overwhelming majority of low-income black families displaced by public housing redevelopment moved to other segregated neighborhoods. [45] The policy designers may have considered that unfortunate, but it was exactly that feature of the program that ensured its ongoing viability.

Finally, the third significant feature of the program is that it involved significant and dramatic physical redevelopment of sizable parcels of land typically located in the core areas of central cities. In many cases, the redevelopment triggered or unleashed rapid gentrification and neighborhood change that resulted in significant increases in land value and private-sector investment.[46] Thus, the scale of public housing redevelopment and its longevity is attributable in main to the fact that its most lasting legacy is not integration at all, but rather the dissolution of previously black communities that had come to be seen as troublesome for many reasons and their replacement with new communities much more acceptable for speculative private investment.

On Program Effectiveness

Integrationists often criticize community development for being ineffective, if not counterproductive. Yet it is easily possible to make the same argument against programs designed to achieve and maintain integration. The typical argument against affordable housing / community development is that it fails to produce community-level impacts. When critics attack efforts to improve life in disadvantaged core neighborhoods, what they find lacking in these efforts is that they have too often not reversed the downward spiral of decline and that they have not altered the neighborhood's position in the hierarchy of places within the region. The critics may point to continuing high levels of poverty, or high levels of segregation, or unemployment, private-sector disinvestment, or perhaps crime. It may well be a combination of many of these. Affordable housing and community development are, in other words, typically judged by their community-scale impacts. There are other scales at which they might be judged, however. They might be judged by the number of decent, safe, and affordable housing units made available to families who needed them. Community development might be judged by the reduced instability of those households, or the number of jobs created or saved in commercial development. Community development might be judged by the enhanced access to services that is made possible through the co-location of housing and social services in some affordable housing developments. Affordable housing and community development might also be judged by the greater feelings of safety resulting from a revitalized section of the neighborhood. The discourse of concentrated poverty and neighborhood effects, however, has devalued these lower-scale benefits to the point that they are frequently completely overlooked in assessments of affordable housing and community development.

The evaluation of integration initiatives, on the other hand, typically exhibits the opposite bias. Housing mobility programs such as Gautreaux and MTO are judged by whether the individuals who participate in them report individual-level benefits. Both of these programs have produced volumes of research aimed at uncovering such benefits. Fair share housing programs and impaction rules are judged by the number of units they produce in various communities or the degree to which they channel development to "opportunity areas." They are not, however, judged by the impact that they have either on the segregated neighborhoods of disadvantage in core areas (i.e., have they contributed to the desegregation of such places, and to what extent?) or on the exclusionary "opportunity" neighborhoods in which they produce housing (i.e., have they contributed to the integration of such places, and to what extent?). This is, of course, a fabulous double standard. Affordable housing and community development are deemed failures if they do not succeed in reversing massive flows of private and public investment that have disadvantaged the very neighborhoods in which community developers operate.[47] Against this standard of success, the Gautreaux and MTO dispersal programs are expected to show only that the families who (a) volunteered for them, and (b) received housing subsidies through them, personally benefited in any number of different ways. Our assessments of community development and dispersal would look very different were we to apply the same standards to each.

Do community development practitioners bring such assessment upon themselves by making claims about revitalization that are unrealistic? This undoubtedly happens in some cases. Yet, generally, community developers are quite circumspect about the benefits they promise. Community-level effects, to the extent that they are claimed for affordable housing projects, tend to be made for fairly small-scale areas—the revitalization of one block, or a street corner, or the reduction in crime at specific addresses. Importantly, however, community development practitioners also claim benefits at the individual level, even though such claims are often ignored and virtually never measured by critics.

The evidence on the actual operation of integration programs suggests that they are deficient at two scales—they are unlikely to achieve desegregation on any appreciable scale, and they tend not to deliver the range of benefits for individual families that the integrationist advocates suggest.

Little Impact on Settlement Patterns

The effort to reduce or cease subsidized housing development in central neighborhoods in order to create more such housing in suburban areas is unlikely to desegregate central neighborhoods for several reasons. The argument is that such units in suburban areas will help with fair housing goals of reducing racial segregation and other goals related to deconcentrating poverty.[48] The fair housing argument is based on the belief or hope that the units built in suburban areas will result in the movement of households of color out of segregated central city neighborhoods into nonsegregated suburban communities. The deconcentration argument is based on the hope that a low-income family will move into a low-poverty, "opportunity" neighborhood. Such outcomes are unlikely for several reasons. First, many low-income families already reside in suburban areas. In fact, nationwide there are more poor people living in suburban parts of metropolitan areas than in central cities.[49] Second, most of these families live in housing that is not affordable to them. For example, in the Twin Cities, the regional planning body, the Metropolitan Council, estimated at the end of the century that there were fifty thousand suburban households earning less than $20,000 per year and spending more than 30 percent of their income for housing.[50] This pattern is repeated across the country. Third, providers of subsidized and affordable housing options in suburban areas already have long waiting lists of families needing subsidized housing units.[51] Given the residency preferences used by many suburban affordable housing providers, new units of subsidized housing will almost certainly be filled by low-income families who are currently suburban residents, and not by central city families moving out to the suburbs. Finally, there simply may not be enough "opportunity neighborhoods" of the sort that integrationists see fit as receiving neighborhoods for minority households.[52]

That much of the new affordable housing built in outlying areas is not inhabited by families moving out of segregated, high-poverty, inner-city neighborhoods is a pattern noted by John Goering as early as 1986.[53] Sometimes, however, the lack of integrative (or deconcentrating) moves is the result of lack of interest among low-income families of color in relocating to distant suburban communities. Housing built in Washington County, Minnesota (suburban Minneapolis–Saint Paul), as a result of the consent decree in *Hollman v. Cisneros* was almost exclusively inhabited by people coming from the Washington County waiting list, despite an explicit effort to market those units to low-income families from Minneapolis, and despite reserving the units for those families.[54] Those units, and others built in suburban communities that would have represented an integrative move for the Minneapolis families, were simply undesirable to those families for many reasons. In other cities, one-half of low-income families given vouchers to move out of poverty neighborhoods moved again very shortly, returning to neighborhoods that were more like the ones they had initially inhabited.[55]

The first HUD initiatives dispersing subsidized household (the Areawide Housing Opportunity Plans and other efforts) produced very little movement of assisted households out of the central city.[56] Even the shift in subsidy type from project-based assistance to tenant-based vouchers that began in the early 1970s has failed to disperse assisted households to an appreciable degree. The nation's largest fair-share housing program aimed at opening up suburban communities to more subsidized housing (the Mount Laurel program in New Jersey) has shown almost no movement of African American families out of central cities and into suburban communities.[57] Finally, despite HOPE VI demolitions, the largest nationwide program aimed at deconcentrating poverty, concentrated poverty in American cities has increased and currently stands at its highest recorded rate.[58] Of course, this lack of impact at the national level is perfectly consistent with the predominant pattern of relocation in HOPE VI projects—moves from one racially segregated and economically disadvantaged neighborhood to another.

There is *a significant need for subsidized affordable housing in the suburbs.* The magnitude of the need justifies greater efforts to produce affordable housing outside the core. The affordable housing movement acknowledges this need and supports efforts to address it. But at the same time it must be understood that such housing will likely not produce significant housing opportunities for central city households, and thus *should not be pursued as a replacement* for continued efforts to provide decent, safe, and affordable housing for those living in the core neighborhoods of metropolitan areas. Those who argue for a cessation of subsidized housing construction/rehabilitation in the central cities in favor of more decentralized development ignore this already existing demand in outlying suburban areas. The development of affordable housing units in the suburbs is most likely to benefit low-income households already living in those suburban communities.

Not only are the ultimate goals of integrationists unlikely to be met; they are ill-defined in the first place. How do we determine what integration means? Should all neighborhoods look alike? What threshold of people of color within a neighborhood is necessary to satisfy integration objectives?[59]

Limited Benefits

Finally, the evidence to date suggests that the individual-level benefits of integration are not as widely experienced as integrationists hope. On this point one can look at the many studies of relocated families in Gautreaux, MTO, and other mobility programs, as well as the studies of families displaced through the HOPE VI program. This literature has been extensively reviewed and summarized elsewhere. Generally speaking, however, while families report benefits related to feelings of safety, there are no demonstrable impacts on financial self-sufficiency, employment, or income,[60] mixed and limited impacts on health and education outcomes, and evidence that dispersal actually damages important sources of social capital and informal support upon which disadvantaged groups heavily depend.[61] The disappointing performance of dispersal and mixed-income efforts are seen in other contexts as well. The British dispersal policies of the 1970s and 1980s "forced Blacks out of clustered living situations into neighborhoods not of their choosing, but for the most part without improving the quality of their housing."[62]

Recent research (what has come to be known as "the Chetty study" after the lead author, sociologist Raj Chetty) shows that economic benefits *do* occur from deconcentration, but that the benefits appear only among those who were children younger than thirteen years old at the time of relocation. The authors show that these children, when they enter the labor force as young adults, earn on average 31 percent more than their counterparts in the control group.[63] The authors also find greater college enrollment among the thirteen-and-under treatment group compared to their age cohort in the control group.[64] The release of the study in 2015 was received with enthusiasm by many, in part because it was the first study among many to demonstrate a positive economic impact of deconcentration. The evidence of benefits to smaller children of moving to lower-poverty neighborhoods reinforced for many the advisability of moving people out of their neighborhoods into areas with greater "opportunity." Thomas Edsall in the *New York Times* placed the study's findings squarely within the debate about whether "federal dollars [should] go toward affordable housing within high-poverty neighborhoods, or . . . to move residents of impoverished communities into more upscale" areas, and argued that the study "challenges" community development policy.[65]

As promising as the findings are, they are balanced by several other considerations related to the MTO program and its operation. First, along with the positive impacts for young children, Chetty et al. also find "that, if anything, moving to a lower-poverty neighborhood had slightly *negative* effects on older children's outcomes."[66] The study also confirmed the previous evidence of no economic impact for adults. Second, MTO was a *voluntary* program of mobility. Enrollment in the program indicated a desire on the part of families to move away from their current circumstances. These findings, as important as they are in identifying some economic benefit for young children, are not generalizable to all households of color, or to all residents of segregated or disadvantaged neighborhoods. Third, as Chetty et al. note, most families in the MTO program could not make the program work for themselves; MTO had only a 48 percent "lease up rate," meaning that fewer than half of the families participating were able to successfully use the housing choice voucher to move to another neighborhood. Finally, among those who did move, a sizable number moved back to higher-poverty neighborhoods. Within ten years, MTO treatment group movers living in neighborhoods with less than 20 percent poverty dropped from 90 percent to 60 percent.[67] Only 25 percent of the treatment group movers lived in a neighborhood with poverty below 10 percent less than ten years after the program began. An Urban Institute study of three MTO cities indicated that in 2004, eleven years after the program began, only 27 percent of treatment group movers lived in neighborhoods with poverty rates below 20 percent, "and only 17 percent were living in neighborhoods with less than 10 percent poverty."[68] All these consider-ations strongly suggest that voluntary mobility programs are not for everyone and that considerable work remains to tailor such programs to the families for whom benefits will occur, and to address the obstacles to successful implemen-tation for those families. Questions remain about what to do for families not wishing to volunteer for mobility programs and those who quickly move back to higher-poverty neighborhoods, questions that are not resolved by the findings of Chetty and colleagues.

The city of Chicago's extensive efforts in producing and operating mixed-income communities reveals that these integration efforts have not, for the most part, produced living environments that are supportive of lower-income people of color.[69] Policy analysts Robert Chaskin and Mark Joseph studied the degree to which the mixed-income developments that have been the core of decon-centration and desegregation efforts from the early 1990s onward have realized their stated goals. In general, they conclude that they haven't. The authors note that the residential management regimes put in place to address the needs of market-rate residents who could easily move elsewhere have "generated new forms of exclusion and new dynamics of marginalization" for the public housing residents, "rather than promoting integration of the poor into well-functioning mixed-income neighborhoods."[70] The central aim of these mixed-income devel-opments, to foster cross-class relationships and even to benefit the lower-income residents through the establishment of relationships with middle-class neigh-bors, is largely unrealized. The "divide, particularly between lower-income rent-ers and owners, is in some cases a source of middling discomfort, informed by subtle cues and quiet assumptions about race and class. In other cases it generates considerable tension."[71]

They also found "little evidence of inclusionary democracy" resulting from these efforts. Residents' lack of civic engagement beyond the development itself was disappointing to the program architects. The "neighborhood associational mechanisms, whether intentionally or not, marginalize low-income renters, and associations designed to promote inclusion have been largely ineffective."[72]

Individual-Level Benefits of Affordable Housing

What, on the other hand, can be said about the benefits of community devel-opment and affordable housing? We can say, in fact, that affordable housing development provides a range of direct benefits to families, from increasing the economic security of low-income families to improving the physical living envi-ronment and increasing residential stability.[73] The link between affordable hous-ing and positive health outcomes is also strong.[74] Children of low-income parents living in subsidized homes have a higher chance of meeting "well child" criteria than children in similar families that do not live in subsidized housing.[75] Children in low-income families lacking affordable housing are more likely to suffer from underdevelopment resulting from malnutrition and iron deficiencies compared to those living in subsidized, affordable housing.[76] In fact, recent research shows that children who grow up in both voucher-assisted housing and in public housing experience higher earnings and lower incarceration rates than their peers who did not have access to assisted housing.[77]

The reasons for these outcomes are twofold. First, as noted above, affordable housing simply frees up more resources for families to meet other needs such as health care and nutrition. For example, adults who have subsidized rent are more likely to have health insurance than those who do not live in subsidized housing.[78] Alternatively, having enough money for food allows for a better-balanced diet for children and adults, avoiding illnesses stemming from malnutrition.

Affordable housing can reduce stress levels for adults and children by lessening the financial pressure of market-rate rents and providing a stable housing environment. Difficulties in keeping up with house payments have been shown to lead to lower levels of psychological health and greater rates of engagement with medical systems.[79] Residential instability, eviction, and doubling up induced by lack of affordability have been linked to adverse psychological outcomes.[80] In the case of the extreme instability of homelessness, a number of adverse psychological outcomes appear in both adults and children.[81]

Aside from benefits that arise from the extra income that subsidized rent facilitates, affordable housing contributes to bettering the health of residents directly through the physical environment that safe, stable housing provides. For example, safe housing can decrease exposure to environmental factors that affect health, such as allergens, neurotoxins (e.g., lead paint), rodents, or insect pests.[82] Affordable housing also reduces the incidence of overcrowding, which can facilitate the spread of infectious disease and can contribute to stress in the home.[83]

A stable home environment is important for the educational performance of children. Lack of affordable housing produces instability in housing for low-income families with children. Hyper-mobility can have a negative effect on children, resulting in stress, behavioral problems, and poor performance in school.[84] Frequent interruptions of educational instruction make progressive learning difficult.[85] Schools located in areas with a hyper-mobile, often low-income population need to tailor their work to these kinds of students, and must focus more on reviewing previously covered topics, slowing down educational progress overall.[86] Research has also shown that children's cognitive achievement is higher for low-income families living in affordable housing and that lower-income families spend more on child enrichment when living in affordable housing.[87]

Creation of Jobs, Economic Stimulation, and Public Revenues

Development of low-income housing can have effects on the community in multiple ways, most directly by creating jobs for skilled construction laborers.[88] The National Association of Home Builders estimates that the building of one hundred Low-Income Housing Tax Credit (LIHTC) units for families can create 120 jobs.[89] The multiplier effects of construction can also benefit local businesses when local suppliers are used. Local businesses can also benefit from the increased consumption of construction workers. Residents of affordable housing projects will experience an increase in their residual income after paying for housing, which can also contribute to the local economy.[90] New housing construction and rehabilitation also generate revenues to local and state governments through fees and costs associated with zoning, permitting, and providing utilities for developments[91] and through increases in sales, income, and property taxes from the housing project.[92]

In addition to providing revenue for the state or city and community surrounding the affordable housing development, low-income housing options can also prevent the local government from losing money by decreasing the likelihood of foreclosure for tenants that may have had difficulty remaining in a market-value home without assistance.[93] Avoiding foreclosure also means avoiding declines in property taxes and utility revenue, and promotes stability of the housing market.[94] The rehabilitation of vacant and abandoned properties brings them back on the tax roll and, as research has shown, increases property values nearby and can produce fiscal benefits that meet or exceed the cost of the rehabilitation subsidy.[95]

Creation of more affordable housing options will draw both employers and employees to the community. Employers view adequate affordable housing stocks as an advantage when determining where to locate business, as a shortage of affordable housing can prevent employees from staying with a company for an extended period of time.[96] This suggests that building or maintaining low-income housing developments may draw potential employers to the community by providing adequate, stable, and safe housing for potential employees. A recent study showed that the lack of local options for affordable housing was linked to slower employment growth.[97]

Crime and Property Values

When community development corporations purchase problem properties for the purpose of rehabilitating and operating them as subsidized housing, there is a great potential for neighborhood improvement. The replacement of an overwhelmed or disinterested private landlord with a community-based non-profit owner can improve management of the building, reducing the nuisance behaviors on and around the property. The upgraded physical condition of the building achieved through rehabilitation, combined with the reduction in nuisance behaviors, can produce benefits for the community.[98]

Determining the true impact of a subsidized housing development on property values is difficult because many projects are sited in neighborhoods that already have a less dynamic housing market. Thus, what appears to be a negative impact of the subsidized housing (property value declines or slower than average increases) is in fact not a result of the development being located nearby but rather the reason why the development was placed there in the first place. In the end, the impact of subsidized housing on neighborhoods depends on a number of factors, including the type of subsidy program involved, the size of the development, and ownership and neighborhood characteristics.

Generally, studies have shown that Low-Income Housing Tax Credit properties tend to have a positive effect on neighborhood property values.[99] The role of nonprofit developers appears important in determining the ultimate impact of subsidized projects. In New York City, for example, although both non- and for-profit complexes have produced positive impacts on nearby property values, the nonprofit developments had a sustained positive impact over a longer period when compared to the for-profit projects.[100]

The experience is much more mixed with older forms of subsidized housing such as public housing and Section 8. Studies have shown positive, negative, and no effects of these forms of subsidized housing on neighborhood property values.[101] Project size may be an important factor in the impact of public housing and Section 8. Small projects in New York City and Denver have had a positive effect on the neighborhood property values, whereas a large public housing project in New York City has had a negative effect.[102] Tenant profiles can also produce differential effects; small public housing for the elderly produced a positive effect in New York City, whereas small projects for families had no impact on property values.[103] Part of the positive impact of community development, of course, is the result of removing or improving existing land uses that are disamenities.

The housing rehabilitation efforts of local community development corporations that focus on single-family homes also have positive impacts on nearby property values. The rehabilitation of vacant properties increases property values nearby and can produce fiscal benefits that meet or exceed the cost of the rehabilitation subsidy.[104]

The Question of Choice

The issue of choice is at the core of the integration question as it has evolved in the fair housing movement. The working assumption of the movement is that given the choice, people of color will move into integrated settings. This has proven, in setting after setting, to be unfounded. The experience of the recent generation of mobility programs, for example, both the forced and the voluntary programs, show in some cases a reluctance to move to the prescribed areas and in other cases a noted tendency on the part of program participants to move back into more segregated and lower-income neighborhoods over time.[105] The programs have also suffered, in some places, a lack of demand and even outright resistance to moving.[106] Perhaps the most consistent and clearest lesson coming out of the studies of forced and voluntary mobility is that the desire for integration among lower-income people of color does not match what has been imagined by the integrationists.

Whose Preferences Matter?

The question of choice presents integrationists with a number of difficult issues.[107] The first is a practical one. Thomas Schelling's game theoretical work on residential integration shows that high levels of residential segregation can arise solely from whites and blacks acting on the basis of their integration preferences.[108] Research has shown fairly consistently that blacks and whites have different ideas of what the ideal racial breakdown of neighborhoods should be. Preferences as stated in survey research show that most blacks would prefer a neighborhood that has roughly equal parts black and white.[109] The majority of whites, however, see the ideal racial mix of a neighborhood they would consider living in to be closer to 75 to 80 percent white and thus no more than 20 to 25 percent black. As Schelling shows, the outcome in a setting in which blacks and whites act on these preferences is a high degree of segregation. First, there are too few whites with a preference for majority black neighborhoods to shift those neighborhoods out of segregated status. Second, blacks with a higher tolerance for white neighbors will be the first to move into predominantly white neighborhoods. As the percentage of whites declines, more blacks will move in, and this would continue presumably until the 50/50 balance is achieved. Except that once black occupancy reaches 20 percent, whites for whom this level of black occupancy is intolerable (i.e., the majority of whites) will begin to leave the neighborhood. Their exit will continue until only those whites with a higher preference for diversity remain. And, as with the first example given, that number is too few to prevent resegregation.

This 20 percent threshold is sometimes referred to as the neighborhood "tipping point"—the proportion of racial/ethnic minority population that will trigger white flight from a neighborhood. Research has shown that this point will vary from one urban area to the next and will also vary over time. It is, in effect, an index of white prejudice or intolerance.[110] Thus, from a practical standpoint, blacks are often faced with only two residential options—either a segregated black neighborhood or a neighborhood in which they are part of a very small minority.[111]

The dilemma for integration efforts is that if everyone is given full choice about where to live from the standpoint of neighborhood racial composition, integration will not be achieved. Thus, what to do about it? The answer for integrationists has been to constrain the choices of people of color. However, as one observer notes, "What is missing in [such an] argument is an explanation of how ... [to] convince Blacks to change their preferences on the kinds of neighborhoods in which they prefer to live."[112] Where some integration advocates are silent on the issue of black preferences, others address the conundrum directly and conclude forthrightly that policy must for practical reasons accede to the preferences of whites, "otherwise, efforts to achieve deconcentration either will be frustrated by community opposition or lead to the exodus of white households."[113]

The lesson is clear: for the integrationists to achieve their goals, blacks must sacrifice their residential preferences. Put differently, the narrow pursuit of fair housing integration must relegate the choices of people of color to a position behind those of whites, and in some cases actively restrict the exercise of choice by people of color.[114] This happens in at least two ways. First, the integration imperative specifically calls for restricting affordable housing development in black and/or high-poverty neighborhoods. Thus, those who wish to occupy new affordable units are limited in their choices to moving out of core neighborhoods (or not moving into them).

This restriction of choice is most obvious in cases of redevelopment and the forced displacement of lower-income people of color. The demolition or conversion of over 250,000 units of public housing in the United States since the early 1990s has disproportionately affected people of color and forced their relocation whether or not they desired to move. The engineers of this displacement seem quite comfortable in asserting their choice over even the expressed opposition of families who did not want to move. President Bill Clinton's first secretary of HUD, Henry Cisneros, presided over the policy changes that led to the mass demolition of public housing and displacement of hundreds of thousands of low-income, mostly black public housing residents. He dismissed the opposition to this displacement on the part of the tenants: "Although even residents living in horrible conditions had mixed feelings about leaving neighborhoods where they had developed bonds of friendship and mutual support, *it was our judgment* that conditions in the most distressed public housing developments were so bad that replacement was the only reasonable course" (emphasis added).[115] The second means by which the fair housing imperative constrains choice is illustrated by attempts to manage neighborhood composition to the liking of white residents. The programs of integration management of the 1970s and 1980s, for example, allowed only a certain number or percentage of minority families into communities in order to maintain the desired level of diversity and to avoid triggering white flight. The disappointing irony of all this is that these programs place "constraints on black housing choice in addition to those imposed by overt discrimination."[116]

The various mobility and dispersal programs set up to desegregate lower-income blacks rarely, if ever, incorporate the neighborhood racial characteristics preferred by blacks. Neighborhoods with a 50/50 black-white split (the expressed preference of most blacks surveyed) are not what participants are offered in the various programs that engineer their relocation. Under *Gautreaux*, African Americans are obliged to move to neighborhoods that are at least 70 percent white. In the consent decree that governed the integration of public housing residents in Minneapolis, the approved neighborhoods had to be at least 71 percent white. In Allegheny County, Pennsylvania (Pittsburgh), the target neighborhoods had to be more than two-thirds white. In other mobility programs the neighborhoods approved for their residence are defined by poverty rate, but once that definition is applied, the de facto racial prescription is for neighborhoods that are typically at least two-thirds white. Take the MTO program as an example. Participants in that program were obliged to move to neighborhoods with poverty rates below 10 percent. The 1990 census shows that these census tracts were very unlikely to have the 50/50 racial composition that most black families prefer. In fact, across the five cities participating in the MTO program, only 6 percent of all census tracts in the metropolitan areas had poverty rates of less than 10 percent and white populations between 40 and 60 percent. Only 6.6 percent of all housing units in those five metropolitan areas were in those neighborhoods. In short, the various programs and legal remedies being offered do not incorporate the preferences of most blacks with regard to integration. The black/white balance that drives these initiatives reflects other considerations and other calculations.

The "Complex Subjective Web" of Housing Choice

Of course, housing mobility choices are almost never a reflection only of neighborhood racial composition. Instead, settlement patterns are the result of complex and multiple causes that integrationists often either fail to understand or simply ignore.[117] People choose housing on the basis of a wide range of considerations, and for some very low-income people the very concept of housing choice is inappropriate for explaining mobility.[118] People may hope to maximize their proximity to place of employment, or seek particular schools for their children. Some will choose to move toward or remain close to family and friends.[119] Those who are transit dependent will prioritize transit access, and some will look for particular kinds of neighborhood amenities. One of the most important considerations in housing choice, obviously, is cost. In short, there is a "complex subjective web that helps guide people's choices" in housing.[120]

Fair housers will point out, accurately, that housing choices are framed by the public policies that determine the spatial distribution of the factors important to people. For example, the transit-dependent are limited to those parts of a metropolitan area with acceptable transit service. In most metropolitan areas transit access is focused in the central city and immediate suburbs. Government support of highway development opened up vast suburban tracts for habitation, and this choice is one that middle-income families can make. Various public policies in the past have concentrated affordable housing in core parts of metropolitan areas, while local exclusionary zoning has actively kept it out of developing suburban areas. Thus, the choice of low-income people is constrained, of course, by cost and the spatial distribution of affordable housing and the spatial distribution of infrastructure and amenities that they most value. In addition, the continued influence of racial discrimination in housing importantly constrains choice. As previously noted, integrationists will often explain the reluctance of blacks to integrate with reference to their desire to avoid the direct racial animus of whites.

For the integrationists, the serious constraints on choice faced by lower-income people of color are of central importance. They question, for example, whether the choices that members of disadvantaged groups make to stay in a community or to return to a mostly segregated community are a true expression of preference. The decision of low-income people to locate or remain in less advantaged neighborhoods, they argue, is not a full and free choice. As Squires and Kubrin write, "All too frequently such decisionmaking is framed and limited by a range of structural constraints. Individuals exercise choice, but those choices often do not reflect what is normally understood by the term 'voluntary.'"[121]

So, the argument goes, how much does choice really mean when it is not full and free choice? Does the absence of free and full choice in housing relieve us of concern about whether choice is served by integration efforts? Would low-income families choose to remain in their communities if they had full and free choice?

In the end this is a fruitless path. The answer to what housing people would choose in the absence of all constraints is as unknowable as the conditions of "full and free choice" in housing are unattainable. We can agree that full and free choice in housing is not available to lower-income people of color. However, we must also be prepared to agree that it is not available to affluent whites either. When one buys a house or rents an apartment, one is getting not just the unit but the neighborhood in which it is set. That neighborhood has an existing endowment of institutions and amenities, and an existing pattern of land use. In other words, an entire social and physical environment accompanies each home. Though these can change over time, typically they do not change quickly. So the neighborhood one "buys" along with the housing unit is the neighborhood one must negotiate on a daily basis for the foreseeable future. Full and free choice in housing is available to no one because, simply, no metropolitan area has neighborhoods available with every possible combination of school quality, transit service, retail amenity mix, housing affordability, and so on. Of course affluent whites are much better able to maximize their preferences because their choices are much *less* constrained than those of lower-income people of color. This observation provides us then with what should be the guiding principle of fair housing advocacy: *the maximization of choice* for disadvantaged groups. Fair housing advocacy should be about providing more choice, not constraining it. And, importantly, choice includes the decision to remain where one is, whether integrationists deem that location to be a good one or a bad one.

The first station of fair housing spatial strategy, the opening up of exclusionary housing markets, meets the standard established above. Opening up exclusionary communities will provide another housing option for people of color and low-income people who had been kept out through a combination of regulatory restrictions. The second and third stations of fair housing spatial strategy, preventing further segregation and dismantling existing segregation, too often violate this principle. These efforts can involve (a) limiting the development of affordable housing where it is needed; (b) in the case of integration maintenance, denying entry of families of color to communities in which the current degree of diversity has been deemed optimal; or (c) forcing the relocation of families who have no desire to move. In these cases, the options of people of color are artificially and unnecessarily limited out of a desire to achieve an approved level of integration.

Affirmatively Furthering Community Development

More than thirty years ago, geographer Ceri Peach made a distinction between "good segregation" and "bad segregation." More recently Peter Marcuse has differentiated between what he calls ghettos and ethnic enclaves.[122] Peach and Marcuse make essentially the same basic point, that not all cases of racial/ethnic clustering are to be condemned or seen as evidence of oppression. What makes segregation objectionable is not the spatial concentration of a particular ethnic group, but rather the forms of oppression and structural inequalities that produce it or are attendant to it.[123] Examples of healthy and functional ethnic enclaves are easy to identify. Similarly, disempowered ethnic ghettos are just as clearly delineated by the weight of social problems and physical decline they exhibit. Furthermore, and somewhat obviously, the acknowledgment of the benefits of clustering does not require a belief that all clustering is voluntary.[124]

It is not the concentration of minorities that distinguishes enclaves and ghettos, but rather the power inequalities, economic deprivation, stigma, and structural disadvantage. Iris Marion Young, after acknowledging the conditions of segregated ghettos, then asks, "What norms and ideals ought to guide policies and actions aiming to reverse these harms?"[125] Her answer is not integration that imposes a spatial remedy with an "ideal" population mix in the "proper proportions."[126] Instead she calls for "an alternative ideal of social and political inclusion" that she calls "differentiated solidarity." Differentiated solidarity, she argues, "affirms the freedom of association that may entail residential clustering and civic differentiation" while simultaneously establishing the basis for principles of justice across groups.[127] Integration, she argues, tends wrongly to focus on patterns of group clustering while ignoring more central issues of privilege and disadvantage.[128] Thus, Young defends "group differentiation [as] both an inevitable and desirable aspect of modern social processes."[129]

Tommie Shelby distinguishes between segregation (the spatial pattern of racial clustering) and "the diverse social factors that contribute to bringing it about or maintaining it—discrimination, institutional racism, private residential choices, street crime, urban renewal policies, economic inequality, and so on."[130] Efforts to address the racial injustices inherent in segregation should therefore address the various factors that produce segregation. Integration, Shelby concludes, is not a requirement of a corrective response to racially unjust segregation.

In essence, the choice between fair housing integration and community development, to the extent that it must be made, is a choice between the values of diversity and equity. In Susan Fainstein's *The Just City*, she argues that of the two values, diversity is the lesser. She concludes that "Iris Marion Young's formulation of relatively homogeneous neighborhoods with porous boundaries" is therefore preferable to efforts to manage settlement patterns to achieve the "proper proportions."[131]

Political scientist David Imbroscio employs a somewhat similar argument critiquing integrationist efforts.[132] Like Young, Imbroscio condemns the injustices associated with race and class segregation, and he, too, sees the solution in something other than integration.[133] Imbroscio assigns integrationist urges to a larger "politics of liberal expansionism."[134] Liberal expansionism, in Imbroscio's eyes, "combines a liberal political philosophy (in the contemporary, American political sense of 'liberal') with the idea that the social and economic problems of America's central cities can only be solved by . . . 'crossing the city line'" and incorporating metropolitan area-wide solutions.[135] Thus liberal expansionism is essentially the same as what others refer to as new regionalism.[136]

Subordinating Protected Class Interests

The pursuit of integration as idealized by fair housers and regionalists tends to leave the dominant group relatively undisturbed. Integration programs privilege the white position and reproduce white domination.[137] Integration efforts that limit the number of blacks in a neighborhood in order to avoid "tipping" tacitly accept and accommodate white racism but also have the perverse effect of limiting choices for disadvantaged groups. In effect, this reproduces housing market processes of discrimination and segregation.

Sociologist Mary Patillo points out that integration entails both a "celebration of Whiteness" and presents white communities as the normative model for success. This is a point, she notes, that Derrick Bell makes in the context of education integration and the *Brown* decision.[138] As she further argues, "Integration dwells on and is motivated by the relatively problematic nature of Black people and Black spaces, and posits proximity to Whiteness as the solution."[139]

Furthermore, the desire for residential clustering rarely reflects a wholly separatist orientation, and most disadvantaged groups actively seek integration into labor markets and political institutions regardless of residential pattern.[140] "Social group distinction," writes Iris Marion Young, "is not wrong." Further, what we should be seeking, according to Young, rather than a mechanistically applied spatial quota designating approved mixes of majority and minority groups, is "to balance values of inclusion and respect with more particularist and local self-affirmation and expression."[141]

As a result, Young argues for "movements of resources rather than that of people."[142] She claims that policy that "aims to move resources to people addresses directly the inequalities of material privilege and disadvantage [that] processes of segregation produce" and thus is a more direct and effective means of achieving racial equity.[143] In a like manner, Imbroscio argues for "the normative superiority of addressing urban problems where they currently exist rather than using . . . measures to foster a spatially oriented solution."[144]

Young and Imbroscio echo, in a more generalized manner, the concerns of housing advocates who suggest that the focus of the fair housing movement on housing integration ignores the more pressing issue of housing inequality and the poor housing conditions faced by lower-income people of color. The privileging of integration rejects the validity of people's desire to live and associate with others for whom they feel particular affinity. However, the privileging of integration also leaves intact fundamental inequalities. As Patillo writes, "integration is a strategy to achieve equality, not the substance of equality itself."[145] The solution to the problems of "lack of fairness, opportunity, justice, equality, and recognition of shared humanity" that lie at the bottom of American race relations, she argues, "cannot be realized through the co-location of Black and White bodies alone, but must include the real stuff of equality."[146]

Social and Cultural Benefits of Neighborhoods

Virtually all social observers acknowledge that at least some of the social and racial "sorting" that characterizes American housing markets is due to "self-segregation" or the desire to live with others who share one's sociocultural-racial identification. Place identification can be very strong for some families, and the desire to remain within a neighborhood and to see that neighborhood improved is as legitimate an aspiration as is the desire to move away to a different and "better" neighborhood. Furthermore, the impulse to self-segregate can reflect the "need of individuals to develop psychologically healthy and mature racial identities."[147] Racial clustering, "when its purpose is mutual aid and culture-building among those who have affinity with one another," is defensible, according to Young, "as long as the process of clustering does not exclude."[148] Shelby argues that black self-segregation is fundamentally different from what is seen in exclusive white neighborhoods. Rather than an attempt to hoard resources and deprive nonblacks access to the advantages of black neighborhoods, he writes, "black solidarity is . . . instead a component of an ethic of resistance to injustice."[149]

Lower-income people tend to rely on informal safety nets to obtain needed services such as child care and transportation.[150] Such informal support networks are built up over time and depend on close, interpersonal relationships between neighbors, friends, and family members. Lower-income households rely on these informal networks for a range of goods and services that they are unable to purchase on the market. This informality is a central feature of their lives and can extend to basic needs such as housing and employment as well as to supportive services. Access to this type of social capital requires residential proximity and thus can influence the housing and neighborhood decisions of lower-income households. Kinship ties and social networks reduce the mobility of families, especially among low-income households.[151]

Integrationists frequently argue that the bridging social capital that would be available to blacks in integrated neighborhoods is more useful for economic advancement than the bonding social capital of informal support networks. But as Shelby points out, given white resistance to integration there is little guarantee that bridging would actually occur.

> The social capital argument also makes integration a particularly distasteful remedy for ghetto poverty because of its racial dimensions. Such an approach to corrective justice would reinforce the symbolic power that whites hold over blacks by encouraging whites to see their relationships with blacks not as intrinsically valuable forms of interracial community but as an avenue for blacks to share in (not abolish) white privilege. Because such relationships cannot be coerced but must be entered into voluntarily, whites are free to dole out this dubious privilege to whomever they see fit and, crucially, to withhold it at their discretion. This puts blacks in an untenable supplicant position.[152]

Further, some neighborhoods are more accepting of informal economic activity than others, making them locations where income generation is easier for those participating in informal economies.[153] Indeed, neighborhoods, as noted above, are endowed with a set of physical, social, and economic characteristics. Neighborhoods contain differing arrays of jobs and job opportunities, shopping options, and market-based services such as Laundromats. They also vary by the type of public service infrastructures that exists, including public transportation facilities and social service agencies. As a result, studies have documented the fact that lower-income families frequently put emphasis on improving their existing communities rather than favoring a dispersal strategy in which they are forced or given an option to move to another community.

As with the social and cultural benefits of neighborhoods, the contention that some neighborhoods provide an array of services attractive to lower-income people is not an argument against integration, but rather an argument for choice and specifically for the choice of moving to or remaining in a neighborhood that integrationists find problematic on the basis of racial mix.

Political Power

It has long been observed that one of the outcomes of residential clustering is the development of electoral power among minority groups. The main argument is that residential clustering allows for the creation of so-called "majority minority" districts in which communities of color are more easily able to elect representatives from their own community and thereby build a tradition of political leadership. This basic dynamic was of course a fundamental element in the black power and community control arguments of the 1960s, but it is also a truism of local politics.[154] In contrast, patterns of perfect integration would establish minority groups as a permanent electoral minority in all political jurisdictions and subdivisions.

Elizabeth Anderson, in *The Imperative of Integration*, relegates this notion to the status of "conventional wisdom" and ultimately dismisses its importance, suggesting somewhat paradoxically that only when minority groups are spread throughout all districts within a given polity will their interests be truly considered by the political elite. The bulk of political thought, however, suggests otherwise. Minority status within broader political arenas dominated by whites is more likely to create the conditions for ongoing political marginalization.[155] Spatial clustering has led to a rise in the number of minority representatives and increased minority political participation.[156] Aggressive desegregation efforts, were they to truly reduce concentrations of ethnic settlements, would necessarily reduce the political power of minority groups.[157]

Young, too, argues that "policy change to undermine structural inequality is more likely to occur if subordinated groups are politically mobilized."[158] This is more likely to happen where minority groups are able to build political leadership through successful electoral strategies. Integration consigns minority groups to perpetual minority status, making political development more difficult. Finally, spatial racial clustering has also led to the creation and emergence of political leadership and power within communities of color. This is an effect that even Anderson acknowledges, noting that minority districts have "arguably provided the foundation for a black political leadership which . . . has fostered a racially integrated, coalitional style of politics."[159]

In the end, political empowerment of disadvantaged groups is a precondition for effective integration in any case. Groups must operate from positions of equality if integration is going to be anything other than tokenism.[160] Contact theory suggests in any case that integration will improve race relations only under conditions of equality.

Those Who Do Not Move

Integration programs offer no solution to the conditions of segregated communities. Implied in the integration model is the idea that segregated communities will simply wither away as their inhabitants move to other places. As we have seen, however, the programs are unable to generate the degree of mobility that would be necessary for such a sea change in settlement patterns. What is left is the very selective out-migration of a few households with no discernible impact on the rest of the community.[161] To the extent that those households that move out are carefully picked in order to maximize the potential for their success (an admitted element of the Gautreaux mobility program, for example), then the communities left behind are even more concentrated in poverty and disadvantage.

Were real deconcentration to occur and were integrationists able to produce real change in the targeted core neighborhoods, the likely outcome would be rapid neighborhood gentrification and the spillover displacement of disadvantaged groups. Again, the one deconcentration effort that has occurred at a significant scale, the dismantling of America's public housing system, is frequently associated with gentrification-style turnover. The possibility that dispersal and redevelopment are simply preludes to gentrification has been an ongoing concern for several decades now. John Calmore, for example, wondered in 1980 whether dispersal efforts were not a prelude to gentrification. Indeed, many observers have noted how income-mixing efforts in previously low-income neighborhoods have been a form of Trojan horse penetration of housing markets ripe for revalorization.[162] Integrationists have not been particularly guarded in their support for such wholesale change and the community disruption it brings. Indeed, this kind of change is the point, according to some.[163] Though gentrification is seen as a problem by affordable housing advocates because of its deleterious impacts on housing affordability, it is seen as a positive outcome by fair housers because it changes the income (and often racial) dynamics within low-income, segregated communities.[164]

Regardless of their impact on segregated communities, one must acknowledge that integration programs that force mobility have done an exceedingly poor job of achieving integration in white middle-class neighborhoods. Indeed, the more common outcome for low-income people of color participating in mobility programs, voluntary and involuntary, has been reconcentration or no change.[165] A majority of Gautreaux and MTO participants could not even successfully use their voucher subsidies and thus moved nowhere. Among those who did move, a portion have returned to neighborhoods more like the one they left than the first one they moved to. Families involuntarily displaced through HOPE VI overwhelmingly moved to other segregated, low-income communities. Should isolated families make it out of the core neighborhoods and into predominantly white neighborhoods, they frequently face social isolation. Gautreaux advocates celebrate the fact that program participants faced overt harassment only in the early years of the program, and note the disappearance of active hostility after a period of time. However, the greater concern for low-income families who moved into "opportunity" neighborhoods is the loss and ongoing absence of an informal network of support that allows them to make ends meet.[166]

This is not to say that affordable housing built in suburban areas is a failure. Affordable housing in the suburbs has been shown to successfully provide stable, clean, and affordable housing to disadvantaged households. It has been shown, furthermore, to operate in ways that do not damage local property values, or disrupt "quality of life," two concerns that opponents of affordable housing frequently verbalize. For those families who do find their way out from central cities, affordable housing in the suburbs can work very well.[167] Such housing fills an important need, and it works. For this reason it should be pursued aggressively. It does not, however, desegregate central neighborhoods. And for that reason it should not be a substitute for continued affordable housing efforts in the core.

"The Stuff of Equality"

The counterargument to integration as a policy objective is not an apology for segregation. Critiques of dispersal, mixed-income housing schemes, and deconcentration do not constitute a tacit acceptance of segregation or spatial inequalities. The choice between committing to the integrationist ideal on the one hand or surrendering in the fight against segregation on the other is a false one.

The community development movement, at its basis, expresses an ideal different from that of integration. It suggests that a fundamental objective in the pursuit of racial justice is the desire to achieve "the real stuff of equality," as Patillo calls it. This means greater political and economic power for people of color, the kind of power that produces and maintains good schools and safe communities wherever they are located, and provides economic security to residents. It also means the pursuit of decent living conditions independent of the number of white people living nearby.

The systematic forms of oppression visited upon black communities are rendered invisible when the focus is on how many people of color are clustered together. An emphasis on neighborhood demographics produces integrationist solutions that, as will be detailed in the next chapter, focus on managing and restricting the entry and exit of people into and out of neighborhoods to maintain acceptable color/ethnicity mixes. What is acceptable, furthermore, has always been determined by what the white majority will tolerate. Success in such endeavors would have the effect of ensuring black minorities in *all* communities and enshrine the tipping point as a guiding principle of urban policy. Thus do integration initiatives ratify white racism.

As a result, Iris Marion Young argues that housing should not be distributed "according to some integrated patterned outcome decided by allocators."[168] The community development position, it should be pointed out, does not mean a retreat from public-sector responsibilities in monitoring and regulating housing-market processes and outcomes. Responsibilities related to enforcing antidiscrimination in the private sector and reducing exclusionary and discriminatory behavior within the public sector remain central to ensuring equitable patterns of regional development.

The fair housing / community development tension has been playing out since the 1940s. It has been present in varying degrees ever since the federal government became involved in building affordable housing for lower-income households. The next chapter looks at the early years of this debate and how it was perceived by African American leaders in the 1940s and '50s, and how the debate evolved through the civil rights era.

THE "HOLLOW PROSPECT" OF INTEGRATION

The integration and community development debate is as old as federally subsidized housing for lower-income families. In the United States a concerted effort to provide subsidized housing for the poor was initiated with the public housing program in 1937, and the first units began to be occupied as the 1930s came to a close. Before that program was ten years old there was debate within the black community about where such housing should be built and whether its primary effect was to provide much-needed housing for the community or to perpetuate patterns of residential segregation.

Both fair housing activism and community development evolved from racial activism of the mid-twentieth century. In fact, the evolution of this debate unfolds in the overlapping threads of three movements: the civil right campaign led by blacks demanding equality of opportunity and integration in all phases of life, the open housing struggle concerned with breaking down barriers to residential integration, and the black nationalist movement that stressed self-sufficiency and community control for the black community. As each of these movements matured and gained its greatest influence in the mid-twentieth century, the spatial debate in affordable housing crystallized. In most respects, the open housing movement was an echo of the larger civil rights effort, asserting the larger movement's integrationist objectives within the context of both housing markets and government housing strategies. Black nationalism contested the integration ideal of the civil rights movement, arguing for black self-sufficiency and, in its more radical forms, a degree of separatism and independence from white society.

In terms of housing strategies this meant achieving goals of adequate and afford-able housing within the black community rather than relying on the strategies of dispersal and integration. It also meant community control of housing as an economic asset that would help enhance the economic capacity of the black community.

The mid-twentieth century American ghetto was the central fact around which these opposing positions were formed. For integrationists, the ghetto represented the constraints placed on blacks by the larger white society. The ghetto was a physical manifestation of racial oppression in the country and the chief means by which racial inequality was maintained and recreated. As such, the ghetto was an institution to be done away with. Equal rights and civil rights demanded the dismantling of the ghetto and the entry of blacks as equal actors into all communities. Black nationalists also, of course, recognized the racial oppression that was behind the inferior public and private services that char-acterized the ghetto, and the blatant and violent forms of discrimination that created and reproduced the poverty and marginalization of the ghetto. Nev-ertheless, they also saw the ghetto as the indispensable home to black cultural life and community, and thus defined the objectives of racial justice in terms of improving housing and economic conditions there, while enhancing self-sufficiency, building political and economic power, and preserving the identity of the community.

Early Voices

As long as there has been federal policy related to low-income housing, there has been a debate within the black community about what such policy would mean for it. As long as there have been large-scale efforts, federal or otherwise, aimed at redeveloping the nation's urban areas, blacks have been concerned about what such efforts would do to their communities. The issue of race has dominated both housing policy and urban redevelopment policy from the outset. Large-scale efforts on the part of the federal government to influence the housing mar-ket and to provide housing assistance to the poor began in earnest during the New Deal era of the 1930s. The New Deal programs of support for homeown-ership, notably the FHA and VA programs that introduced federal backing for mortgages and led to a vast expansion of homeownership during the 1930s to the 1950s, explicitly incorporated racially discriminatory guidelines that system-atically disadvantaged black communities.[1] The New Deal program of support for lower-income rental housing, the public housing program, also incorporated explicitly racial guidelines that ensured segregation.[2] Beyond the program guide-lines, however, the issue of race dominated the way in which the public conceived

of the programs, the ways in which intended beneficiaries experienced the programs, and the ways in which the programs affected American cities during the
mid-century period.

Within the black community the questions regarding housing and redevelopment have focused on whether such programs should be encouraged as a source
of much-needed investment from a government that more typically ignores conditions within black neighborhoods, or regarded as further efforts to maintain
systems of segregation, discrimination, and oppression. Similarly, was urban
renewal to be seen as a way of breaking down segregation and expanding neighborhood choices for blacks, or was it an attempt to displace blacks from valuable
inner-city areas? Descriptions of mid-century black urban politics reveal these
debates within the black community.[3]

In Chicago, for example, there were clear lines between factions on these issues.
Robert Weaver, who would go on in 1965 to become the first African American
to hold a cabinet-level position in the federal government as the first secretary
of HUD, was a prominent member of what Preston Smith III calls a black policy
elite that pushed the integrationist agenda. This group included other federal
housing officials such as George Nesbitt and William Hill. The integrationists
in Chicago felt that they were responding to what they regarded as the "vested
interests of the ghetto defense faction."[4] The "ghetto defense faction," according
to the integrationists, included local black politicians who owed their position
to the unified voting bloc of blacks that resulted from residential segregation of
the population, black business leaders who feared integration because it would
mean greater competition and loss of business, and "the lower-income and tenant masses" whose shortsighted perspective (in the eyes of the integrationists) led
them to favor black concentration.

On the issue of redevelopment, there was little expectation among members
of either side of this debate that renewal efforts would provide housing needed by
working-class and lower-income blacks. In fact, the predominant pattern at that
time was for urban renewal and redevelopment to reduce the amount of housing
available to such groups. Thus, among black leaders, redevelopment was assessed
more for what it would mean for residential patterns. Non-integrationists, those
labeled the "ghetto defense faction" by Weaver and his allies, were concerned that
renewal would mean displacement and removal of the black community from
the urban core. These leaders felt the need to mobilize the community "to con-
solidate [its] position near the heart of American cities."[5] Indeed, even a strong
integrationist like Weaver in 1948 called redevelopment in Chicago a triple threat
to the black community in that it could displace blacks, break up strong but
racially identified neighborhoods, and further restrict the living space available
to blacks in northern cities.[6] In the end, however, Weaver was influenced more by

the "opportunity" that he felt redevelopment provided, thinking that it would, in the end, open up new settlement areas for blacks and help to relieve the spatial pressure of the ghetto.

At the time, the only form of subsidized low-income housing was the federal public housing program, and so it was in the context of this program that debates about the impact of subsidized housing and about where it should be placed began. By the 1950s, local public housing authorities in Chicago and elsewhere were building much public housing in predominantly minority neighborhoods as part of slum clearance efforts. As the program was becoming more racially identified through the 1950s in cities across the country, there was opposition to its placement in white areas or in greenfield locations on the periphery of cities.[7] James Q. Wilson's study of black political leadership in Chicago in the late 1950s captures the dilemma faced by the black community leaders in these years who recognized the need for better housing among its residents, but also feared the long-term impact of concentrating such housing within the community. Chicago public housing was heavily clustered in black neighborhoods.[8] Some in the black political establishment objected to this (as well as to what they felt were sterile and unattractive designs that contained those units within mostly high-rise buildings) even as housing needs were so great. "Such a choice—to oppose further public housing and to work instead for desegregation that would permit it to be scattered—is a hard one," wrote Wilson, "and most Negro leaders are not prepared to make it. Most hope that both ends can be served simultaneously, but if they cannot, then one must take what one can get."[9]

Thus, leaders in the black community "found it difficult to reject much-needed low-income housing" even when it was placed within the ghetto.[10] Though Chicago is the paradigmatic example of how local politics concentrated public housing in black neighborhoods, the pattern was repeated in most U.S. cities.[11] Another of James Q. Wilson's Chicago sources said, "If I had to make a choice, and I don't always think you do, between more public housing or putting it in integrated areas, I would favor putting up more housing. . . . There is a real need."[12] Wilson quotes a black newspaper editor: "We think that public housing is wrong the way it's being handled. . . . But if we come out against it hard, then they'll just not build it anywhere, and that would be worse. So what do we do? We just mumble about it."[13]

The tension between further housing in black neighborhoods or dispersal strategies hinged mostly on the issue of immediate needs versus devotion to a longer-term vision of integrated residential patterns. The idea that building housing in the black community could be more than simply a means of meeting desperate needs, that it in fact might be part of a positive strategy of building community capacity, of protecting and maintaining the unity and strength of the community, would not emerge fully and strongly until the 1960s.

Open Housing, Fair Housing

The fair housing movement, the political struggle to combat racial discrimination in housing and end blatant practices of residential segregation, began in the 1940s. It was in its earliest stages a highly decentralized movement of activists working at the local level in communities across the nation.[14] Fair housing emerged at a time when overt racial discrimination was a routine part of the housing market, when racially defined ghettos were a central feature of most American cities, and when the suburbs were homogeneously white and middle class. The movement reflected these three realities. The goals of the movement were often expressed in terms of phrases like "open housing," which was meant to describe a situation in which skin color, ethnicity, or religion would not preclude anyone who had the desire and the resources to do so from entering any community. "Open housing," furthermore, referred to the goal of breaking down the exclusionary barriers that communities erected in order to maintain racial and class homogeneity. From the 1940s into the 1960s, such barriers were widespread, including restrictive zoning and land-use regulations, and the common practices of real estate professionals in maintaining the color lines in American communities.[15]

Thus, at the outset the effort was known as the "open housing" movement.[16] The strategy was twofold: the elimination of discrimination in housing markets that kept African Americans largely clustered in racially identified neighborhoods, and the accessibility of black families to neighborhoods that were predominantly white, neighborhoods that through discrimination had been essentially off-limits. These two elements, nondiscrimination and integration, were for almost two decades assumed to be equivalent. The diagnosis of racially dual housing markets that preoccupied the movement throughout its early history was that they were created and maintained by discrimination. The end of that discrimination, it was assumed, would produce integrated living patterns. Throughout the 1950s there was not a sense that these two objectives were independent of each other or that they may, under some circumstances, conflict. In fact, it can be said that from the outset the movement had a discrimination focus with integrationist assumptions. The earliest policy prescriptions advanced by national and local activists were to simply ban discrimination. There was faith that this would lead to integration.

The open housing movement achieved its first successes at the local level. According to a historian of the movement, Juliet Saltman, the most active and advanced early efforts took place in New York City. New York is, in fact, where the campaign experienced its first major success when, in 1951, the New York City Council passed an ordinance banning discrimination in city-assisted housing. New York City was, at the time, building a large number of subsidized units under its own auspices, and thus the ban was not mere window dressing, but applied to the largest subsidized housing initiative in the nation. Early open housing advocates wanted to make federal funding of local governments contingent upon local commitment to open housing. In the 1950s they proposed to withhold federal funds and assistance from local governments that practiced or supported racial segregation in housing and public facilities.[17] Both these ideas would eventually become part of federal policy, illustrating a common dynamic in fair housing policy in which practices first emerge at the local level and become national policy only after years of operation in a more decentralized manner.[18]

An early success of the movement was its victory convincing the developer of Stuyvesant Town, a large residential development on Manhattan's east side, to adopt a nondiscriminatory rental policy, allowing blacks to compete for all the units. In the end, blacks did not exactly embrace that particular opportunity, foreshadowing a problem that the integrationist agenda would face many times as the decades wore on. As historian Nicholas von Hoffman reports, "tenant leaders had assumed 'that blacks would welcome the chance to step up into a white world,' but they later realized that 'evidence contradicted the myth.'"[19]

Over time, the focus on "open communities" took on a third dimension as the discourse surrounding black ghettos began to stress social pathology, and the ghetto was depicted as the location where the negative outcomes of enforced racial oppression were manifest and spatially concentrated. By the end of the 1950s and more so during the 1960s, the black ghetto became something that required a solution. Indeed, the open housing movement at this time made reference to "the establishment of a community-wide pattern of open occupancy *as the only answer to the ghetto*" (emphasis added).[20] Activists directly attributed the deplorable living conditions within the ghetto to discrimination.[21] It was the substandard housing, inferior or nonexistent public services, and employment discrimination and inequality within the American ghetto that most directly mobilized the racial justice efforts of this era.

The movement created a national organization in 1950 when the National Committee against Discrimination in Housing (NCDH) formed. It was an umbrella organization of fifteen groups that had been working on the issues of housing discrimination and segregation, including the American Civil Liberties Union (ACLU), the National Association for the Advancement of Colored

People (NAACP), and the Anti-Defamation League. Though NCDH provided a national infrastructure for open housing advocacy, the movement remained a highly decentralized effort for most of the 1950s and 1960s.[22] Indeed, by the time a federal fair housing bill (the Fair Housing Act) was passed by Congress in 1968, there were 153 fair housing laws across the nation at the state and local levels. Even in the first three months *after* the 1968 Fair Housing Act, 100 more local laws were passed.[23]

The earliest accomplishments of the open housing movement locally were in influencing the actions of public-sector housing agencies. Despite the legislative successes at the local level in the 1950s, there remained during this time widespread political support for allowing property owners to dispose (by sale or rent) of their properties as they deemed fit, including allowing for the intentional differential treatment of people according to skin color, religion, and other characteristics. In the face of these entrenched beliefs, those in the open housing movement redirected their efforts to seek to address discrimination in publicly assisted housing. NCDH, for example, claimed during this period that federal housing programs, chiefly public housing and the FHA mortgage insurance programs, were reinforcing segregation. President John F. Kennedy's Executive Order 11063, issued in 1962, the first major federal policy proclamation in the fight against racial discrimination in housing, was a response to the advocacy efforts of NCDH.[24]

The momentum for targeting white communities and the private housing market picked up during the second phase of the open housing movement, which Saltman places between 1956 and 1964. In this period NCDH successfully pressed for passage of city and state laws banning discrimination in both publicly assisted and private housing. In 1956 only three states and fourteen cities had laws prohibiting discrimination in housing, though other cities had narrower laws focused on assisted housing or redevelopment areas. As the 1950s wore on, NCDH began to focus on the need to pry open previously white-only neighborhoods in order to provide greater housing choice to minorities, to loosen the grip of the ghetto on black families, and to create more integrated living patterns.

The focus on open housing during this period also began to implicate suburban communities in the larger metropolitan-wide pattern of segregation that characterized most regions. In the late 1950s, for example, the Detroit NAACP organized protests against racial segregation in the region's suburban communities. In October 1959, NCDH's newsletter, *Trends*, called for county-level action and the reduction of barriers to black residency in the suburbs.

The movement remained largely a local one as the 1960s started, with the continued formation of grassroots organizations across the country promoting integration and open occupancy.[25] The question of open housing, however, was pulled into a bigger debate within the black community, a growing schism between the integrationist goals of the mainstream civil rights movement and the community-control orientation of black nationalism.

Civil Rights and Black Nationalism

The U.S. civil rights movement first began to emerge in the 1940s. Of course, efforts to achieve greater racial equality date back many years before that. W. E. B. Du Bois organized the Niagara Movement in 1905 as a reaction to the more accommodationist strategies of some black leaders at the turn of the century. The NAACP formed in 1909 and began its efforts to achieve justice and integration for blacks in all aspects of American life. In 1916 Marcus Garvey began to spread his message of racial unity and black pride, introducing in the process a model of racial equality that did not depend on integrationist aspirations.

The 1930s and '40s saw an increasing rate of direct action on behalf of civil rights and labor concerns.[26] Sit-ins and boycotts, tactics that would become a staple of the movement twenty years later, were first pursued during the '30s and '40s.[27] The organizational capacity of black civil rights activism was also growing during this period, laying the foundation for the mass movement that was to come. The NAACP initiated its legal strategy aimed at dismantling the web of laws and customs that made up the bulwark of segregation in the mid-1930s, and in April 1942 activists in Chicago formed the Committee of Racial Equality (CORE) to fight racial discrimination using nonviolent tactics.[28]

Concrete examples of progress, however, were few. Episodes of racial violence and the use of firebombs, mob intimidation, bricks, and gunshots to enforce the strict racial boundaries of segregation were common at the time.[29] The year 1943 alone saw over 225 incidents of racial violence across the country, including a three-day battle between whites and blacks in Detroit, and a one-day riot in Harlem, again triggered by the arrest of a young black man by local police.[30] Entering the 1950s, then, blacks in American cities of the North and the South could recite a familiar litany of poor housing conditions, job discrimination, and segregated public facilities as central realities of life. Throughout the 1950s, black civil rights activists pursued their agenda and continued to build their organizational capacity. Successful bus boycotts in Baton Rouge and Montgomery drew media attention, as did the overblown violence of the southern white reaction. By the early 1960s there were four significant organizations pursuing civil rights for blacks across the country—the NAACP, CORE, the Southern Christian Leadership Conference (SCLC), and the Student Nonviolent Coordinating Committee (SNCC).

Black Nationalism

Another strain of black thought related to racial inequality was developing during the 1940s and '50s. Activists driven by core ideas of self-sufficiency and self-determination and the development and empowerment of the black community were operating largely within the black neighborhoods of northern cities. As historian Peniel Joseph recounts, "In the 1950s, black nationalists stalked Harlem like itinerant Baptist preachers in search of wayward flocks."[31] None gained the notoriety or following equal to that of the Nation of Islam.

NOI leaders stressed dignity, strict personal behavioral guidelines, and modeled a type of racial identity and pride that was directed not at integrating into the larger white society but at developing a parallel black nation that would provide a different route to economic security and political self-determination. Malcolm X, first appointed as an officer of NOI in 1953, became the most widely recognized spokesman for NOI, and by extension the most widely recognized face of black nationalism. As Malcolm X's following grew, the ideas of black nationalism began to spread within the black community. By 1959, Malcolm X had been speaking widely on the themes of racial pride, dignity, separatism, and self-sufficiency. Malcolm X's rhetoric departed sharply from the integrationist ideas of the mainstream civil rights groups at the time. While perhaps jarring to whites, the important differences between the self-sufficiency orientation of nationalism and the integrationist perspective were old features of racial politics for black activists and had been debated internally for years. Malcolm X gave black nationalism a national and charismatic spokesman who would help launch the movement into the wider consciousness of the black community and onto the larger political agenda as well.

Malcolm X's views on racial justice exhibited a specific local geography, according to historian James Tyner. Malcolm X regarded integration as "a deception"— a kind of political sleight of hand that diverted attention from more fundamental questions of power. "Integration without a change in the underlying attitude of a racist society, for Malcolm X, was a hollow prospect."[32] Malcolm X felt that integration was "another tool of the oppressor, one that retained the basic inequalities in society."[33] As Tyner writes, for Malcolm X "an uncritical acceptance of integration as either a method or an objective served only to reify white supremacy."[34]

Yet Malcolm X fiercely attacked the injustices of segregation as well, identifying in it the core dynamics of racial exploitation and oppression. While a spokesman for NOI, Malcolm X talked about separatism, a physical separation of races that would form the basis of black self-determination. After his split from NOI, however, Malcolm X conceived of separatism as more of a political, economic, and cultural project than as one that required strict physical separation. Physical separation was not necessary, he felt, to achieve the goals of racial equality. What was important for social justice was "control of communal resources."[35] Signaling his emphasis on dignity and power over any particular geography of race, Malcolm X said in 1964, "We don't want to be integrationists. Nor do we want to be separationists. We want to be human beings."[36]

Tensions within the Civil Rights Movement

Black Nationalist and mainstream civil rights leaders were solidifying their respective positions on both the appropriate aims and tactics necessary to bring about racial justice. Not only did the nationalists differ with the integrationist aims of the mainstream civil rights movement; they tended to support more aggressive tactics, including self-defense and the possibility of militancy in defense of racial equality. The two movements reflected generational and regional divisions within the black community. The black nationalist movement was largely a northern and urban phenomenon, while the strength of the civil rights movement was in the South and was primarily rural. As the decade wore on, the generational split would become accentuated, with younger activists leaning toward the nationalist ideology while an older generation of activists maintained their integrationist objectives. But even as the decade began, the rift between these two arms of the growing black movement had become widely evident and public, so much so that when SNCC was created in 1960, where it stood on issues of goals (integration or separatism) and tactics (the continued nonviolence of the SCLC and the patient legal strategies of the NAACP on the one hand, or increasingly confrontational rhetoric and direct action on the other) were critical questions for its organizers.[37]

The unabated violence, however, of white backlash to peaceful civil rights protests, violence that was most often condoned if not abetted by local police authorities, began to eat away at the solid commitment to nonviolence among black activists. White aggression and the hesitancy of white political leaders to support civil rights contributed to a strategic crisis within the movement. Leaders of both CORE and SNCC began to question the fundamental strategy of the civil rights movement of working with the federal government and with white liberals.[38] The messages of black pride, self-sufficiency, and resistance to white violence voiced by Malcolm X and other black nationalist leaders began to resonate more widely as civil rights activism was met by continued white intransigence. By the end of 1964, CORE and SNCC had begun to reject not only nonviolence, but the very goal of integration as well.[39]

In fact, criticism of the mainstream civil rights movement and its leaders became more common among those contemplating a different and more nationalist approach to racial equality. Manning Marable notes that in 1963 "many black nationalists targeted [Martin Luther] King and other more conservative Negro leaders with personal and even physical abuse. In Harlem, black separatists tossed eggs at King after his appearance in a local church."[40] Intellectuals within the black nationalism movement considered the mainstream civil rights movements stalled and lacking answers for the violent intransigence of whites and the hesitancy of public officials.

After reconsidering its position on nonviolence in the year prior, CORE made a break with its white membership in 1964 and shifted to black control.[41] That was also the year when the Mississippi Freedom Party went to the Democratic National Convention to challenge the state's all-white delegation.[42] As Joseph notes, the denial of credentials to the Freedom Party delegates provided great clarity for many in the civil rights movement; it was for many a bitter illustration of the limits of working within national political institutions for racial change and equality.[43]

Black Power

In June 1966, Stokely Carmichael, the twenty-five-year-old chairman of SNCC, was jailed in Greenwood, Mississippi. Carmichael had been with other civil rights leaders on a march through the South. On June 16, he emerged from jail and made a speech introducing a new slogan that was to dominate the rest of civil rights era in the United States, saying to his fellow marchers that from that point forward, their objective was "black power." The phrase proved to be a lightning rod, generating immediate and intense reaction from both blacks and whites. Among many whites, and in the context of widespread urban unrest, the phrase generated fear. The white media seemed interested above all in what specific objectives were embodied by the phrase, and pressed leaders for explanations of what it meant.[44] Although some have criticized the phrase for being too vague, blacks, as Robert Allen notes, "grasped its essence easily."[45] For black activists, black power was a rallying cry, and a précis for the movement. At the CORE convention in the summer of 1966, the group adopted the phrase as its official slogan and announced its independence from the larger, mainstream civil rights movement. SNCC activists also adopted the phrase and, like CORE, considered the importance of a black-led movement with all that implied for working with white allies.

Black power suggested a strategy for civil rights that celebrated the black community while simultaneously identifying the bases of economic and political domination that produced and reproduced racial inequalities. The imprecision of the "black power" phrase allowed much to be read into it. It could accommodate interpretations that emphasized self-sufficiency, whether expressed as political power or economic self-determination; black power, however, was powerful also for its cultural message and content. It expressed racial pride and generated the development of cultural expressions, including a rapid expansion of literary, musical, and artistic output that celebrated blackness in a society that otherwise largely devalued it.[46]

For their part, the mainstream civil rights leaders were vocal in denouncing black separatists as impractical extremists, suggesting that their efforts were merely the outgrowth of impatience and the result of the slow pace of progress toward racial equality. The SCLC and the NAACP attempted to fight the radicalizing developments of black nationalism, the aggressive rhetoric of Malcolm X, Stokely Carmichael, and others who emerged around this time such as Huey Newton, H. Rap Brown, and Eldridge Cleaver. The civil rights mainstream did not embrace this vision but instead continued to insist that integration in both a broad and narrow sense was the only way of achieving economic and political parity. The mainstream questioned the idea of "separate but equal" that was implied in the black power vision. Civil rights leaders Roger Wilkins, Martin Luther King Jr., and Andrew Young publicly dissociated themselves from the black power movement, fearing in part that the increasing militancy of the movement was damaging the cause of racial inequality rather than serving it.[47]

In many ways, however, the appeal of black power had eclipsed the efforts of mainstream civil rights activism. Indeed, Robert Allen considered the mainstream civil rights movement to be "in its death throes" by the middle of 1966. On the West Coast, the Black Panthers were founded in the fall of 1966 in Oakland, California, adopting a message of black self-sufficiency as well as an image of militancy and armed self-defense.[48] The Panthers offered a ten-point platform of demands for racial justice and adopted an aggressive public persona, including armed patrols that would monitor police action in the black community. In Los Angeles, another nationalist group, US Organization, emerged in 1965 pursuing a strongly cultural version of black nationalism. The mood of the times and the enthusiasm of black activism were with the idea of black power. As Joseph notes, "as the decade proceeded, Black Power, rather than civil rights, framed public perception" of the black movement more generally.[49]

Before too long, the representatives of the older, mainstream wing of the black movement came to see power in the slogan, and acknowledged its importance in engendering and celebrating black pride. By the end of 1967, both Dr. King and the SCLC as an organization had embraced the themes of racial pride and cultural expression.

More urban riots, which had been taking place with regularity since 1964, occurred in 1967, including significant ones in Newark, Detroit, and Minneapolis.

In the following year the riot season, which had typically been from June to September, moved forward two months when the assassination of Martin Luther King triggered widespread rebellions across the country.[50]In May 1968, armed Black Panther members protested outside the California capitol building. The FBI ramped up efforts to disrupt the black power movement and to sow dissent within it.[51] Rivalries and violence within the movement were fomented and aggravated by the FBI, and armed confrontations occurred between activists and police, and between rival groups of activists.[52]

Armored Tanks and Think Tanks

The path of the civil rights movement, its internal debates as well as the emergence of black power as an organizing concept, was conditioned in part by the response of white citizens and leaders. The reaction of white residents of the nation's cities was to use the choice available to them in the housing market and remove themselves from large portions of the central city.[53] The response of many whites to black power and the increasing resistance of the black community to continued oppression was fairly typical of the actions of a dominant group in the face of increasingly violent actions of an oppressed minority: fear. The white population fell precipitously in most cities during the 1960s and well into the 1970s.[54] This development was a continuation of postwar trends of suburbanization that initially were about the growing housing opportunities of suburbs versus older city neighborhoods, but quickly came to be about the flight of whites away from growing concentrations of blacks in the urban core. During these years, then, the dominant geographic pattern of American metropolitan areas came to be a significant minority population in the center surrounded by largely lily-white suburbs.[55] This "doughnut" pattern was mirrored by the pattern of private and public investment as the movement of jobs also accelerated outward, and suburban shopping malls were built to service the changing geography of purchasing power within metro areas. The population within many U.S. cities declined as whites moved out. Schools, parks, transportation (typically roads and highways) investment in suburban areas replaced urban investment. It was this "white noose" around the central cities that became the subject of much political and social concern, and indeed the target of the fair housing movement, as the 1960s ended and as an uneasy peace settled upon the black ghetto.[56]

To public officials, the rapid development of black nationalism represented a more threatening set of objectives and strategies than those of the more traditional civil rights movement. The riots of the 1960s only added to the jitteriness of white politicians and white residents of urban areas. The policy response nationally and locally, then, was a mixture of restrictive criminal justice and military reactions to actual and potential urban unrest and racial violence on the one hand, and, on the other, programs aimed at ameliorating poverty based on the latest thinking of social scientists about the cause and spread of race-based inequality. It was, in a phrase, a mixture of armored tanks and think tanks.

The deployment of National Guard troops and the heavy martial presence brought down on American ghettos included the movement of troop carriers and tanks. Robert Allen notes that "after the 1967 rebellions, the development and production of antiriot and exotic weaponry became a booming industry."[57] The response to urban riots included the modification of armored personnel carriers for police use. The first deployment of National Guard troops in a northern city was in Rochester, New York, in 1964. Troops were also deployed in the 1965 Watts rebellion, and over the next three years in Cleveland, Omaha, Detroit, Minneapolis, Newark, Baltimore, Chicago, and Washington, DC. Local governments also resorted more often to control tactics such as curfews to manage the local population.

While military tanks patrolled some American cities during the period of unrest, think tanks were taking their aim at the ghetto as well. A range of policy experiments and philanthropic efforts were being developed at this time, incorporating new ideas for delivering services to the poor, increasing the participation of the recipients of government aid, and empowering poor residents of ghetto neighborhoods. Many of these ideas were incubated by philanthropies before finding their way into federal policy. The leading effort in addressing the conditions of ghetto poverty was undertaken by the Ford Foundation. Its Gray Areas program, begun in 1961, experimented with alternative ways of delivering services in poor, urban neighborhoods. The foundation also made program investments in economic development and community development initiatives throughout this period, innovating ideas related to job training, minority business development and ownership programs, and support for community development corporations. Ford had committed itself to the "task of achieving full domestic equality for all American Negroes."[58]

Community Control and Development

Provisions for "community control" contained in several of President Lyndon Johnson's "War on Poverty" programs aligned closely with calls for greater black community control over the economic and political resources that were shaping ghetto conditions. Theories of poverty had long contained the idea that a lack of "community competence" contributed to the development and reproduction of poverty.[59] Policy reformers both inside and outside the federal government adapted that idea by experimenting with notions of the participation of "indigenous" populations in programs designed to address the social and economic needs of ghetto residents. The Ford Foundation's Gray Areas program encouraged community participation while still retaining a very top-down flow of resources and program authority. But in the political ferment of the early 1960s, the idea of indigenous participation took hold and grew beyond its original and limited form. In part this was because it aligned well with the growing activism of minority groups in U.S. cities across the nation. When Johnson declared his War on Poverty in 1964, ideas of community action animated many of the programs. In the fall of 1964, the newly created Office of Economic Opportunity made its first round of Community Action Program grants, aggressively funding organizing efforts in the nation's poorest communities as an integral part of its antipoverty objectives. But community action meant different things to different actors. Social service providers tended to see it as a means of co-delivery of services, blurring the client-expert distinction in hopes of more effective service provision. Local politicians saw community action as a means of building consensus without necessarily sacrificing the top-down flow of program control and authority. But for activists, community action was an opportunity to organize political power within the community, to challenge the sclerotic and exploitive power relations that they felt had contributed to extreme conditions of deprivation within low-income and ghetto neighborhoods.[60]

Community Development Corporations

The creation of community development corporations (CDCs) was one concrete manifestation of these efforts to experiment with community action and community control.[61] In 1966, Congress passed an amendment to the Equal Opportunity Act called the Special Impact Program (SIP). SIP provided for a new type of organization, one that would combine the political goals of community control and local leadership on the one hand with the ownership and control of economic and financial assets on the other. The goal of these CDCs was to improve conditions within black communities. These activists enlisted images of community strength and self-determination in which blacks would own the economic assets of land and capital, replacing absentee and exploitive ownership with a system in which local ownership, consisting of local activists and accountable to local residents, would invest and reinvest within the community, channeling and recycling assets for the benefit of local residents.

The SIP program was the brainchild of New York senator Robert Kennedy, and it constituted Kennedy's alternative approach to Johnson's War on Poverty.[62] Indeed, by 1966, the central Johnson administration initiative related to community action, CAP, had sparked enormous controversy and political struggle in dozens of localities across the country, and was immediately reined in by program architects. Some of the early organizing efforts of CAP, including the funding of black street gangs to lead antipoverty efforts, generated significant political backlash and negative press coverage for the agency. By the end of 1965, support for community organizing had been de-emphasized in favor of a more mainstream service provision model and local government control.[63]

The community development corporations created by SIP would do more than simply implement federal antipoverty programs and do more than channel services to low-income people. They were meant to move beyond the clientelism of the War on Poverty to generate new economic power in disadvantaged neighborhoods, a power based on economic strength, controlled by community members and deployed on behalf of objectives aimed at further developing and consolidating the political and economic self-sufficiency of ghetto neighborhoods.

In the beginning, then, CDCs were equal part political and economic entities. Their existence and their agenda called forth a new vision of antipoverty work, one that would replace absentee landlordism that extracted profits from the community and provided subpar (if not outright dangerous and unhealthy) housing with responsive ownership and management that provided better-quality and more-affordable housing while keeping the wealth generated by landownership within the community. It meant new businesses oriented toward employing residents, providing job and career skills training. The CDCs were, according to John T. Baker, "efforts of leaders within low-income, predominantly black communities to create institutions through which residents of low-income communities could exercise control over important social, political, and economic resources both within and beyond the boundaries of their communities."[64] This formula came the closest of any federally sponsored antipoverty program to operationalizing the black power agenda. Stokely Carmichael's definition of the phrase emphasizes, above all, black control and leadership over the institutions affecting daily life. "Black people must lead and run their own organizations," he and Charles Hamilton wrote in *Black Power*.[65] But beyond the visibility of black leadership, they wrote, "the power must be that of a community, and emanate from there."[66] While much of Carmichael and Hamilton's book is devoted to political power, strategic political objectives, and the repositioning of black political activism within the structure of electoral politics, Carmichael and Hamilton also describe the colonial economic relationships between black communities and the larger white society. They accept Kenneth Clark's description of economic colonization of black communities, described in his book *Dark Ghetto*, that highlights the white ownership of assets within the black community and the flow of assets out of the community as whites "take their profits home."[67]

Within the black power movement there was a debate over economic strategy. While more radical elements within the movement advocated a rejection of both white economic domination and capitalist domination, other elements within the black movement of the 1960s focused more narrowly on the development of economic power within the black community and greater black participation in the economy. There were those who located black oppression in the exclusion of the black community from effective participation in the economy. For these people, greater levels of black economic ownership and activity, what came to be called "black capitalism," was the answer. CORE, for example, was an early adopter of the notion that the black community needed to build its own economic power, and the Ford Foundation was a significant funder of economic initiatives aimed at building black capitalism.[68] In 1968, the two organizations joined efforts to pursue redevelopment efforts in the Hough neighborhood of Cleveland.

At the same time, however, a significant part of the black power movement had adopted a more radical economic analysis, suggesting that black oppression was part of a larger and systematic framework of oppression constructed by the capitalist system itself.[69] Nishani Frazier argues that CDCs emerged as a middle ground between those who favored greater black participation in the existing economic system and the more radical and anticapitalist Marxist views that represented another strain of black power thought.[70]

First-Generation CDCs

The initial generation of CDCs emerged in the major urban areas of the North. The Bedford Stuyvesant Restoration Corporation (BSRC) in New York City was the first. BSRC was supported by the initial allocation of funds under the SIP program. While it did a significant amount of work to renew and improve physical conditions within the neighborhood, BSRC emphasized community organizing and the development of shared ownership models.[71] Other first-generation CDCs emerged where significant urban uprisings had occurred, including the Hough Area Development Corporation created in Cleveland after the six-day riot in that neighborhood in 1966, and CDCs in Newark in the aftermath of the 1967 riots there. As with the BSRC, these CDCs focused on business development and on improving physical conditions within their neighborhoods while simultaneously expressing the community organizing and political development objectives of the black power movement.[72]

These early CDCs worked in multiple arenas, pursuing economic development and job creation as well as housing development. The focus was on controlling capital and investment within the neighborhood in ways that would immediately improve the lives of residents, upgrade neighborhood conditions, and lay the foundation for growing economic self-sufficiency and build capacity for political self-determination. The CDC model aligned well with black power objectives, but it also embodied an indictment of top-down, government-led urban renewal initiatives, which were seen as ineffective in black communities and, in many cases, actually detrimental to local black interests and resident concerns.[73]

CDCs were also an attempt to take the initiative in improving living conditions within the ghetto away from government renewal agencies that were seen as impersonal and distant. As many critics have pointed out, both during the era of urban renewal and since, government renewal efforts were frequently regressive and tended to damage local communities, sometimes eradicating them, rather than supporting and strengthening them. The urban renewal program specifically worsened housing conditions within the ghetto and destroyed more low-cost housing than it ever produced. Its displacement effects on black households became in fact its defining characteristic. CDCs were the preferred method for many in the racial equality movement to address the substandard conditions of the ghetto.

The first generation of CDCs, thus, was located within the politics of black power and as a response to ghetto marginalization and the political and economic position of the black community. Housing was central to the CDC formula and was pursued because it produced three benefits of value to black activists. First it provided an important upgrading of physical conditions and living environment within the ghetto. Second, it provided a concrete benefit to ghetto residents in the form of affordable and safe housing, both of which were greatly lacking. Finally, it was a form of development that created economic assets that could be owned and controlled by and within the community rather than by absentee, external, and typically white investors.[74] Hill and Rabig call CDCs "one of the Black freedom movement's most enduring legacies."[75]

Kerner Commission

Facing a fourth consecutive summer of ghetto rioting in America's cities, President Johnson in 1967 appointed a National Commission on Civil Disorders. Known as the Kerner Commission after its chair, former Illinois governor Otto Kerner, the eleven-member body was charged with examining the scale of rioting that had been occurring since 1964 and determining the causes and possible means of preventing the disorders. The commission took note of the two prevailing ideas about how to deal with conditions in black communities: ghetto enrichment and residential integration. In general, while noting the value of enrichment activities, the report's conclusions leaned heavily toward integration as the best solution to riots and to the state of race relations in the country. The commission famously concluded that "nation is moving toward two societies, one black, one white—separate and unequal."[76] Thus, it favored what it called the only policy option that conceives of the possibility of a single, unified nation, and that was the integration option. In fact, the commission considered enrichment suitable only as a short-term strategy that could ameliorate conditions within the black ghetto while the business of integration was proceeding. Furthermore, the commission was aware of the effect that federally subsidized housing had had on patterns of segregation and called for "a new thrust" in federal housing programs "aimed at overcoming the prevailing patterns of racial segregation."[77]

In this respect, then, the commission's report was in line with the mainstream civil rights movement and mainstream thought within the fair housing movement. The commission's report was published in March 1968, less than one month before the assassination of Martin Luther King and subsequent passage of the Fair Housing Act.

Housing and Civil Rights

Throughout the period in which the civil rights movement had emerged and grown, the fair housing movement had largely tracked it. Open housing activists mirrored the larger civil rights movement in calling for an end to sanctioned discrimination in housing, the racially dual housing market, and for the end of government actions that supported or deepened patterns of racial segregation. The working assumption of the movement was that rectifying private and public acts of discrimination would lead to integrated living patterns—that is, the two objectives were not only compatible, but in practice the same. The assumption that blacks would choose integration when given greater housing choice was largely unquestioned, until the emergence of black nationalism and the black power movement.

Black Power and the Housing Question

Paradoxically, housing was both a central part of the civil rights movement and in some senses quite peripheral. The scourge of residential segregation was reflected, of course, in the development of the black ghetto and in the limited housing choices available to blacks, and these were among the most central animating concerns of blacks in the civil rights era. The Kerner Commission noted, for example, that inadequate and sometimes dangerous housing conditions were among the important grievances that gave rise to the ghetto rebellions of the decade. In another sense, violence over the maintenance of the color line in residential patterns, violence that was typically initiated by whites, had been common for decades.[78] The strict spatial containment of housing that was available to blacks, and the poor conditions of that housing, were the baseline and background reality that conditioned much of the interaction between whites and blacks in northern cities. Yet, at the same time, very little of the mainstream civil rights activism was aimed at housing issues. Sit-ins over access to public facilities were quite common, but direct action to assert housing rights were less so. Jill Quadagno reports that of 181 protests related to segregation by civil rights organizations between 1966 and 1970, only 12 focused on the issue of housing.[79] The housing issue to those preoccupied with equal access and the end to segregation was, it seems, a fairly simple matter. SCLC, in fact, stated in 1967 that the problem of housing discrimination would be easily solved by a presidential administrative order making it illegal.[80]

The most prominent example of where the larger civil rights movement and open housing came together was in Dr. King's open housing campaign in Chicago in 1966–1967. Called the Chicago Freedom Movement, it brought together local activists and organizers from SCLC, and focused both on improving conditions in the city's slums and on opening up the housing market in exclusionary communities.

Though civil rights in the arena of housing had for years been defined as the pursuit of integration and the opening up of new communities for black settlement, as the 1960s wore on the integrationist/nationalist debate began to be reflected within the open housing movement. The ideas of community control, black nationalism, black power, and black pride undermined the unquestioning pursuit of integration and suggested that upgrading housing within the black community was an equal if not preferred civil rights objective. Thus, as the civil rights debate transformed into a discussion about the legitimacy and self-sufficiency of the black community, the open housing movement similarly detoured from a focus on discrimination to questions of the status of the black ghetto.

The major fault line within the black community, as always, was on the question of where assisted housing should be placed. For integrationists, the priority for assisted housing was to see it move out of the ghetto and into predominantly white communities. For black power advocates, better housing was needed to preserve and enhance black communities. Insofar as the black power movement questioned the very desirability of integration, the black power position on the housing question was rich with conceptual and strategic questions about the contribution of good housing to community vitality and strength. For Malcolm X, Stokely Carmichael, and others, the cause of community decline was "exploiters [who] come into the ghetto from outside, bleed it dry, and leave it economically dependent on the larger society."[81] This includes those who own and manage critical assets such as the housing stock of the ghetto, which is allowed to be maintained at a substandard level, although residents are required to pay more than whites in other parts of the city. Black power advocates made a strong call for self-reliance and building economic power within the ghetto. This meant black ownership of housing assets and businesses.

Black power also critiqued the larger civil rights movement for its acceptance of "the middle-class values and institutions of this country . . . without fully realizing their racist nature."[82] "The goals of integrationists," wrote Stokely Carmichael and Charles Hamilton in *Black Power: The Politics of Liberation in America*, "are middle-class goals, articulated primarily by a small group of Negroes with middle-class aspiration or status. Their kind of integration has meant that a few blacks 'make it,' leaving the black community, sapping it of leadership potential and know-how."[83] This class dimension of the black power movement pushed it toward new forms of economic and political participation. Businesses that simply replaced white owners with black owners but continued to perpetuate the same economic oppression over ghetto residents were not the answer, according to black power leaders. Similarly, black politicians who did not challenge the basic nature of political power in the city were "not examples of black power," wrote Carmichael and Hamilton. "The power must be that of the community, and emanate from there."[84]

Black power leaders felt that integrationist goals were

> based on complete acceptance of the fact that in order to have a decent house or education, black people must move into a white neighborhood or send their children to a white school. This reinforces, among both black and white, the idea that "white" is automatically superior and "black" is by definition inferior. For this reason, "integration" is a subterfuge for the maintenance of white supremacy. . . . Such situations will not change until black people become equal in a way that means something, and integration ceases to be a one-way street.[85]

"Decent housing, fit for shelter of human beings," for example, was a prominent element of the Black Panthers' ten-point program for self-determination: "We believe that if the white landlords will not give decent housing to our black community, then the housing and the land should be made into cooperatives so that our community, with government aid, can build and make decent housing for its people."[86]

Open Housing

The latter half of the 1960s also saw the emergence of advocacy strategies by the leading fair housing group, the NCDH, that would become very significant in subsequent years. The first was a challenge to the siting practices of government housing programs. The second was to draw attention to the land-use and zoning practices of local governments that had the effect of limiting housing for blacks. An important part of the NCDH strategy was to challenge the siting pattern of federally and locally subsidized housing. Open housing advocates felt that through assisted housing, government was complicit in the creation and mainte-nance of segregated black ghettos. The solution was to change the geography of subsidized housing. Although this effort had its greatest impact in the 1970s, it was initiated during the 1960s.

This concern about the siting of federally subsidized housing, debated within the black community for two decades, became the subject of fair hous-ing action during this period. The NCDH and the NAACP filed a legal protest with state and federal officials in 1967 over a plan in Greenburgh, New York, just north of Yonkers, to use $8.7 million in urban renewal funds to build low-rent public housing for relocates in areas the plaintiffs argued would simply extend the ghetto.[87] The organizations called on federal and state offi-cials "to stop using public funds to entrench and extend segregation."[88] In Michigan, the state's Civil Rights Commission also worked to guide the sit-ing of public housing units so as to achieve more integration. The commis-sion worked with local governments across the state and with HUD to adopt siting guidelines "that would contribute to the desegregation of homes and schools."[89]

As the 1960s wore on, NCDH became more vocal about how, in its eyes, the federal government was contributing to racially segregated housing pat-terns. In 1965, NCDH sponsored a conference on "how to break up the ghetto," and in 1967 it published a report on "how the federal government builds ghet-tos." The report analyzed patterns of assisted housing placement and argued that the clustering of such units in black neighborhoods concentrated lower-income blacks in small geographic areas, reinforcing segregated residential pat-terns within metropolitan areas. The 1967 report called the U.S. government a "ghetto builder" for the way in which its programs were "undergirding a ghetto system" in the nation's cities.[90] The paper laid out seventeen specific charges against the government, focusing on its lack of will in pursuing desegregation.[91] In 1968 NCDH also began another effort that highlighted local regulatory bar-riers to affordable housing that had the effect of limiting black occupancy in suburban areas.[92] Those efforts were a continuation of the open housing move-ment's focus on expanding housing opportunities for blacks beyond the walls of the ghetto.

Yet during the 1960s, and as a result of the influence of black power, the open housing movement began to consider the question of the importance of upgrading housing options within the black community. David Goldberg argues that in Detroit, for example, the open housing movement aimed certainly to open up exclusionary white suburban areas of Royal Oak, Dearborn, and Grosse Pointe, but was also concerned with eliminating discrimination within the city. In 1964 and 1965, the local offices of CORE and the NAACP helped create more than fifty tenants' rights organizations to address the poor housing conditions faced by black residents of the city—as well as to build leadership among residents. Goldberg argues that this local activism was driven by the realization that the "legal and political struggles for open housing in the city's outskirts or suburbs did little to address the realities and problems faced daily by poor and working class Blacks" in Detroit.[93] In fact, Michael Danielson argues that blacks had been only moderately involved in the open housing movement and that some black leaders vehemently opposed it. City leaders, according to Danielson, harbored "doubts about any urban strategy that emphasizes suburbs."[94]

By the end of the '60s, the question of whether to work to improve ghetto areas was on the agenda within the housing rights movement as it had never been before. Movement historian Juliet Saltman notes that the NCDH newsletter, *Trends*, contained an average of thirty-seven references to integration each issue in 1956. By 1970, the average issue used the term only twice.[95] In its place was a growing emphasis on revitalizing the ghetto and discussion of the merits of multiple strategies. The debate consumed the movement for several years. As Saltman recounts,

> The Chicago national conference in 1971 revealed a deep concern with this issue, as indicated in the summary of the proceedings; . . . debate, which was never resolved, included the following points: 1. The desirability of dispersing the ghetto as opposed to extending equal opportunity in housing, 2. whether the focus should be on improving the quality of housing everywhere rather than anything else, 3. should the goals be a strengthening and rebuilding the ghetto as opposed to open housing, 4. to what degree do the goals, however defined, extend to groups other than negroes.[96]

Debates about revitalizing the ghetto were played out within the movement. The integrationists argued that the impacts of enrichment—at that point urban renewal and early War on Poverty programs—had been too limited. The NAACP and other open housing activists found the enrichment strategy "dangerously shortsighted."[97] Others within the movement were not so quick to dismiss enrichment. Open housing activists were more likely to conceptualize the debate as one between integration on the one hand and greater choice and access to housing on the other. While understanding the terms of this tradeoff, open housing advocates often found it difficult to make a choice. Saltman describes local open housing activism across the country and its ambivalence about this issue. She reports activists in Denver who worked "to provide every citizen of the metro area freedom of choice but in practice they encouraged everyone to make integrative moves."[98] In Los Angeles, she reported, "the immediate goal was to allow people out of the ghetto, but the long-term goal was related to freedom of choice," while in Seattle activists prioritized desegregation and at the same time the director indicated that the intent was "first, last, and always, a free and meaningful choice in housing for everyone everywhere." In these respects, then, open housing activists were attempting to pursue both objectives, and preferred to think of the two objectives as mostly complementary rather than conflicting. Still, there was awareness that this construction of events did not always hold. Activists in the Seattle open housing movement in 1969 "faced two alternatives: use existing staff to aggressively recruit and move middle class Negroes and minority families, thus accelerating the abandonment of the core city to the poor and powerless, or change our program strategy and direct it towards opening access to the existing supply of low and moderate priced housing while at the same time moving to increase the inadequate supplies in this category. We had little difficulty in opting for the second alternative."[99]

In Akron, Ohio, the fair housing movement evolved away from integration and toward housing choice as the main objective.[100]

The Clash of Integration and Community Development

The early history of the open housing movement, as well as the early history of the broader civil rights movement in the United States, was characterized by a widespread commitment to integration. Integration was initially considered the chief objective of civil rights (and fair housing) activism and in all cases consistent with the effort to eliminate racial discrimination in housing. Almost from the outset of government efforts in the area of assisted housing for the poor, however, a debate arose within the black community about the relative importance of pursuing integration on the one hand and pursuing improvements in housing conditions within the black community on the other.

This debate magnified during the 1960s with the emergence of important voices within the black community that argued forcefully in favor of community development and against the privileging of integration within the civil rights movement. In part, the growing resistance to integration among some civil rights and black power activists was meant to address what some felt was a fundamental flaw in much of the integrationist agenda—the fact that most housing integration efforts produce tradeoffs for African Americans. These tradeoffs range from simply the disruption of having to move to a new (and integrated) neighborhood, to exposing themselves to the enmity of new neighbors when they made such moves. Furthermore, as Christopher Bonastia argues, these tradeoffs in the pursuit of housing integration are often more costly than the tradeoffs that are required to achieve employment or educational integration. Housing desegregation efforts, he writes, "are likely to subject African Americans to some form of hardship and hostility, [and] the direct sacrifice of more housing."[101] That is to say, the pursuit of housing integration typically imposed a *burden*.

The "enrichment/integration" debate also redefined the issues facing fair housing in another way. Up until this point there was no general distinction made between the objective of enhancing residential choice and achieving residential integration. The black power movement revealed, however, that these were in fact separable goals, that it was possible to pursue the expansion of housing choice for people of color without necessarily advocating for integration. The choice to remain within an ethnically or racially defined community was legitimized by the black power movement. If integration was not the only or the inevitable choice of people of color, then it followed that there was an important distinction between the goals of antidiscrimination and integration. It was clear in the wake of the black power challenge to traditional fair housing advocacy that *greater choice*, not integration, was the direct and inevitable outcome of antidiscrimination efforts.

Thus, nearing the end of the 1960s, the fair housing movement was faced with a divide that was actually three different questions, the first related to the desirability of enriching and developing black communities on the one hand or working to eliminate concentrations of people of color on the other, the second related to whether nondiscrimination or integration should be the primary goal of the movement, and the third being whether the achievement of greater choice in housing for minority groups should be the objective of the movement, or if facilitation of a particular choice (dispersal and integration) was to be the chief pursuit.

Passage of the Fair Housing Act in 1968 would mark a transition in this debate. Congressional action on the question of housing discrimination could have provided definitive answers to some, if not all, of the questions facing the fair housing movement. In fact, the Fair Housing Act and the circumstances of its enactment and subsequent implementation have not, in the main, provided clarity on these questions. It is to this issue that we turn next.

THE THREE STATIONS OF FAIR HOUSING SPATIAL STRATEGY

Fair housing advocacy in the 1960s was driven by two realities. The first was the existence of exclusionary, white communities that relied on a combination of legal, political, and violent means to keep blacks and people of color from entering as residents. These were both neighborhoods within central cities that clung tightly to their "ethnic purity," as President Jimmy Carter would famously call it in 1976, but also the "white noose" of suburbs that circled the central cities of American metropolitan areas. It was to these communities, closed to minority occupancy, that the open housing movement was chiefly oriented. But the other side of the exclusionary coin was the impoverished urban ghetto, and conditions within the ghetto also importantly drove fair housing and more generally civil rights activity during the 1960s. Conditions in the black ghetto and the maltreatment of blacks, manifest in the housing conditions within the ghetto, the lack of jobs, the inferior public services, white-on-black violence, and police-community relations, repeatedly animated black activism during the decade. From the first uprising in 1964 through the end of the decade, the ghetto was the central reality that framed civil rights and fair housing politics.

The urban uprisings of the mid-1960s were, in fact, one of the defining domestic political issues of the decade. An important aspect of the grievances felt by blacks at this time was the malign neglect of and active disinvestment within black neighborhoods, problems that were long-standing. As Stokely Carmichael and Charles Hamilton observed in *Black Power*, "the problems of Harlem in the 1960s are not much different from those of Harlem in 1920."[1] Thus, the quickly escalating scale of racial politics in the 1960s was not simply a response to contemporary conditions of the ghetto, but was also a release of resentment and indignation over decades of racial oppression, forced segregation, and abuse. The uprisings of the mid-1960s came to dominate politics at both the local and national levels, affecting the course of urban policy under three presidents, forcing programmatic experimentation in participatory methods of policy making and implementation, and accelerating the pace of civil rights legislative activity. The rebellions are even credited for hastening white flight from American cities and contributing to the breakup of the New Deal coalition between white working classes and nonwhite voters.[2] As city after city burned in successive summers from 1964 through 1968, and as cities seemed to teeter on the edge of outright warfare between swaggering, largely white police forces and gun-carrying Black Panther Party members, the policy atmosphere was gripped by what Alexander von Hoffman calls "ghettophobia."[3]

It was in this environment in early 1968 that Dr. Martin Luther King Jr. was assassinated in Memphis, triggering yet more rebellions, and in which Congress finally passed a fair housing law. The bill's language focuses on describing the penalties for housing discrimination and the processes by which the law would be enforced. Rather quickly a consensus emerged that the law addressed two related but nevertheless distinct objectives: the elimination of housing discrimination so as to ensure equal access to housing, and support for integrated living patterns that would lead to the ultimate elimination of both the exclusionary white neighborhood and the isolated black ghetto.

Upon passage, the bill was used vigorously by fair housing advocates to attack private discrimination and to challenge the way in which public-sector housing programs were contributing to patterns of racial segregation. As fair housing activism evolved, advocates began to rely on an interpretation of the law that privileges the integration objective, maintaining that in cases where the pursuit of equal access to housing and the pursuit of integration are in conflict, the integration objective is paramount. This issue remains the basis of the unresolved tension between housing and fair housing advocates.

Title VIII of the 1968 Civil Rights Act

The Kerner Commission's report, published in March 1968, prominently reviewed the question of whether ghetto revitalization (enrichment) or integration was the more promising avenue for redressing racial inequalities in American metropolitan areas. The pursuit of integration and the pursuit of ghetto revitalization, of course, mean the deployment of very different sets of policies. Urban renewal, the community action program, model cities, and the rest of the

urban initiatives of the 1960s Great Society programs were aimed at ghetto revitalization and empowerment, although, of course, there is disagreement about
the effectiveness and even the true intent of some of these programs. They were,
however, targeted to central city communities and at least rationalized on the
basis of their potential benefits for improving declining and deteriorated inner-
city neighborhoods. Fair housing initiatives were a separate set of policies, and
focused on (1) how the private real estate market worked, (2) managing the
inflow and outflow of racially defined groups, and (3) the land-use controls used
by local governments to influence housing market outcomes. The push to adopt
fair housing legislation at the national level did not, therefore, activate the latent
tension between integration and revitalization.

An Act of Ambiguity

Fair housing legislation was considered by Congress in 1966 and 1967. The resistance of conservative southern Democrats to any bill establishing equal rights in
housing ultimately killed the effort in those years. Though Congress had enacted
a raft of civil rights laws over the previous three years, no agreement could be
reached on the issue of housing. Reintroduced in 1968, the bill was passed by the
Senate shortly after the Kerner Commission issued its report on the urban riots
of the previous years. Despite the Senate's work, opposition in the House made
1968 seem no different from previous years with respect to the prospects for full
passage of equal housing legislation.[4] However, Dr. King's assassination in Memphis, Tennessee, on April 4 and the subsequent rioting in cities across the country
jolted the House into action. Within three weeks the 1968 Civil Rights Bill was
passed by both chambers and signed into law. Title VIII of that bill constitutes
what has come to be known as the Fair Housing Act.

The bill was passed in a hurry by a Congress whose greatest motivation was
not so much to create landmark legislation related to housing rights as it was to
respond to rioting and violence across the country. Most observers agree that passage required such extensive compromise on the part of the bill's advocates that
the resulting law was weak in a number of ways. In fact, advocates and Congress
set about to amend the law very soon after its passage in an attempt to strengthen
many of its provisions.[5] In the end, these efforts took twenty years to bear fruit,
resulting in a fairly comprehensive set of amendments in 1988 that expanded
coverage of the law and also strengthened several implementation features.

The record of legislative debate on the bill is not extensive. In fact, there is little
in the congressional debates that can be used in retrospect to divine the intent of
Congress on several specific and important issues. This is important because the
legislation itself is vague on several critical issues, including what the definition

of "fair housing" is, what the explicit intent of Congress was in terms of the multiple objectives that might constitute fair housing, and on the exact nature of the government obligations related to fair housing in the implementation of its own programs of housing and urban development.[6]

Of greatest importance in terms of the ambiguities in Title VIII is the lack of certainty relating to what is precisely the mandate of fair housing. There is widespread agreement that the act has two overriding objectives: the elimination of discrimination in housing, and the achievement of integration.[7] The exact nature of these two objectives and their relative importance, however, generate debate among scholars. Whether and how Congress conceptualized the goals of the Fair Housing Act are debatable. The only goal explicitly identified in the language of the bill is the equal access goal—that is, the elimination of discrimination. The goal of integration, in contrast, has been read into the act, repeatedly, by the courts.[8] The act never explicitly specifies the broader social goals of ending segregation or even of promoting integration.

The text of the law and the congressional record bear out the contention that integration has been read into the act by the courts. The words "integration" and "segregation," for example, never appear in Title VIII; nor is there any direct statement of policy or intent that suggests that by passing Title VIII Congress intended to achieve residential integration. In fact, Congress never explicitly addressed the distinction between the two goals. Jean Dubofsky's insider account of the passage of Title VIII does not even mention the issue of discrimination versus integration.[9] This is not to say that members of Congress did not mention both goals. Indeed, many integrationist fair housing advocates (and the courts) have made repeated references to statements during congressional debate by then-senator Walter Mondale of Minnesota, the floor leader for the bill on the Senate side, regarding the need for "truly integrated living environments." Members of Congress acknowledged the twin objectives of equal access (nondiscrimination) and integration, but they never distinguished the two. Instead, lawmakers conflated them. It seems from the available evidence that it was assumed by Congress, as it had been by fair housing activists for years, that *the end of discrimination would result in integrated living environments*. This much can be gleaned from the congressional testimony. The bill itself, however, focuses on the elimination of discrimination. Thus, following Lake and Winslow, and Rubinowitz and Trosman, it is clear that the "best understanding of the statute is that it is aimed at reducing barriers" to equal access in housing and that integration was thought to be an outcome that would result from greater choice in the housing market.[10]

More indisputable is the fact that there is, as Lake and Winslow argue, "nothing in the statute [that] suggests that restrictions on choice are justified to achieve integration."[11] That is to say, in those cases where the two objectives are actually in conflict (e.g., where full housing choice for minorities might result in resegregation of an integrated community), there is nothing in the law or in the congressional debate to suggest that the integration objective is privileged over the equal access objective. This is critical because subsequent court rulings addressed this very issue, as did a raft of "integration maintenance" initiatives across the country.

Contemporary civil rights attorneys active in the fair housing movement, while maintaining that integration and nondiscrimination are the dual objectives of the act, go to great lengths to justify the importance, if not primacy, of the integration goal.[12] Florence Roisman, for example, asserts that integration is the main objective of Title VIII. She notes that the "floor debates in the Senate in 1968 were very focused on allowing blacks to move to the suburbs."[13] She also quotes the secretary of HUD at the time, Robert Weaver, as saying, "our non-white citizens must feel free to find their homes both in our central cities and our suburbs if the enforced racial ghetto is to be eliminated."[14] The quote most widely used to support the notion that Congress was intentionally acting to integrate communities through Title VIII is the one Walter Mondale said during the debate over passage of Title VIII. Mondale argued that the "reach of the proposed law was to replace ghettos with truly integrated and balanced living patterns."[15]

Remarks by Attorney General Ramsey Clark and Senator Charles Percy of Illinois are also enlisted in the effort to show that integration was the agreed-upon objective of the legislation.[16] Furthermore, there is some evidence that the fair housing advocates of the time saw their efforts in terms of specific spatial outcomes—integration and desegregation. Political scientist Mara Sidney notes in her history of the floor debate that supporters of fair housing repeatedly emphasized that fair housing would enable members of the black middle class to escape the ghetto.[17] Roisman also points to the subsequent actions of HUD secretary George Romney, whose major efforts in fair housing were to move toward integrating suburbs that had erected exclusionary barriers, as evidence that integration was the central objective of the act.

Still, there is ambiguity in the statute and in the congressional record. There is reason to believe that the ambiguity in Title VIII is purposeful, the result of legislators' unwillingness to grapple with a difficult issue of defining exactly the boundaries of fair housing. The repeated failure of fair housing legislation in the years running up to April 1968 speaks to the controversial nature of the bill, and the quick passage in the days following King's assassination points to the desire of Congress to minimize civil disorder. Indeed, the nature of the congressional debate preceding passage of the bill reflects a desire to avoid fundamental questions about integration and settlement patterns, not agreement on them. The absence of guidance in the statute itself likely reflects avoidance of these issues, not their resolution.

There is also some evidence that the law's ambiguity was as much a failure of imagination as it was a failure of will. The congressional debate on the issue, as well as the stated objectives of the fair housing movement at the time, evince a somewhat careless conflating of two distinct objectives, ending discrimination on the one hand and promoting integration on the other. Most actors at the time simply assumed that ending discrimination and producing integration were one and the same, or that the former would lead inevitably to the latter.

Given the prominence of the black power challenge to integrationist ideals that was in full bloom at the time of the 1968 debate on the Fair Housing Act, congressional actors were surely aware of the enrichment/integration debate. Indeed, the Kerner Commission explicitly and prominently referenced these two different strategies for achieving racial justice. Mondale's statement can be interpreted as support for the integration approach, possibly even a statement expressing preference for that approach. There is also evidence that Mondale was worried about the influence of the black separatist argument. He was very conscious of the signals being sent from white communities regarding fair housing, saying that if black America thinks that whites won't end segregation, then black separatists will gain.[18]

Yet other evidence strongly contests the notion that integration was the primary goal of Congress when it created the Fair Housing Act. Lake and Winslow, for example, argue that antidiscrimination is clearly the focus of the bill; "the language of the statute itself, as well as statements made in the Senate debate, strongly suggest that the protection of equal access is the primary intent of the FHA."[19] Others have noted that Senator Mondale made additional statements about the bill that seem to contradict the notion that it was about anything other than enhancing choice on the part of disadvantaged populations. In reference to Title VIII, Mondale said, "Obviously [the act] is to be read in context with the entire bill, the objective being to eliminate discrimination in the sale or rental of housing. . . . Without doubt, it means to provide for what is provided in the bill. It means the elimination of discrimination in the sale or rental of housing. That is all it could possibly mean."[20] Mondale also said that "the basic purpose of this legislation is to permit people who have the ability to do so to buy any house offered to the public if they can afford to buy it."[21]

The senator's statements about integrated and balanced living patterns seem to express a belief that given the choice, blacks would overwhelmingly choose to integrate. Speaking about the impact of the law, Mondale also said, "There will . . . be the knowledge by Negroes that they are free—*if they have the money and the desire*, to move where they will" (emphasis added).[22] How do we reconcile these statements by Mondale, some suggesting an explicit intent to integrate, others indicating that equal access is the goal of the law? The interpretation that fits these disparate statements is that the equal access and integration objectives were assumed to be one and the same—that equal access would, perforce, produce integration. Mondale's statements suggest that he believed that the act would accomplish an extension of choice for African Americans and that that choice would lead to integrated living patterns. There is nothing in this record acknowledging that the two objectives might conflict, nor is there evidence one way or the other about the primacy of one of these goals over the other.

What Is It to "Affirmatively Further" Fair Housing?

Another issue on which the congressional record and the language of the bill itself provide little guidance is what the federal government's obligations are in the operation of its own housing and urban development programs. Section 808(e)(5) of Title VIII requires the secretary of housing and urban development to "administer the programs and activities relating to housing and urban development in a manner affirmatively to further the policies of" the act. This has become known as the duty to affirmatively further fair housing (AFFH). Unfortunately, this is the only reference to this duty that exists in the legislation, and neither "affirmatively further" nor "fair housing" is defined in the statute. As Sidney notes, "Whereas the fair housing statute was quite detailed in its delineation of the enforcement process for remedying discrimination in the private sector, it offered no guidelines on how HUD was to incorporate fair housing into its own housing programs."[23]

The original or even subsequent intent of Congress related to affirmatively furthering fair housing remains obscure because, despite the passage of more than fifty-five years since enactment, Congress has never moved to define the phrase.[24] In 2015 the Obama administration issued a set of regulations aimed at clarifying the AFFH obligation. The regulations require local bodies to perform specific analyses related to the geographic location of assisted housing and patterns of racial/poverty segregation in local housing markets, but the regulations do not offer specific guidelines related to the implementation of assisted housing programs. The regulations do not resolve the issue related to the relative importance of equal access and integration in Title VIII. In fact, the words of HUD secretary Julian Castro made it clear that in the wake of the AFFH rule setting, the agency was not endorsing integration over community development: "I agree with folks who say that, just because these neighborhoods are distressed and they're minority neighborhoods, that [doesn't mean] we shouldn't invest in them. We should invest in them. We shouldn't forget about them. They do have value. And so we can't just have a policy of trying to get people out. There are a lot of people who don't want to move, and we have to improve their neighborhood, too."[25]

Interpreting the Act

In the current debate about the relative place of community development and integration in the nation's housing policy, two things must be established. First, regardless of whether Congress intended or even recognized two distinct objectives of fair housing—antidiscrimination and integration—is there evidence in the bill or the legislative record that integration is the privileged objective? Second, does the law or the congressional record suggest in any way that Congress envisioned or sanctioned the imposition of burdens upon disadvantaged groups in order to serve integration objectives? The answer to both of these questions, it must be concluded, is in the negative.

As to these questions, I have already argued that the language of the act itself is unambiguously focused on eliminating discrimination in the private housing market and on describing the penalties and procedures adhering to such discrimination. The integration goal is entirely unspecified in the act. Nor can reference to legislative intent sustain the integration-first argument. What the record shows is a mix of statements, some referencing choice as the major intent of the bill, some highlighting equal access, others mentioning integration and solving the problems of the ghetto. What the record lacks is a definitive statement that privileges integration over equal access, or evidence that Congress envisioned the sacrifice of choice for individual members of minority groups in order to serve integrationist goals.

Into the breach created by this ambiguity the courts have stepped. In a series of rulings since passage of Title VIII, the courts have offered their interpretation of the law, frequently weighing in on the issue of the relative importance of equal access versus integration. On the government's AFFH duty, the courts have exercised greatest discretion in interpretation. Over the years, courts have referenced AFFH to direct the federal government to restrict subsidized housing in predominantly minority neighborhoods and to redirect Low Income Housing Tax Credit funds away from central cities and to suburban areas, and, in one legal case frequently referenced by fair housers (*Otero v. NYCHA*), explicitly privileging integration over equal access. Here, too, fair housing advocates argue that the record supports aggressive integrationist strategies. Florence Roisman, while acknowledging the statute's silence on the issue of segregation and integration, nonetheless suggests that the Supreme Court of the United States recognizes the spatial goals of the law.[26] Such an interpretation undergirds a spatial strategy of fair housing that focuses on integration and desegregation.

Since passage of Title VIII, the fair housing movement has developed its spatial strategies in increments that are ever more aggressive. Its proponents point to judicial sanction of such strategies legitimized in *Traficante v. Metropolitan Life Insurance Co.* (1972) in which the U.S. Supreme Court ruled that Title VIII defined fair housing harms as not only the direct suffering from discrimination, but also the suffering of community members, white and nonwhite, who are deprived of integrated housing environments. Roisman and others argue that this decision establishes integration as one of the chief objectives of the act. This interpretation is further supported by the opinion in *NAACP Boston Chapter v. HUD* (1987), in which the First Circuit Court explicitly held that the Fair Housing Act went beyond merely directing HUD to not discriminate in the operation of its programs, but ruling that it must take active steps to further integration.[27] Other judicial rulings have interpreted the law in important ways, generally with the effect of elevating the goal of integration as national policy in ways that the law itself did not.[28]

The Three Stations

I have argued thus far that the opening up of exclusionary communities was the way in which the fair housing movement first conceptualized itself. In practice that meant eliminating public and private acts of discrimination that were maintaining the racial lines in America's urban centers. Phrased in this way, as it most frequently was by fair housing activists, the objective of the movement entails two dimensions. The first is equal access to housing, and this has no inherent spatial implications. The elimination of discrimination in housing is a universal objective, to be pursued in segregated or integrated environments. The second dimension of the fair housing mission is explicitly spatial. That is, "open housing" referred to breaking down patterns of segregation that limited people of color to racially defined neighborhoods. In this formulation, the strategies of the fair housing movement were to explicitly facilitate a spatial reorganization of races and ethnic groups to achieve more integrated living environments.

Opening Up Exclusionary Communities

The spatial strategies of fair housing as they have evolved have reflected three general goals. The first station of fair housing's spatial strategy is to break down the barriers of white exclusion. This objective is aimed at removing the obstacles for people of color in moving out of the ghetto and into predominantly white communities. As there is little conflict between fair housing and community development on this strategy, we do not dwell long here.

In the first decade after passage of the Fair Housing Act, the bulk of nationally noted legal suits focusing on housing involved the issue of exclusionary zoning or land use control.[29] In practice, this meant challenging the land-use regulations of suburban communities that limited the amount of affordable housing that could be built within their jurisdictions. In fact, however, litigation challenging the exclusionary practices of suburban governments was pursued even prior to Title VIII. Much of the litigation surrounding suburban exclusionism took place at the state level and resulted in a string of legal victories that saw regulations for large lots struck down in some areas, and other zoning provisions such as minimum floor areas, building sizes, restrictions on number of bedrooms or number of apartments interpreted as exclusionary and invalidated.[30] The federal courts have also contributed rulings that have struck down restrictions on low-cost housing construction in white neighborhoods, and prohibitions on multi-family housing.[31]

THE BRIEF ROMNEY INTERREGNUM

The Fair Housing Act was less than one year old when Richard Nixon was elected president and appointed George Romney to head the Department of Housing and Urban Development. Romney was a liberal Republican and governor of the state of Michigan who had been a public supporter of desegregation and, as Nixon noted in making the appointment, passionate about fixing the problems of inner cities.[32]

Romney identified most of the problems of central cities in the widening disparities between the largely white suburban communities and the increasingly disadvantaged urban core disproportionately inhabited by blacks. Romney acted quickly and assertively in attempting to bring federally subsidized housing to predominantly white suburban communities. Several initiatives were launched in a short period of time to penetrate these communities. One tool was Operation Breakthrough, begun in 1969, which incentivized the development of affordable, factory-built housing. The program resulted in exactly one suburban project.[33] The Open Communities program was an attempt to use the leverage of federal funding to influence suburban governments to accept subsidized housing. The program conditioned HUD water, sewer, and other infrastructure grants on the acceptance of subsidized housing. The agency withheld funding from a handful of localities after they refused subsidized housing.[34] When Romney moved to impose the same requirements on the Detroit suburb of Warren, Michigan, the vitriolic response of this working-class community ended not only the program, but also Romney's tenure as secretary of HUD and, ultimately, the federal government's affirmative efforts to force suburban communities to accept federally subsidized housing.[35] As Bonastia reports, "In the wake of Warren, the White House instructed all federal agencies to hold off on pro-residential integration policies until the administration had settled on a uniform policy."[36] Months later the administration announced that it would not pursue "forced integration" and would discontinue the policy of withholding funding from communities that oppose subsidized housing. Nixon was quite explicit about the "new" policy, noting that "it is not the policy of this Government to use the power of the Federal Government or Federal funds in any other way, in ways not required by the law for forced integration of the suburbs. I believe that forced integration of the suburbs is not in the national interest."[37] Nixon was especially sensitive to appeasing a suburban constituency that was partially responsible for his election in the first place, and held the key to reelection hopes.[38] The grand federal experiment in aggressively implementing an expansive view of fair housing by using the influence of federal funding lasted less than two years and produced next to nothing in actual desegregation for the nation's urban areas.

The almost total retreat from efforts to spread the development of subsidized housing to suburban areas was especially remarkable given the political environment of the late 1960s. The Kerner Commission had noted the need for opening up exclusionary white communities; public opinion polls reflected a mix of support and acceptance of integrating suburbs that was unprecedented in the nation's history; and a wide range of politicians were supportive of the effort, as were important business constituencies such as the National Association of Home Builders and suburban employers in search of an appropriate workforce for their expansion.

Leaders of the black community in many metro areas, however, saw HUD's efforts to disperse subsidized housing in a different light. Michael Danielson notes that "blacks in cities across the nation bitterly protested the new federal emphasis in the early 1970s on locating subsidized housing outside lower-income black areas."[39] In part, this was due, he argues, to the fact that in the early 1970s, "most blacks and black leaders [did] not yet consider exclusionary zoning a gut issue. They do not feel it every day like they do job discrimination," school segregation, and public facilities discrimination.[40] On the one hand, part of the concern was that facilitating the flow of households and resources out of the central city would further impoverish those central cities. On the other hand, some argued that the main beneficiaries of expanded subsidized housing opportunities in the suburbs would be whites and that very few black families would be desegregated in this manner.[41] Danielson suggests that black leaders felt that the question of the location of subsidized housing was a zero-sum game, and given "meager benefits . . . the principal effect of emphasizing the improvement of housing opportunities in suburbs would be to shift resources away from the inner city where most blacks live, where housing needs are the greatest, and where blacks, because of their strength in numbers," have greater potential to influence public policy.[42] There was also concern that dispersal had the potential to undermine political support for subsidized housing by activating a strong white resistance to HUD activity.[43]

This position was not universal. The National League of Cities and the U.S. Conference of Mayors strongly backed the idea of "fair share"—that all communities within a region provide affordable housing opportunities. The NAACP, furthermore, strongly opposed the position of those who criticized dispersal.[44] Once again, within the black community the tradeoff was apparent: either critical needs within the community might be met, or progress in desegregation might be achieved, but there was little to no expectation that both could occur simultaneously.

REGIONAL FAIR SHARE

Not all the action was taking place at the federal level. Some metropolitan areas were taking the initiative on dispersing subsidized housing. The creation of regional fair share allocation plans in several metro areas opened up the possibility of meaningful dispersal of affordable housing. Specially constituted regional bodies had authority to review local proposals for federal infrastructure grants. This "A-95 review" power, named for the U.S. Office of Management and Budget circular that outlined this policy, invested in regional bodies the authority to review local applications for federal grants and to recommend them for eventual federal funding. More than a hundred federal aid programs and planning grants were covered by A-95.[45] Although A-95 review was originally designed as an environmental review, a 1972 amendment expanded it to incorporate an examination of the civil rights implications of federally funded projects. This allowed these regional bodies to accomplish what HUD had backed away from in 1972, the conditioning of federal funds on progress made in regionalizing affordable housing. A-95 review was the basis for several regional fair share housing initiatives.

In the end, however, the regional approach never went far. Suburban resistance to regional bodies that wished to impose subsidized housing requirements was as strong as it had been to the federal government. The regional agencies had little political or institutional power of their own and, like the federal government, were unwilling or unable (or both) to challenge suburban voters on the issue of integrated housing and the widespread dispersal of subsidized housing.

USING TENANT-BASED SUBSIDIES TO
OPEN UP THE SUBURBS

In 1974, Congress created a new housing subsidy tool that was seen as having potential to further disperse subsidized households. The Section 8 certificate, a housing subsidy that is attached to the household and not to a particular unit, was created by the Housing and Community Development Act of 1974. If getting suburbs or some city neighborhoods to accept "housing projects" was proving to be difficult, perhaps subsidized households could be better dispersed on an individual basis. Families holding the certificate would find a unit in the marketplace and then enter into a lease using the Section 8 certificate to pay a portion of the rent. In fact, the expectation of greater dispersal for tenant-based subsidies like the Section 8 certificate (now somewhat euphemistically called the housing choice voucher—HCV) has been borne out. Nationally, households receiving tenant-based subsidies are more dispersed than those in project-based subsidized housing.[46] At the same time, the degree of dispersion achieved by tenant-based assistance has disappointed those who hoped it would be a vehicle of integration. From the outset, Section 8 did very little to achieve desegregation. Observing the program's earliest years, Saltman concluded that "what has happened to housing allowances and subsidies for the poor has thus created the usual pattern of segregation."[47] This basic assessment of the program has not changed over the years. Analysts continue to document the fact that housing vouchers achieve only an incremental increase in dispersal compared to project-based assistance, but not enough to generate any real racial or class desegregation.[48] These patterns are typically attributed to the constraints and rules by which the program operates. As a result, several attempts have been made to create special versions of tenant-based assistance that would facilitate greater dispersal than the basic program.

During the Carter administration, three pilot programs were initiated to achieve greater dispersal of tenants in the Section 8 and HCV programs. The Areawide Housing Opportunity Program was a voluntary program designed to encourage municipalities within metropolitan areas to collaborate in planning for low-income housing and to facilitate the regional mobility of voucher holders. The Regional Housing Mobility Program (RHMP) was created in 1979 to facilitate the "porting" of Section 8 certificates from one jurisdiction to another, in the hope that those who receive their subsidy from a housing authority in the central city would be able to use that subsidy in a suburban community. RHMP was succeeded by the Section 8 mobility demonstration program, which operated in a different manner to achieve the same dispersal outcomes. These programs were never scaled up to any appreciable degree, and their dispersal impacts were minimal.

Despite the limited success of these 1970s efforts to enhance the dispersal impacts of Section 8, the idea did not go away. Congress and HUD continued to tinker with the program to allow greater choice for tenants, assuming that greater choice would lead to integration. This led to the addition of vouchers to the original Section 8 certificates to allow families the ability to pay more in order to enhance choice. Congress increased the portability of Section 8 subsidies, first across city lines within the metropolitan area, then to the state and national level.[49] Finally, voluntary "special mobility programs" were designed to facilitate relocation out of disadvantaged neighborhoods. As noted, the assumption behind increasing the portability options within the HCV program is that, given the chance, families would use the voucher to move from lower-opportunity areas to higher-opportunity communities. Program officials envisioned a movement out of central cities and into suburban areas, a pattern that does not always occur.[50]

Because this dimension of fair housing spatial strategy does not restrict choice for disadvantaged groups, nor does the implementation of this strategy place any burden on members of the disadvantaged groups, there is little conflict between fair housing goals and affordable housing goals in the pursuit of greater housing opportunities in exclusionary communities. The creation of an administrative apparatus for achieving greater affordability in suburban areas, such as a regional governance of fair share housing efforts, will have the effect of increasing housing choices for low-income people region-wide. It may allow disadvantaged groups to settle more widely if they so choose, although the greater income and racial diversity in suburban areas of the United States has largely occurred without the assistance of fair share housing. From the viewpoint of affordable housing activists, however, regional strategies to increase the availability of low-cost housing are important because they increase the supply of affordable housing, and there is demand for such housing in suburban areas.

Yet this first station of fair housing's spatial strategy is not entirely without issue for those who put greater value on community development efforts. When resources are scarce and participants perceive of the spatial question as a zero-sum game (i.e., greater investment in suburban areas means reduced investment in the core), conflicts can occur. The notion of a zero-sum game is one that both sides of the debate accept.[51] The potential for conflict exists in periods of scarcity when choices must be made about where to allocate meager resources. As shown in the response by some black leaders to HUD's efforts to promote suburban subsidized housing, the perception of zero-sum tradeoffs can generate conflict between fair housers and affordable housing providers.

Preventing Further Segregation and Resegregation

The second station of fair housing spatial strategy consists of efforts to prevent further segregation or resegregation. These efforts are most clearly seen in rules that restrict the siting of subsidized housing and in various programs aimed at maintaining integration. The siting restrictions, or what are sometimes called impaction limits, have come about largely as the result of court decisions. In these decisions, various courts have ruled that individual projects sited in minority neighborhoods would have the effect of perpetuating segregation and so have upheld actions that have denied approval of such projects.

SITING GUIDELINES

Restrictions on the placement of subsidized housing are authorized by the "affirmatively furthering" requirement of Title VIII. The courts have interpreted that clause to mean that the U.S. Department of Housing and Urban Development must operate its programs in a way so as to achieve spatial goals in the allocation of assisted housing. The courts have interpreted that to mean that there must be a limit on the number of assisted units placed in segregated or "impacted" neighborhoods. Roisman points out that the concept behind impaction rules actually predates Title VIII by two years. The argument in *Gautreaux v. CHA*, filed in 1966, for example, called for guiding assisted housing according to the racial makeup of neighborhoods, limiting the development of subsidized units in neighborhoods where it is thought to reinforce segregation.[52] Other efforts in New York and Michigan were also aimed at limiting the siting of assisted housing in ways that would reinforce patterns of racial segregation, prior to passage of Title VIII.[53]

Fair housing advocates continued to litigate on this issue after Title VIII was enacted, using the AFFH clause as their foundation. In 1970, plaintiffs in *Shannon v. HUD* sued HUD over a proposed housing development in Philadelphia. Interestingly, the original proposal called for homeownership units, and the lawsuit was filed only after HUD had approved a revision to the proposal that changed the housing from owner to rental.[54] The plaintiffs argued that the rental housing would mean more minority residents in what had already been a minority area. The central finding in the case is that HUD did not have in place any process for judging the impact of a proposed development on the pattern of racial occupancy in the affected neighborhood and that this constituted a breach of the agency's obligation to affirmatively further fair housing. The court directed HUD to create a policy and procedure for making siting decisions.

The *Shannon* decision is predominantly a procedural one. The court did not say that HUD *must limit* subsidized housing in minority neighborhoods, only that the agency must have a policy to review the racial impacts of its siting decisions. As Michael Vernarelli notes, "Although the court identified affirmative fair housing as an important goal of national housing policy, it recognized the existence of other important, competing goals: 'There may be instances where a pressing case may be made for the rebuilding of a racial ghetto. We hold only that the agency's judgment must be an informed one; one which weighs the alternatives.'"[55]

HUD responded by creating siting policies for its development programs in 1972 that generally limited development in minority neighborhoods unless comparable housing opportunities already existed outside those neighborhoods or the project in question met overriding housing needs that would not have been possible to meet otherwise.[56] Those advocating community development regarded the siting guidelines as damaging to efforts to meet housing and reinvestment needs of core neighborhoods. Black politicians and community activists feared that the dispersal of assisted housing would dilute black electoral power and ignored the preferences of people of color who wished to remain in core neighborhoods and needed housing assistance. When HUD applied their siting restrictions to a proposed project in Kansas City, and denied approval for a 280-unit project in an African American part of town, community leaders regarded it "as a slap in the face to local community development efforts."[57]

These siting guidelines, while reflecting concerns about reinforcing segregation, were nevertheless criticized by many as a form of government-directed redlining that limited reinvestment in predominantly black neighborhoods. Given the unyielding opposition of whites to the placement of subsidized housing within their communities, both political activists and officials within HUD worried that the siting guidelines would reduce the overall amount of assisted housing that HUD would be able to produce.[58] These worries echoed those of leaders in the black community during the 1940s and 1950s who feared a tradeoff between the quantity of needed housing and its location in predominantly white neighborhoods.

HUD policy and congressional input on this issue have followed something of a wandering path since *Shannon* was decided. In the first ten years after *Shannon*, HUD revised its siting guidelines twice, first to acknowledge rehabilitation and reinvestment needs in core neighborhoods and then again to introduce even greater flexibility in agency decision making. In 1978, HUD was criticized by the U.S. General Accounting Office for not doing enough to deconcentrate its assisted housing. HUD secretary Patricia Harris responded by arguing that the agency had multiple objectives and was simply balancing dispersal objectives with "equally important legislative goals such as neighborhood revitalization."[59] Just two years later Congress, urged on by members representing urban areas, moved to prohibit HUD from denying housing proposals based solely on the impaction limits and called for greater flexibility in siting decisions.[60] Members were at that time worried about whether the guidelines were keeping affordable housing out of communities where it was greatly needed. "Congressmen representing urban areas strongly opposed HUD's site selection criteria that resulted in housing going to areas that did not want it rather than to areas that needed it the most."[61] Though the amendment did not become law, HUD responded and softened its criteria the next year.

SITING RESTRICTIONS—*GAUTREAUX*

Few court decisions in the fair housing field have had the impact in either duration or scope of the decisions in the *Gautreaux* cases. In 1966 lawyers from the American Civil Liberties Union filed class action lawsuits against the Chicago Housing Authority (CHA) and the U.S. Department of Housing and Urban Development.[62] Predating the 1968 Fair Housing Act, the two *Gautreaux* cases claimed that the way in which CHA and HUD operated the city's public housing program violated Title VI of the 1964 Civil Rights Act as well as the equal protection clause of the Constitution. The case against the CHA was decided first with the presiding judge Richard B. Austin ruling that the agency had discriminated in selecting sites for public housing and in tenant selection in ways that perpetuated racial segregation in the city. The judge ordered the agency to build the next seven hundred units of public housing and three out of every four additional units outside minority neighborhoods. For the purposes of implementing this order the city was split into "limited" and "general" areas. The limited area included all census tracts with 30 percent or more African American residents, and all census tracts within a one-mile buffer zone. The general area was the rest of the city. The court's order, which was essentially written by the plaintiff's attorneys, put a binding limit on the number of public housing units that could be built in the limited area.[63]

If implemented, the court's order would have resulted in a large, scattered-site public housing program and spread public housing to predominantly white neighborhoods in the city. The resistance of white neighborhoods to receiving public housing, however, was strong, and the will of the CHA to scatter the units was quite weak. The result was that CHA stopped building new public housing. In the five years following the order, no new units were built, and only a handful were constructed after that. In 1987, Judge Austin appointed a receiver, the Habitat Company, to take over CHA's development program and carry out the intent of the court's remedy.

After the case against the CHA was decided in 1969, the judge took up the case against HUD. Interestingly, Austin at first dismissed the case, invoking a variant of the conundrum dealt with in this book. He argued that "HUD had to continue funding the discriminatory program or deprive low-income families of much-needed housing."[64] Appeals took the case all the way to the U.S. Supreme Court, which decided in 1976 that HUD was responsible for supporting a metropolitan-wide program to remedy the segregation that the agency had allowed through its continued funding of the CHA.

By this time, of course, the Fair Housing Act had been passed (in 1968), requiring the agency to affirmatively further fair housing, and the 1974 Housing and Community Development Act had created the Section 8 program that gave HUD a new way of providing housing subsidies to low-income families. The remedy for this case was a metropolitan-wide mobility program that provided Section 8 certificates to Chicago public housing families to move to predominantly white neighborhoods in the city or suburbs. The same general area / limited area distinction used in the CHA case was used to guide the relocation of families in the mobility program. The Gautreaux mobility program was voluntary; public housing families had to sign up to participate in the program and had to meet program criteria before being enrolled.

The scattered-site program that resulted from the CHA lawsuit operates as a form of siting restriction for HUD-assisted housing in Chicago. Although initially applied only to public housing, the Section 8 new construction program was also brought under the same geographic restrictions of the court order in the 1970s, as were HOPE VI funds in the 1990s. In each case, the use of these federal housing subsidies in black neighborhoods was strictly limited and made contingent on the development of HUD-assisted housing in the predominantly white, "general" areas of the city.

These restrictions were objected to almost immediately by leaders of the black community in Chicago. In Andrea Gill's cogent and comprehensive analysis of the debate in Chicago generated by *Gautreaux* she documents the extensive objections of black community leaders to the restrictions imposed by the court.[65] The court orders in both *Gautreaux* cases offered integration as the remedy to CHA's discriminatory actions. The CHA case was decided in 1969, just as calls for self-determination and community development were dominating local politics in cities across the nation. As Gill notes, the Nation of Islam, the Black Panther Party, and PUSH were all strong presences in Chicago, as were local community organizations stressing black community development. She writes: "Before the ink had dried on the order [in the CHA case], other activists mounted a challenge to [lead *Gautreaux* attorney Alexander] Polikoff's integrationist approach, which flattened racial justice to a process of relocating poor African-Americans."[66]

Opponents of the order included the Chicago chapter of the national civil rights organization the Southern Christian Leadership Council. The opponents objected to the difficulties that the order would impose upon efforts to revitalize black neighborhoods in the city. Gill quotes the Reverend A. I. Dunlap, director of the United Coalition for Community Action, as arguing that the effect of the order is "to force us out toward the suburbs, and Black people don't welcome that any more than White people welcome us coming."[67]

The issue broadened when federal Section 8 new construction funds were brought within the purview of the court's order in 1975. Within three years "PUSH, the local NAACP chapter, and the Chicago Urban League [had] formed a task force to modify the [court] order to exempt all developments in areas expected to undergo racial transition and to permit the use of rent certificates in subsidized developments built before 1969."[68]

Illinois congresswoman Cardiss Collins called a congressional hearing in her West Side district to examine the effect of the *Gautreaux* court order on housing production in Chicago. A major concern aired at the hearings was the continued decline in the housing stock in the "limited" areas of the city (census tracts with more than 30 percent African American population) because of arson and private-sector disinvestment. Collins began the hearing by noting that "much of the blame for the inadequacy of Chicago's housing stock in these devastated neighborhoods has been placed on the *Gautreaux* decision."[69] The court order made reinvestment in the housing stock there contingent on subsidized housing development in white areas. The continued resistance of white communities to such housing left the black neighborhoods without it as well. Collins noted that "residents in these areas are in a Catch-22 situation. They find themselves in critical need of new housing . . . and yet, they cannot get new units until communities outside their neighborhoods agree to accept Section 8 funding."[70] Real estate agent Ronald Laurent was even more direct: "The *Gautreaux* decision as handed down is directly responsible for the lack of decent and affordable housing in the City of Chicago. It has prevented the construction of new units in black areas with few or rare exceptions." He likened the order to a kind of inverted restrictive covenant.[71] Congresswoman Collins pointed out that *Gautreaux* is "preventing those who wish to remain in their present neighborhoods from enjoying better housing."[72]

Gautreaux attorney Polikoff also spoke at the hearing, pointing out that the court order "does not prohibit new construction of subsidized and assisted housing in minority neighborhoods." He argued that such construction can occur, provided that units are first built in white neighborhoods. "The problem," continued Polikoff, "is that there has been virtually no construction of subsidized and assisted housing in white neighborhoods of the city."[73] Though others agreed that the housing was not getting built in white neighborhoods, they saw the problem as being that better housing in their own neighborhoods was being "held hostage" to the willingness of whites to accept it in their communities.[74]

In 1981 the *Gautreaux* order was modified to allow HUD-assisted housing in "revitalizing areas" of the city. This would allow subsidized housing to be placed in limited areas of the city that were in the process of changing economically and demographically. In neighborhoods such as these, which were becoming gentrified, the provision of subsidized housing would likely produce the integration that the fair housers sought. But Polikoff was not convinced and felt that the "acceptance of the revitalizing area concept was a reluctant concession to frustrated black developers, strongly backed by HUD."[75]

A few years later, when the CHA began to think about rehabilitating some of its housing stock and introducing "mixed-income" approaches, the *Gautreaux* attorneys were there, ready to extend the reach of the siting restrictions to rehabilitation as well as to the new construction that was the target of the original court order. The logic of the *Gautreaux* attorneys was that such rehabilitation "amounted to rebuilding segregated high-rises in a black neighborhood."[76] Though the presiding judge in the case, now Marvin Aspen, did not extend the order as the plaintiffs desired, the reach of the *Gautreaux* siting restrictions *was* extended to the redevelopment of public housing that began in the 1990s.

SPECIAL MOBILITY PROGRAMS

The *Gautreaux* siting restrictions have proven to be of enduring importance, created in the 1970s but still affecting affordable housing development in Chicago forty years later. As important as this element of the *Gautreaux* decisions has been, the other aspect of the *Gautreaux* remedy, the mobility program, has arguably had greater national influence on questions of housing policy. The allocation of thousands of Section 8 vouchers to members of the *Gautreaux* plaintiff class, and the restrictions on the use of those vouchers to neighborhoods with a limited African American population, introduced an important new development in integrative housing policy—the Special Mobility Program (SMP). This type of program is important because it attempts to achieve greater dispersal and integration by confining the use of vouchers to neighborhoods that meet a program-defined level of acceptable integration. That is, it attempts to enhance the variety of neighborhood choices made by participants in the voucher program by limiting those choices to neighborhoods that will desegregate. This model was adopted in other desegregation lawsuits pursued by fair housing advocates in several metropolitan areas across the country, and it served as the basis of the national demonstration program, Moving to Opportunity, created by Congress in 1992.

SMPs have some generic characteristics. First, they are voluntary programs. Second, SMPs attempt to desegregate by restricting the neighborhoods in which the vouchers may be used. The Gautreaux program operated by restricting the use of the vouchers to neighborhoods that had fewer than 30 percent African Americans. Other lawsuit-based SMPs adopted a variant of that, either defining the acceptable neighborhoods in terms of race (i.e., specifying the maximum allowable percentage of people of color in program-eligible neighborhoods) or class (i.e., specifying the maximum allowable poverty rate in program-eligible neighborhoods) or both.[77] SMPs also typically incorporate enhanced tenant counseling in order to assist families in finding and leasing units.

The treatment of choice in SMPs is complex. SMPs are, by definition, voluntary programs, so that all who participate have expressed the choice to do so. Once participants are admitted to the program, however, their choice is restricted in that the voucher subsidy may be used only in certain neighborhoods and not others. It should be noted that constraints on neighborhood choice are an inherent part of the voucher program in the sense that eligible units are typically concentrated in certain neighborhoods. This is the very factor that most analysts agree has limited the integrationist impact of the program. But the concentration of program-eligible units within certain neighborhoods can be regarded as a feature of the regional housing market. SMPs impose an additional limit on whatever market constraints exist by restricting families to renting in neighborhoods that meet the dispersal criteria. Special mobility programs are, of course, subject to the same zero-sum considerations as any other programmatic initiative. Resources devoted to SMPs might be used otherwise, and thus, although they are voluntary, they represent funding that privileges one spatial outcome over others.

INTEGRATION MAINTENANCE PROGRAMS

So-called integration maintenance programs are initiatives that are aimed at preserving racial diversity in communities where it does exist, and at keeping communities that have diversified from resegregating through a combination of white flight and the in-migration of people of color. Integration maintenance programs are usually undertaken by suburban communities to manage the racial composition of their populations to maintain a desired mix. Such management includes "discouraging additional black occupancy" in neighborhoods that have a preferred level of integration.[78] The "preferred level" is typically just below the percentage of people of color that would induce white families to move out. In some cases, integration maintenance programs have included incentives for white families to remain in a community that is changing, or it can consist of attempts to attract white in-movers. In these instances the programs work by attempting to influence the residential choices of families. Whether it is by discouraging further black entry into neighborhoods or incentivizing whites to move in, sociologist Harvey Molotch characterizes these efforts as "competing for whites."[79] The normative standard for integrated neighborhoods is the white neighborhood, and integration means attracting a few, but not too many, people of color, while trying "to maintain a physical environment conducive to middle-class white residency."[80]

One type of integration maintenance program, however, worked by more actively limiting housing access by people of color in order to limit their numbers within a community to a prescribed level. Again, the concern in these quota-based approaches was the imperative to avoid activating white fear and prejudice, and thus avoid white flight and complete racial turnover. By restricting housing opportunities for people of color to an approved percentage within a predominantly white community, these programs involved a form of purposeful discrimination in the service of integration when families of color were denied housing opportunities on the basis of their skin color. Quota-based integration management programs rather starkly revealed the potential conflict between the fair housing goals of choice and access on the one hand, and the achievement and maintenance of integration on the other. Such programs, as Wilson and Taub point out, "violate the letter of the 1968 Fair Housing Act by limiting the housing options of racial minorities."[81] They also violate many local housing ordinances, and thereby forced some communities to modify their nondiscrimination ordinances to allow such action.[82]

There are several notable features of integration maintenance schemes that work by means of such constraint and coercion. First, this constraint on equal access is acceptable, according to integration advocates, because it preserves larger patterns of integration that are good for "the community."[83] Thus, it places a purported community good in front of the good of individual people of color. This is a principle that was espoused forcefully in *Otero v. NYCHA*, as I point out below.

Second, the strategy works by requiring "the victims of past discrimination to carry the burden" of integration efforts.[84] Its mechanism is coercive in that people of color are actively denied housing opportunities. This is in contrast to how integration maintenance programs treat white households. To the extent that white households are targeted by such programs, they are *incentivized* to either remain in a community or move to it. No coercion or limiting of choice is directed toward white families.

Third, integration maintenance programs ensure—actually mandate—black minorities within the residential communities in which such programs operate.[85] Because these programs assume a "tipping point"—a level of black in-migration that will trigger white flight—they typically limit black residence to a small minority hypothesized to be acceptable to the majority of whites.

Finally, of course, quota-based programs have a discriminatory impact on families of color. That integration maintenance programs require constraints on the choice of individual families was readily acknowledged by those who advocated them. As such, these programs clearly placed the integration objective of fair housing before the equal access objective, a position that, as I have argued, is unsupported by either the text of Title VIII or the legislative record. The courts, furthermore, have ruled that such quotas are illegal, and thus this approach is no longer pursued by integrationists.[86]

OVERRIDING CHOICE: *OTERO V. NEW YORK CITY HOUSING AUTHORITY*

In *Otero v. New York City Housing Authority*, the court broadened its interpretation of the integration mandate of Title VIII.[87] The case focuses on a planned redevelopment in the Seward Park Urban Renewal Area in New York's Lower East Side. The New York City Housing Authority (NYCHA) had cleared land for a 360-unit public housing project and in the process displaced 1,852 low-income families. These families were promised priority standing for units in the new housing development. Demand for the new units among the displaced families, 60 percent of whom were people of color, was greater than NYCHA had anticipated. After 161 former residents were rehoused in the new development, the agency began to lease the remaining units to applicants who were not displacees. The agency did so out of fear that to honor its initial promise of rehousing original residents would be to resegregate the project. Almost 90 percent of the non-displacees on the waiting list were white. According to court documents filed by the plaintiffs, if NYCHA had fully honored its original commitment to displaced families, the new housing development would have become 80 percent people of color and 20 percent white.[88] Had the original residents been allowed back to the site, the development would have been a predominantly minority enclave within a largely white neighborhood; 73 percent of the families in the larger area would be white.

If, on the other hand, the agency had its way and limited the rehousing of displacees, the project would have been 40 percent people of color and 60 percent white, and 82 percent of the families in the larger area would be white. The agency was motivated by concern that to allow the new development to be filled by former residents would trigger a tipping point that could produce racial turnover of the larger redevelopment area and resegregate it.

The plaintiffs sued, claiming that the agency's new policy of maintaining an acceptable level of racial diversity on site had the effect of denying housing opportunities for people of color. The district court agreed, holding that the duty to foster and maintain racial integration "could not as a matter of law be given effect where to do so would be to deprive a non-white minority of low cost public housing that would otherwise be assigned to it."[89] Furthermore, the ruling noted the continued predominance of whites in the surrounding area and agreed with the plaintiff's point that to allow former residents back to the site *would, in fact, integrate the larger neighborhood more* than if they were denied the housing.

NYCHA appealed the decision and won. The case was remanded for a trial, in which the defendants would be able to make the argument, if they could, that returning the original residents to the site would in fact lead to resegregation of the area. The appeals court held that NYCHA be allowed to demonstrate its "tipping point" argument. However, the case ultimately settled, so NYCHA was never actually forced to defend its predictions of tipping.

The appeals court decision in *Otero* reflects all the objectionable elements of integration maintenance programs described above. First, as many have pointed out, it creates a judicial rule based on the idea of tipping points. In this case, the tipping-point argument was an assertion that a predominance of people of color within the 362-unit development was not, in fact, an enclave that would integrate the larger white community, but a "pocket ghetto" that was likely to trigger white flight and a larger segregated community. Rubinowitz and Trosman note that tipping points can be thought of as an index of white racism.[90] In *Otero*, the court allowed for that index to be used to guide housing policy. The decision in *Otero* not only ratifies the notion of tipping; it enshrines it as a guiding principle of housing allocation.[91]

Second, the logic of the appeals court ruling suggests that people of color must always be a small minority within a larger white community. The court essentially defines predominantly minority communities as problems to be avoided and defines healthy, desirable communities as ones in which the vast majority of residents are white. Indeed, by accepting and incorporating the "tipping point" idea to guide the allocation of assisted units, the *Otero* court indicates that what it means by integration is whatever degree of diversity whites will accept.

Third, the decision emphatically elevates the integration imperative of Title VIII above the equal access objective. It does so even though the court wrote, "It is true that the Act was designed *primarily* to prohibit discrimination in the sale, rental, financing, or brokerage of private housing and to provide federal enforcement procedures for remedying such discrimination" (emphasis added).[92] The court makes reference to Senator Mondale's statement that the Fair Housing Act "was designed to replace the ghettos 'by truly integrated and balanced living patterns.'"[93] *Otero* honors the desire of people of color to move where they will only when that desire accords with the court's sense of integration and only when that desire will not invoke a "tipping point" that will trigger white racist reaction. It specifically contravened the housing choice of low-income households of color who wished to return to the newly redeveloped site. In one of its most-repeated statements, the court wrote, "To allow housing officials to make decisions having the long range effect of increasing or maintaining racially segregated housing patterns merely because minority groups will gain an immediate benefit would render such persons willing, and perhaps unwitting, partners in the trend toward ghettoization of our urban centers."[94]

Fourth, the court ratifies the pursuit of integration even when it imposes specific burdens on people of color. In *Otero*, NYCHA's fear of tipping meant that families of color who were promised rehousing on site if they so desired were in fact denied it. As the court maintained, "The affirmative duty to consider the impact of publicly assisted housing programs on racial concentration and to act affirmatively to promote the policy of fair, integrated housing is not to be put aside whenever racial minorities are willing to accept segregated housing. The purpose of racial integration is to benefit the community as a whole, not just certain of its members."[95]

As Lake and Winslow point out, the court's position here assumes "the existence of widespread housing options for blacks," a condition that does not hold in many metropolitan areas.[96] Furthermore, the court is suggesting that the preferences of "certain of [the community's] members" are simply to be sacrificed in favor of the preferences of others who desire integration. It is notable that the judges of the Second Circuit made this ruling in the context of the choices made by people of color. This is not a mandate that any judge or group of judges has ever been willing to make concerning whites. We still await the court ruling that so readily dictates to whites the housing choices they can and cannot make.

For all the aggressiveness and commitment to integration reflected in this decision, there is also an unreflective acceptance of white domination through both the concept of integration offered by the court—one that essentially defers to the tolerance level of whites—and in the willingness to impose dictates on people of color related to the legitimacy of the housing choices they can make. While *Otero* proclaims the cause of racial justice, it operates through mechanisms that accept and perpetuate racial oppression.

Since *Otero*, according to Relman et al., subsequent rulings have retreated from the blanket endorsement of integration over choice.[97] *Starret City* ruled that a quota system in the service of integration violated nondiscrimination standards in the Fair Housing Act, thus limiting the application of *Otero*. In 1982, in *Burney v. Housing Authority of Beaver Co.*, the court struck down an integration maintenance program because it limited housing opportunities for blacks.[98] In *U.S. v. Charlottesville Redevelopment and Housing Authority*, the "court struck down ... tenant assignment program as a violation of the FHA, concluding that the duty not to discriminate has priority over the duty to integrate."[99]

Dismantling Existing Communities

The final station in the spatial strategies of the fair housing movement is in many ways the most aggressive and involves the purposeful dismantling of existing communities that integrationists find to be unacceptably segregated. This strategy is carried out through mandatory desegregation orders applied to individual public housing communities, and through federal housing programs that fund the demolition of public housing and the forced displacement of the very low-income residents, predominantly people of color.

This effort to desegregate public housing communities, consistent with so many integrationist initiatives, imposes burdens on people of color that do not apply to whites. The "disestablishment" of segregation is a concept that seems to apply exclusively to communities of color. In just over twenty years of trying, more than a quarter of a million units of public housing have been demolished or otherwise removed from service.[100] As with restrictions on choice described above, efforts to disestablish segregated white communities have not proceeded with anything like the speed and efficiency shown in the efforts to desegregate public housing communities. This is so despite the evidence that whites are the most highly segregated racial group in American metropolitan areas.[101]

It is critical to an evaluation of these efforts that in most cases the original residents of the public housing communities redeveloped have not, in fact, been desegregated. The record of those forcibly displaced by public housing redevelopment shows that most are moved to other low-income, predominantly nonwhite neighborhoods.[102] There is, in short, little evidence that these initiatives actually work in achieving desegregation or in deconcentrating poverty, another rationale widely used to justify demolition and dispersal.

PUBLIC HOUSING DESEGREGATION CASES

Since the early 1990s, fair housing advocates have favored efforts to demolish segregated public housing communities. The effort to take active steps to desegregate public housing stems from a 1984 initiative by then-secretary of HUD, Samuel Pierce. HUD called upon public housing authorities to relocate families and use vacancies to desegregate existing stocks of public housing. In the end, this mandate did not produce much in the way of results.[103]

Roisman describes the subsequent national strategy on the part of civil rights organizations to desegregate public housing communities.[104] Law journal articles were written advancing theories of litigation, and training sessions to support such litigation were sponsored by nonprofit legal groups across the country. These efforts led to class-action lawsuits in Baltimore, Buffalo, Dallas, Minneapolis, Omaha, and Pittsburgh against local housing authorities and HUD for the ways in which operation of public housing programs had contributed to residential segregation. Upon taking office in 1993, President Bill Clinton moved to end the active opposition of the federal government to these cases and authorized settlement negotiations.

The settlements that were reached in a number of cities contain several common elements.[105] First, most call for the demolition of public housing projects with a dramatic loss of such units on the site, and in most cases an absolute loss of assisted units overall. Second, subsidies are shifted into housing choice vouchers, portable subsidies that residents can use in the private housing market. The hope is that these tenant-based subsidies will result in a greater dispersal and deconcentration of assisted families. Third, public housing families are forcibly displaced from their communities.

Many will contest whether the displacement is "forced" or not, since the displacement is a consequence of a class action suit, and those relocated are members of the class of plaintiffs. But merely being a member of the class does not indicate agreement with the legal remedy negotiated by attorneys for the plaintiffs. Furthermore, the remedy in these public housing desegregation lawsuits differs from those in many class action suits in two important ways. First, in many other class action suits, the remedy does not impose what some in the class may see as a burden. The demolition of their public housing homes and their forced relocation to other neighborhoods certainly has the potential to be seen by some public housing residents as undesirable, even if many other residents pursue that very outcome. We have seen this in the many studies of public housing redevelopment around the country.[106] Second, in other class action suits, if one is not interested in or not in agreement with the remedy made available, one is typically not forced to engage with it. In the public housing desegregation lawsuits in which projects are demolished and all residents are moved, members of the plaintiff class who may not agree with the remedy are nevertheless forced to participate in it. That some public housing residents subject to these settlements have felt this way has been documented.[107]

PUBLIC HOUSING DISMANTLING AND *GAUTREAUX*

In Chicago, public housing redevelopment has been greatly affected by the *Gautreaux* settlement. The settlement has limited the amount of public housing that has been rebuilt on the sites of former public housing developments. Even when the residents of the public housing have requested more public housing replacement units, the *Gautreaux* attorneys have worked to limit the number. William Wilen and Wendy Stasell of the National Center on Poverty Law have documented the ways in which the *Gautreaux* attorneys have repeatedly resisted rebuilding public housing units on sites where such housing has been torn down by the CHA. They describe the legal battles over redevelopment at three Chicago public housing sites that ring the downtown area—the Henry Horner Homes to the west, Cabrini-Green to the north, and the ABLA project on the south.

In 1991, residents of the Henry Horner Homes on the city's near west side sued the Chicago Housing Authority, alleging that the agency was engaging in de facto demolition by allowing the development to deteriorate and allowing vacancies to go unfilled.[108] At the time the lawsuit was filed, more than half the units at the Horner Homes were empty. Because Chicago had been chosen to host the 1996 Democratic National Convention, which was to take place at the brand new United Center, just blocks away from the Horner Homes, the city had an interest in fixing up the area. The area around the arena was already being upgraded.[109] As Wilen and Stasell note, the CHA's unwillingness to re-rent units that had been vacated, and its unwillingness to stem the physical decline of the project that resulted from so many vacancies, had the effect of pushing more and more residents out.[110] The claim of de facto demolition held that the CHA was accomplishing the same thing as a physical demolition would have accomplished—it was taking public housing units out of service, but without having received approval from HUD as federal law required, and without having to provide one-for-one replacement of the units lost (required by federal law at that time). After two years of legal proceedings, the Horner residents and the CHA came to an agreement that would demolish two high-rises, rehabilitate three mid-rises, and provide for some new units of public housing. The objective for the Horner residents was to place enough public housing units on site so that every current resident who wished to remain on the site could be accommodated.[111]

The Horner site, however, was located in the "limited area" of the city as defined by the *Gautreaux* court order, and thus any development of public housing on the site required the approval of the court. As *Gautreaux* attorney Alexander Polikoff wrote in his memoir, *Waiting for* Gautreaux, "If we were going to recommend . . . approval for Horner we wanted a mixed-income development, not a mid-rise and low-rise version of concentrated poverty."[112] The *Gautreaux* attorneys vetoed the agreement between the Horner residents and the CHA and insisted on a mixed-income redevelopment in which the number of public housing units was limited. Negotiations began between the *Gautreaux* attorney and attorneys for the Horner residents who wanted the number of public housing units on site to reflect the choice of existing residents rather than a limit set by the *Gautreaux* counsel. Redevelopment of the site was held up for months as the parties negotiated a settlement. In the end, more units were added in order to simultaneously accommodate all the public housing residents who wished to return and create a mixed-income development on the site.

Similar scenarios played out in the Cabrini-Green and ABLA redevelopments. In both cases, the residents sued CHA in order to preserve as many public housing units as possible. And in both cases, the *Gautreaux* attorneys stepped in to limit the replacement of public housing units in order to avoid reconcentrations, regardless of the desires of the resident groups. Because the receiver had been given authority over all CHA development, the CHA could not enter into development agreements by itself. This put the *Gautreaux* attorneys and the receiver in the position of determining redevelopment strategies. The residents of Cabrini-Green realized that their desire to preserve as many public housing units as possible was not going to be approved by *Gautreaux* counsel. The residents asked the court to relieve them of the oversight of the *Gautreaux* order, alleging "that *Gautreaux* plaintiffs' counsel did not adequately represent the interest of the Cabrini residents because his goal was to integrate public housing on a city basis, whereas the [residents] sought to 'maximize the ability of current and former Cabrini-Green residents to remain in their neighborhood.'"[113]

The ABLA case proceeded in a similar fashion, with residents trying to influence the redevelopment process as much as possible to preserve public housing options, and the *Gautreaux* counsel advancing its own redevelopment plan calling for fewer public housing units. The extraordinary efforts on the part of the *Gautreaux* attorneys to shape the remedial efforts in these three cases have in each case pitted the attorneys' vision of integration against the desire of the public housing residents to preserve as much public housing opportunity as possible in these three revitalizing areas.

In the meantime, the majority of displaced public housing residents in the city simply moved to other high-poverty, segregated neighborhoods.[114] As Wilen and Stasell argue, "This type of fair housing is in actuality neither 'fair' nor 'housing.'"[115] It is not fair in the sense that the wishes of low-income public housing residents are disregarded in pursuit of a maximum degree of integration, an objective that is not often on the residents' agenda. It is not "housing" in the sense that it rarely produces more affordable housing for lower-income families than existed previously. At best, the settlements may achieve one-for-one replacement, but typically the number of subsidized low-cost units is reduced.

HOPE VI PUBLIC HOUSING DISMANTLING

Passage of the federal HOPE VI program in 1992 (at that time called the Urban Redevelopment Demonstration program), initiated an era of public housing demolition and redevelopment all across the country. Research has shown that most of the residents displaced by such actions have simply moved to other high-poverty, racially segregated neighborhoods. If the desegregation of original residents is the objective of this effort, it has been an absolute and documented failure. Research has also shown that most of the residents displaced by this effort are African American. In fact, their representation as a percentage of those displaced by public housing redevelopment is disproportionate to their residence in public housing.[116] The program originated in a complex policy environment that included emerging theories about how poor neighborhood conditions can affect the life chances and outcomes of residents, and the redevelopment opportunities provided by a reviving real estate market in America's central cities. The program evolved into one of demolition and displacement over the same time period during which the public housing desegregation lawsuits were being settled. What these efforts have failed to produce, however, is widespread and significant benefits for the original residents of the public housing subjected to redevelopment.[117]

HOPE VI was not explicitly an outcome of fair housing advocacy, and thus the negative outcomes for low-income, black public housing residents should not be laid at the feet of the fair housing movement. It is nevertheless the case that at least one prominent fair housing attorney, lead *Gautreaux* attorney Polikoff, has endorsed the program, calling it the necessary "radical surgery" that highly distressed public housing communities need. Polikoff also acknowledges many of the failures of HOPE VI and argues for better relocation counseling and services for residents who, he notes, have all too often been mistreated in the process.[118] Still, he writes, "even if efforts to improve relocation don't succeed, society should continue to tear down its public housing high-rises."[119]

Integrationists' Paths of Least Resistance

As noted in chapter 1, fair housing advocates frequently criticize the development of affordable housing in disadvantaged neighborhoods as a "path of least resistance." Such an argument suggests that affordable housing is placed in low-income neighborhoods because these neighborhoods lack the resources to effectively oppose such housing. Thus, developers and agencies go where they have a higher likelihood of success, and a reinforcing pattern of spatial concentration of subsidized units ensues. Ironically, the second and third stations of the fair housing spatial strategy outlined above also follow paths of least resistance. Integrationists who focus their strategy on stopping or reducing affordable housing development in disadvantaged neighborhoods capitalize on antipathies toward subsidized housing shared by policy makers and middle- and upper-income citizens. It is typically not difficult to enlist opposition to subsidized housing, especially with an argument that certain places have too much of it. Indeed, as I have pointed out elsewhere, the logic of opposition to affordable housing in the core actually provides a rationale for opposition in exclusionary areas. Defining subsidized housing as a community problem only reinforces the resistance of white middle- and upper-income communities.

Similarly, at the third station of fair housing spatial strategy, integrationists who pursue the demolition of public housing and the dispersal of low-income black communities also trade on these attitudes. Additionally, however, the third station of fair housing spatial strategy also activates the considerable self-interest of landowners, developers, and local officials who benefit from demolition of public housing and the economic and land-use transitions that follow.

Convincing some elected officials and property owners that they have received too much subsidized housing is not so difficult a task, especially compared to the difficulties involved in convincing other officials in exclusionary communities that they need to produce more of such housing. When fair housing integrationists add their voices to the array of interests already opposed to subsidized housing, they follow a path of least resistance. While they may succeed in convincing some officials and activists that their communities are being taken advantage of, these efforts do nothing to get housing built in exclusionary communities. What fair housing integrationists repeatedly fail to demonstrate is how shutting off subsidized housing in the core, or demolishing it, will necessarily reduce opposition to the production of subsidized housing in exclusionary communities.

Since the passage of the Fair Housing Act in 1968, the fair housing movement has mounted an increasingly aggressive spatial strategy to achieve integrationist goals. When fair housing integrationists moved to restrict affordable housing in certain communities, and moved to discourage or outright limit black occupancy in certain neighborhoods, they were asserting the primacy of integration over other housing goals such as equal access. The reluctance on the part of the courts, policy makers, and fair housing integrationists to burden the white community with the obligation of integration is a recurring theme in the decades since the passage of the Fair Housing Act.

Though federal government support for dispersal was halting at first, it has been the centerpiece of federal housing policy since the early 1990s. As integrationists have pushed their agenda, they have challenged a growing number of federal policy initiatives. Integrationists have mounted efforts to bring their agenda to the federal government's sustainability initiatives and to efforts to coordinate housing and transportation policy. In fact, several policy advances since the turn of the century have thrust the fair housing / affordable housing conflict into the forefront. We look at these developments in the next chapter.

NEW ISSUES, UNRESOLVED QUESTIONS, AND THE WIDENING DEBATE

Far from resolving itself over time, the tension related to the siting of subsidized housing is as high now as it has ever been. Several dynamics have contributed to the contemporary tug-of-war between community development and the spatial goals of fair housing. The most important is the ascendancy of dispersal as a policy idea. The idea of mobility and moving people out of pockets of concentrated poverty has dominated urban policy in the United States since the 1990s. The story of this policy idea and its recent rise need not be rehearsed again here.[1] It is enough to note that since the 1990s and since the "discovery" of concentrated poverty by social scientists in the late 1980s, the idea of moving people out of disadvantaged neighborhoods has been dominant. Thus, contemporary fair housing goals related to integration are expressed in the language of poverty deconcentration rather than race. The movement has generated an entire vocabulary of terms and concepts that pepper the narrative about high-poverty neighborhoods and the twenty-first-century solution to urban poverty. Central in this discourse is the concept of "opportunity"—indeed, this concept is the lodestar of the dispersal movement. It is used most frequently not as a noun but as an adjective, describing the type of neighborhood that dispersal advocates regard as appropriate for affordable housing development.

Debate over the effectiveness of dispersal is greater within academia than it is within policy circles. Many studies have documented the pattern of modest and inconsistent gains from dispersal, as well as the costs to families of such a strategy. These findings have produced a nuanced understanding of the circumstances under which such efforts might be expected to generate positive and negative impacts for families. In policy circles, however, little of the nuance survives, and the dispersal strategy is rarely so thoroughly debated. Dispersal is the model of the moment and is very widely accepted as the best path forward for dealing with urban poverty. As I have argued elsewhere, this virtually universal enthusiasm for dispersal is in no small measure due to the ancillary benefits to local officials of opening up significant opportunities for renewed investment and gentrification in core parts of cities.[2]

Adding to the complexity of the current debate is the emergence of sustainability as an important objective for urban policy. Successive recent presidential administrations, but particularly Obama's, have stressed the need for coordinating infrastructure investments in ways that reduce energy consumption and produce more sustainable outcomes. Among other things, this has meant an examination of whether housing and transportation investments should be co-located so as to enhance the value of each. Low-cost housing, it is thought, should be placed near to public transportation infrastructure so that the combined housing and transportation costs of low-income families can be minimized, and so that a ready clientele for public transit exists in proximity to the services created.[3] This formulation, however, has been strongly opposed by fair housing advocates who see in it a spatial pattern of investment that will, in their minds, perpetuate segregation and minimize the development of affordable housing in opportunity areas. Within the Obama administration, the contradiction between the pursuit of urban sustainability and the pursuit of dispersal was never fully resolved.[4]

The Obama administration's relative activism on matters of fair housing also elevated the debate on the spatial distribution of subsidized housing. The administration propagated new rules on disparate impact in 2013 and on affirmatively furthering fair housing in 2015 to guide fair housing work. The Supreme Court's 2015 decision in *Texas DHCA v. ICP* has also focused attention on the issues considered here. These policy developments took place, however, at a time in which the landscape of race and income was changing dramatically in American urban areas, necessitating changes in the way in which spatial goals are articulated. Where once city and suburb stood for the enduring divisions of race and class in U.S. metro areas, now more sophisticated spatial analyses are necessary to describe what some call "the geography of opportunity" in American urban areas.

Changing Context of American Metropolitan Areas

Issues of regional equity and racial segregation and integration are complicated by an increasingly complex suburban demography in the early twenty-first century.

The first significant acknowledgments of suburban diversity were analyses of inner-ring suburban decline in the 1980s and 1990s.[5] The rapidly aging housing stock and weak tax base of inner-ring communities, as well as their relatively high levels of poverty, belied the stereotype of the homogeneous, white, upper-middle class suburb that dominated the popular view of American metropolitan areas. Whether or not this stereotype was ever fully accurate, these changes in suburban demographics have forced a new understanding of the American metropolis.[6] As Karen Chapple argues, "Changes in metropolitan structure have overturned the city-suburb dichotomy as poverty has grown in suburbs and the affluent have flocked to cities."[7]

Contemporary American urban areas are a complex landscape of central city revival and gentrification alongside sporadic economic decline and growing economic and racial diversity in the suburbs.[8]

Suburban Diversity

The economic and demographic profiles of American suburbs have changed dramatically since the 1960s. While suburbs were once thought of as places of extreme race and class homogeneity, they are no longer so. In fact, some argue that the race and class uniformity of suburban areas was always overstated; historian Andrew Wiese writes of his colleagues that "historians have done a better job excluding African Americas from the suburbs than even white suburbanites."[9] Regardless, the degree of racial, ethnic, and class diversity has soared over the past several decades. In fact, the degree of diversity within and across suburbs has moved a number of analysts to propose various typologies of suburbs in order to account for the full range of realities beyond the borders of the central city.[10] Unique forms of suburban differentiation have inspired a number of journalistic and academic efforts to capture the variety of experiences beyond the city limits, producing analyses of places called "edge cities," "boomburbs," "exurbs," "technoburbs," and "ethnoburbs."[11] The differences between suburbs, some note, are often more dramatic than those between city and suburb.[12]

Suburban diversity is in part racial. Rates of suburbanization among African Americans have been significant since the late 1960s. At the same time, some cities have seen significant losses in the number of African American residents, Atlanta, Washington, DC, and Chicago notable among them.[13] In major metropolitan areas of the country, more African Americans live in the suburbs than in central cities, and in at least some metropolitan areas, these residents appear to live in a wide range of suburban types.[14] Still, there is a concern that not all suburban communities have become racially diverse and that in fact settlement patterns outside the central city simply repeat patterns of segregation that characterized neighborhoods within the city.[15]

The picture of suburban diversity includes a large and growing number of immigrants, too. The image of new immigrant groups crowding together in central city neighborhoods belongs to a different century. As urban planner Katrin Anacker points out, some immigrant groups are resettling directly to suburban communities, bypassing central cities altogether.[16] By the end of the first decade of the twenty-first century, there were more immigrants living in American suburbs than in central cities.[17]

Finally, suburban diversity also means growing poverty rates extending not only beyond the central city, but also well beyond inner-ring suburbs. Elizabeth Kneebone and Alan Berube note that during the 1990s, the number of persons below the poverty level in American suburbs grew at twice the rate of city poverty, and accelerated even more so after 2000.[18] Inner-ring suburbs as well as exurban areas have relatively higher poverty rates, but there is also growing poverty in the middle suburbs. Suburbs, in fact, are seeing rapidly increasing rates of "concentrated poverty"—a phenomenon historically associated with the most disadvantaged inner-city neighborhoods.[19] The "near poor," those just above the federal poverty level, are even more suburbanized than are persons below the poverty line.[20]

Some central cities are in effect expelling their poor and losing significant numbers of people of color as a result of gentrifying neighborhoods and rapidly changing land and housing markets that have generated extreme affordability problems for low-income households. Cities such as San Francisco, Seattle, Atlanta, Chicago, and Washington, DC, are seeing rapidly increasing rents that are pushing out lower-income households, who are increasingly moving to nearby suburban counties.[21] At least a portion of this phenomenon has been produced by large-scale government gentrification efforts in the form of public housing redevelopment.[22]

The importance of these demographic changes for the enduring debate between fair housing and community development is not so much in the fact that suburbs are declining and cities reviving, but in the very fact of place-based change. Presumably, fair housing advocates will continue to identify concentrations of people of color and argue for their greater integration regardless of whether these concentrations are in central cities or in first-ring suburbs. As long as segregation persists, it will be the target of fair housing remedies, regardless of the particular pattern of segregation within a metropolitan area. What is important is the more basic fact that the "geography of opportunity" is changing at all, and that metropolitan areas are not static entities. Under such conditions, the integrationist is faced with a difficult task in terms of identifying appropriate "sending" and "receiving" communities for integration initiatives. If the central city revival continues at its current pace, will integrationists be looking to "open up" the same communities that they worked to desegregate a generation earlier? And will they be in the position of desegregating communities that had been the target of their integrating initiatives of a previous generation? The changing metropolitan area puts integrationists in the position of forecasting future demographic changes in order to identify the appropriate targets for their spatial strategies. The potential, in such a situation, for chasing one's tail does not seem so remote.

Gentrification and Fair Housing

The rapidly increasing rents and housing values in many American urban areas threaten to force large numbers of low-income residents and people of color out of central cities in the near future. Though not a universal phenomenon, gentrification is increasingly common and has been accelerated since the recovery from the 2007–2010 recession.[23] New York City and San Francisco are the most prominent cases, but the phenomenon has produced significant changes in Chicago, Seattle, Washington, DC, and reaches to so-called mid-level cities such as Minneapolis and Portland, Oregon.[24]

For areas seeing rising prices and displacement, subsidized housing is an important way to preserve affordability and keep people in neighborhoods they would otherwise be forced to leave. In Washington, DC, for example, where gentrification has led to significant displacement of people of color, subsidized housing efforts have been recognized by local officials as an important tool in keeping residents in place as neighborhoods change around them.[25] City officials passed a budget for 2016 that directed $178 million to affordable housing in part to protect residents in gentrifying neighborhoods.[26]

But merely building subsidized housing in gentrifying neighborhoods does not guarantee that existing residents will be lucky enough to benefit from it, especially in cities with very long waiting lists for such housing. This has led some places, such as San Francisco, to provide long-term residents priority access to subsidized housing in gentrifying neighborhoods. In 2016 the city developed a plan to give residents of gentrifying neighborhoods preferential access to subsidized housing in order to help them remain in their communities. Similar efforts, referred to as "neighborhood preference" plans, have been used in the past by largely white communities to exclude newcomers, and thus have been targets of fair housing advocacy for many years. In this case, however, the City of San Francisco wanted to protect households of color from displacement and forced relocation from their neighborhoods that were seeing rapid increases in housing costs. Federal officials initially applied a narrow fair housing interpretation and rejected the San Francisco plan, arguing that it would perpetuate racial segregation despite the obvious demographic changes taking place in the city and in the city's predominantly black neighborhoods. Leaders of the black community in San Francisco reacted, calling the HUD ruling "devastating" and "an egregious injustice against African-Americans in this city."[27] The application of fair housing logic in this case was harming people of color rather than protecting them. The city appealed HUD's ruling, and the federal agency relented somewhat, allowing the preference but requiring the city to expand eligibility to residents from throughout the city and without regard to race.[28]

San Francisco is not the only place attempting to use neighborhood preferences to protect households at risk of displacement from gentrification. Anti-gentrification neighborhood preference has been contested in New York City by those who claim that predominantly white neighborhoods are using it to exclude people of color.[29] The use of preferences by Portland, Oregon, in contrast, has not encountered opposition locally or by HUD.[30]

The issue of gentrification provides another opportunity for the fair housing / affordable housing tension to surface. Fair housers driven by the impulse to desegregate central city neighborhoods are wary of attempts to preserve affordability in what previously had been low-income communities. They may oppose both the construction of subsidized housing in these neighborhoods and the use of neighborhood preferences to target that housing toward existing residents. Affordable housing and community advocates, on the other hand, place a higher premium on protecting low-income households and households of color from involuntary displacement that accompanies gentrification.

Opportunity Is a Place

The concept of "geography of opportunity" emerged in policy circles during the 1990s as federal housing policy was shifting toward the mobility and dispersal paradigm. The term is meant to highlight the spatially differentiated pattern of life chances within metropolitan areas and to reflect the fact that opportunities are unevenly distributed across urban areas. In policy terms, the phrase "opportunity neighborhood" is used to denote locations that are desirable because of the range of private and public amenities they possess and for the advantages they confer upon residents. "Opportunity neighborhoods" are contrasted with disadvantaged neighborhoods, generally defined as neighborhoods with higher levels of poverty and a higher proportion of people of color.[31] On the assumption that residence in opportunity neighborhoods improves the quality of life of targeted populations, federal housing policy shifted during the 1990s to programs that were designed to move federally subsidized households toward opportunity neighborhoods. Opportunity neighborhoods have since become the holy grail of U.S. housing policy, with a range of local efforts across the country, both public and private, adopting the framework.

The "opportunity neighborhood" discourse originated outside of a narrow fair housing framework. In fact, for more than a decade it was carefully associated with the objective of poverty deconcentration rather than racial desegregation. Early policy initiatives within the opportunity neighborhood framework were aimed at moving people around in order to establish a better mix. That is to say, early programs to enhance opportunity were predominantly displacement/relocation/redevelopment efforts. The original framing of the concept of opportunity neighborhoods was hostile to the idea of community development. Many of the proponents of the opportunity neighborhood approach saw the solution to urban problems in the reorientation of policy initiatives away from small-scale, place-based community development and toward facilitating greater access for lower-income populations to areas outside the core. Thus, David Rusk and others argued that even the largest community development efforts have failed at turning around the basic pattern of central city decline.[32] The first wave of opportunity neighborhood initiatives that took place between 1980 and 2000 reflected these ideas and emphasized the geographic mobility of low-income people.

"Opportunity Neighborhood" Initiatives

In practice, early programs at the federal and local level have been aimed at enhancing the access of the poor and people of color to "opportunity neighborhoods" in two ways. First, and most commonly, programs such as the Gautreaux mobility program, the Moving to Opportunity demonstration program, and other deconcentration and desegregation efforts are designed to achieve the desired outcome by moving *people to opportunity* through relocation, either forced or voluntary. Modifications to the longer-standing programs such as the housing choice voucher program have also been considered for their potential to increase the movement to opportunity among assisted households.[33] Second, and somewhat less frequently, programs are designed to bring *opportunity to places* through redevelopment. The HOPE VI program of public housing demolition and relocation worked, according to its proponents, in both directions, first displacing and forcing the relocation of social housing residents and then redeveloping social housing estates into mixed-income communities and triggering a real estate and investment revival in areas that previously had been largely ignored.[34]

The classic expression of the urban "geography of opportunity" has relied on a pair of simple dichotomies. The first of these was the Manichean division of neighborhoods into categories of "good" or "bad."[35] High-poverty and/or racially segregated neighborhoods were inevitably interpreted as possessing and producing problematic socioeconomic processes. They were seen as neighborhoods that people should strive to leave, and, in the case of public housing communities, areas requiring total clearance, demolition, and reinvention. Conversely, opportunity neighborhoods were seen, equally simplistically, as largely free of problematic aspects for low-income households. The second dichotomy driving the early ideas about opportunity neighborhoods is a geographic one that juxtaposes central city and suburb, largely situating opportunity in suburban areas and its opposite in older, core neighborhoods of metropolitan areas.[36]

Initially, opportunity neighborhoods were typically operationalized by racial mix, or by poverty rate (and less frequently, by both).[37] However, if the concept of opportunity neighborhood is meant to illuminate the pattern of life chances and potentialities available across metropolitan areas, and how these correlate with poverty or race, then the concept itself should not be measured by the degree of poverty or race. Measuring the degree of opportunity in a neighborhood by measuring the percentage of people of color or the poverty rate *defines* communities of color as low-opportunity places. The utility of the concept of opportunity neighborhood, if there is utility, should be in allowing an analysis of the types and degrees of opportunity that are available in communities of color or in low-income communities as compared to other neighborhoods. Such analysis is precluded when opportunity is defined according to the race and poverty status of residents.

As time has passed, the inadequacies of such definitions have generally given way to more sophisticated measurements.[38] Measures of opportunity increasingly focus on non-demographic indicators such as proximity to employment, transit, and well-performing schools.[39] As the concept has advanced in use, furthermore, it has taken on complexity in other ways. Most significant was the emergence of a more multidimensional definition of opportunity. Instead of a simple dichotomy, opportunity is understood by some to have several dimensions, including proximity to employment centers, high-quality educational facilities, access to transit, and even environmental opportunity (defined as freedom from nearby environmental hazards). Such multidimensionality should also imply that in some cases the dimensions of opportunity could be cross-cutting and in fact contradictory. Consequently, a third important development in the notion of "opportunity neighborhood" might be the understanding that areas can be simultaneously high in some types of opportunity and low in others. Finally, there is a high likelihood that these more sophisticated geographies of opportunity will vary dramatically from one metropolitan area to the next on the basis of how jobs are distributed throughout the region, the nature and extent of public transit systems, and other characteristics of place and policies.[40]

This more nuanced understanding of opportunity is not universally held, however. One still finds "opportunity maps" that insist on a simplistic single index ranking neighborhoods from low to high opportunity.[41] The 2012 report *Equity, Opportunity, and Sustainability in the Central Puget Sound Region* is an example of the tendency toward a simplistic single index of opportunity.[42] Though the report measures and maps opportunity along five dimensions, it does not discuss the ways in which the five dimensions reflect different geographies and what the mix of opportunities is within different neighborhoods. Instead, the authors forfeit the richness of five different indicators by forcing them into a single composite index. The idea that opportunity can be reduced to a single index and that neighborhoods can be characterized as either having or not having opportunity must give way to the idea that areas differ in the types of opportunity that they provide or lack. Together, these developments in the concept of opportunity suggest a matrix of types of opportunity and places.

While the first wave of opportunity initiatives was focused primarily on housing policy and programs related to the location of assisted households (and assisted units), the second wave has increasingly involved a range of policy areas. Perhaps most notable is the role that transit investments have played in propelling the idea of access to opportunity, as well as in helping to define the elements that make up an opportunity matrix. Some current efforts at measuring and mapping opportunity emerged from regional efforts to plan transit investments.[43] These efforts have been aimed at maximizing the impact of transit on improving accessibility for lower-income, transit-dependent populations. Other opportunity mapping efforts have emerged from advocacy efforts frequently supported by foundations, pursuing the goal of regional equity, itself a concept that is variously defined.[44]

Opportunity and Fair Housing

When opportunity is defined only by race, as in the Gautreaux program, there is truly no distinction between the mobility objectives of the program and the desegregation objectives of contemporary fair housing doctrine. But even when policy makers shifted language from racial desegregation to poverty deconcentration, the overlap between the objectives of the "opportunity neighborhood" agenda and fair housing were obvious and extensive. Fair housing advocates have, as a result, generally been quite supportive of the wave of opportunity initiatives and policy language, seeing in them a means of achieving integration goals. Concentrated poverty in the United States is heavily racialized—African Americans in poverty are many times more likely to live in concentrated poverty than their white counterparts, and the notion of the "opportunity neighborhood" has been embedded in various nonfederal racial desegregation initiatives, including programs that resulted from the desegregation lawsuits settled during the 1990s.[45]

The Siting Controversies of the LIHTC

As the debate between fair housing and community development has renewed and intensified since 2000, fair housing advocates have been aggressive in applying fair housing goals to the nation's largest program of subsidized housing production, the Low Income Housing Tax Credit program. The decentralized nature of the allocation of tax credits under LIHTC and the fact that the federal authority for the program is the Department of the Treasury and not HUD make LIHTC unique among federal housing programs. Fair housing advocates have reasonably and successfully argued that the provisions of the Fair Housing Act are as relevant for LIHTC, a program not operated by HUD, as they are for any program run by the agency. This advocacy has led to a spate of studies about the spatial distribution of tax credit projects and whether they do in fact reinforce patterns of racial segregation. It has also led to legal action challenging the allocation of tax credits in some states. Fair housing advocates argue that the program is being operated in ways that perpetuate segregation by placing too many units in minority and high-poverty neighborhoods.

The Spatial Distribution of Tax Credit Housing

The program operates by providing tax credits to investors in subsidized housing. The program, enacted in 1986, authorized $1.25 per capita in tax credits and allocates these on a state-by-state basis. The amount of credits allowed is currently adjusted for inflation. Each state develops a Qualified Allocation Plan (QAP), which sets out the guidelines for allocating tax credits to developer applicants. These QAPs allow the states to build into the program ancillary policy objectives by incentivizing certain types of developments, such as those near transit facilities, or projects with energy-saving designs, for example. In fact, the federal legislation itself requires that QAPs incorporate additional selection criteria, including whether the project serves populations with special housing needs, provides for eventual tenant ownership, or is energy efficient.[46] The inescapable conclusion from any reading of the statute is that Congress intended LIHTC to serve many policy objectives and that it wanted states to have some flexibility in the prioritizing of those objectives.

Congress went beyond merely suggesting additional objectives to be incorporated into the tax credit program by specifically mandating three such objectives.

The legislation requires preferences be given to projects that serve the lowest-income tenants, that provide assisted housing for the longest period of time, and for projects located in distressed neighborhoods (so-called "qualified census tracts"—QCTs) that contribute to "a concerted community revitalization plan."[47] QCTs are defined in the law as tracts with either a poverty rate greater than 25 percent, or a tract in which more than 50 percent of households have incomes at or below 60 percent of the area median income. The QCT requirement is, in effect, a congressional directive to use LIHTC to support community development projects in disadvantaged neighborhoods. This provision of the program was added by amendments in 1989 and further defined in 2000. Thus, on those two occasions Congress indicated not only that projects in QCTs were acceptable, but that they were to be incentivized.

The QCT requirement is the provision of the law that is most widely opposed by fair housing advocates. Congressional intent is fairly clear in this case, and it is that intent that fair housing advocates oppose. Fair housers generally consider the QCT requirement a mistake, a misguided continuation of housing policies that have led to segregation. As fair housing attorney Elizabeth Julian argues, "When the LIHTC program was created, the legacy of segregation in prior housing programs for low-income people was ignored in both the statute and the regulatory process."[48] Revision of the QCT requirement is a standard recommendation in assessments of the LIHTC program.[49] Frequently, LIHTC implementation is criticized for ignoring the second clause of the QCT requirement, that the housing built in disadvantaged neighborhoods be tied to a "concerted community revitalization plan." That is, LIHTC projects in QCTs are criticized for being one-off projects that only have the effect of locating affordable, subsidized units in a high-poverty neighborhood rather than being part of a larger community development effort. In some cases, the community development objective of LIHTC is simply ignored or dismissed in fair housing analyses of LIHTC. For example, a national analysis of state QAPs, sponsored by the Poverty and Race Research Action Council, begins with this assertion: "LIHTC is most valuable when it does things that choice-based housing vouchers cannot do or do as well."[50] Having established its own standard for evaluating the program, the analysis goes on to say, "therefore, LIHTC developments should provide housing in situations where vouchers are difficult to use."[51] This proposition is then used as the principal, indeed the lone standard for the assessment of QAPs that ensues.

The spatial distribution of tax credit units has, in fact, attracted a great deal of research attention in the past fifteen years.[52] Social scientists have examined the degree to which tax credit projects have penetrated the suburbs, and analyzed the distribution of units according to the demographic characteristics of locations, school quality, and crime rates. The clustering of LIHTC units has been assessed using spatial statistics, too. All this is done to assess the degree to which the program upholds fair housing expectations. The findings of these many studies are converging on a single story: while LIHTC is not integrating communities, it is also not contributing to greater segregation or concentrations of poverty. Researchers have found, for example, "no evidence that the LIHTC program contributes to greater segregation" and in fact find that at the metropolitan level, increases in LIHTC production are associated with declines in racial segregation.[53] Similarly, a study of all projects developed between 2004 and 2009 reports that "concerns that the LIHTC-subsidized development is contributing to substantial poverty concentration . . . are largely misplaced."[54] In fact, LIHTC projects actually decrease poverty rates in high-poverty neighborhoods.[55] The tax credit program does a better job than other subsidized housing programs in building in suburban areas, and LIHTC projects tend to be located in less distressed neighborhoods than other low-income housing production programs.[56]

On the other hand, a study of LIHTC in Dallas found that almost half of all units have been built in disadvantaged neighborhoods, while just more than half are located in neighborhoods that reflect the average social conditions within the region.[57] In Ohio, researchers found that almost half of tax credit units were built in high-poverty neighborhoods, and less than a third built in neighborhoods of "low racial concentration."[58] Another study of ten metro areas found that in most of the regions studied, LIHTC is clustered in central-city neighborhoods with comparatively high rates of poverty and higher percentages of people of color.[59]

In the end, however, the real variety in these studies is not so much the empirical findings as it is the interpretation given to those findings. For example, while some conclude that LIHTC is not deepening segregation or poverty concentrations in the areas studied, others apply a different standard and conclude that LIHTC is not integrating lower-income households.[60] Not addressed in any of these studies is what should actually be expected from a program that has an incentive to contribute to community revitalization built into it and that, from state to state, is enlisted to serve a range of additional policy objectives. Instead, virtually all recent studies of the program focus on one objective only, the spatial dispersal of tax-credit housing.

LIHTC Legal Actions

As posed by fair housing attorney Elizabeth Julian, the challenge for the LIHTC program is to not follow "in the footsteps of its predecessors by agreeing to trade off the civil rights of low-income people of color in order to get the housing."[61] Lawsuits in several states have challenged local practices in order to ensure that outcome. The legal actions have contested QAPs that, fair housing advocates feel, have resulted in too high a concentration of LIHTC units in disadvantaged minority areas.

NEW JERSEY

One of the first major suits of this type was filed in New Jersey in 2003 by the Fair Share Housing Center and the Camden Chapter of the NAACP.[62] The suit challenged the New Jersey Housing and Mortgage Finance Agency's Qualified Allocation Plans for 2002 and 2003. The Fair Share Housing Center "pushed for a ruling from the Court that would prevent any LIHTC allocations in high-poverty, predominantly minority census tracts."[63] The case pitted fair housing advocates against affordable housing providers and community developers. The plaintiffs strongly challenged the idea that building tax credit housing in central neighborhoods had any potential to revitalize the community. Journalist Robert Neuwirth quotes the associate director and staff attorney for the Fair Share Housing Center as claiming that "our case challenges the notion that more or new affordable housing in cities is fundamentally helpful for revitalization. In fact, building affordable housing in the cities has no net revitalizing effect at all."[64] This is part of the larger fair housing argument regarding the ineffectiveness of community development and the contention that affordable housing, in any case, does not contribute to such goals.[65]

Affordable housing developers responded by arguing that the position of the plaintiffs in the New Jersey case, one that would limit LIHTC housing in core neighborhoods, was the equivalent of "condemning poor people to awful living conditions while claiming to fight on their behalf."[66] In the end the court ruled in favor of the defendants, upholding the New Jersey QAP. Since then, however, the state has changed its allocation plan in the direction advocated by fair housing activists and now includes more incentives for development in "opportunity neighborhoods."[67]

DALLAS

In Texas, the Inclusive Communities Project (ICP), a fair housing advocacy group based in Dallas, filed suit in March 2008 claiming that the Texas Department of Housing and Community Affairs (TDHCA), the state allocator of tax credits, was causing tax credit units "to be disproportionately located in the slum and blighted neighborhoods in the City of Dallas."[68] The ICP further argued that TDHCA actions were preventing the development of LIHTC units in white neighborhoods of the region. Statistics showed that 85 percent of LIHTC units in the region were in minority tracts, compared to only 51 percent of all rental housing units, and that Dallas-area LIHTC units were located in "neighborhoods with high crime and high poverty rates and that are blighted by industrial facilities such as illegal landfills."[69] The ICP complaint urged the court to establish balance in the distribution of LIHTC projects, asking for a requirement that the TDHCA "allocate Low Income Housing Tax Credits in the Dallas metropolitan area in a manner that creates as many Low Income Housing Tax Credit assisted units in non-minority census tracts as exist in minority census tracts."[70]

The TDHCA spent over $1 million defending itself in this suit and argued that the spatial distribution of tax credit units in Dallas was due to the choices made by developers and to the QCT incentive. The ICP argued that the over-representation of LIHTC units in minority neighborhoods was caused by the agency denying projects in white areas. The U.S. District Court found in favor of the plaintiffs on the central question and ordered Texas to revise its selection criteria for tax credit projects to emphasize high-quality schools and avoid proximity to disamenities.[71] The State of Texas appealed the case and in the end won when the district court ruled that the ICP had not proven that the Texas allocation system was causing the spatial and racial disparities in tax credit projects in the Dallas region.[72]

MINNEAPOLIS–SAINT PAUL

In 2014, fair housing advocates filed complaints in the Twin Cities of Minneapolis and Saint Paul against the State Housing Finance Agency, the regional planning agency (Metropolitan Council), and the two central cities, claiming that each has operated the LIHTC program in ways that perpetuate segregation.[73] The complaints produced the same battle lines seen in the New Jersey case, with community development organizations lining up strongly in opposition to the filings, concerned that the legal actions were aimed at significantly limiting their efforts in core neighborhoods of the region. Fair housing advocates in the Twin Cities mounted an aggressive attack on community development, to the point of publicizing the salaries of CDC staff, accusing them in essence of enriching themselves at the expense of lower-income people of color in the neighborhoods in which they operate. The attacks were accompanied by analyses of community development projects purporting to show that they do not produce benefits for the community, and that they are overly costly.[74] Joining CDCs in opposition were, of course, the four defendants (the state, the regional planning body, and both central cities), a group of Latino elected officials from the core neighborhoods of the central cities, and a coalition of community organizations and residents working in core neighborhoods.

The Twin Cities fair housing activists were joined in their efforts by the New York attorney who was counsel for the plaintiffs in the *Westchester* case.[75] The actual complainants were a religious-based housing advocacy group, three inner-ring suburbs, and three Minneapolis neighborhood groups. These latter groups joined the complaint because they regarded their own areas as having done their fair share in providing affordable housing. The communities involved, both the inner-ring suburbs and the neighborhoods represented among the complainants, had a large amount of "naturally occurring affordable housing" and, they felt, more than their share of affordable housing.

There was significantly less evidence to support the LIHTC complaints in the Twin Cities compared to the Dallas case. The distribution of tax credit units was roughly proportional to need, and racially concentrated areas of poverty had received less than 10 percent of tax credit units over the five years preceding the filing of the complaint. Even the two inner-ring suburbs that joined the plaintiffs had demonstrably not received an outsized share of tax credit units.[76] In May 2016 both cities settled the complaints with HUD, agreeing to participate in an extensive analysis of impediments to fair housing in the region that would include extensive engagement with community members.[77]

Sustainability and Housing/Transportation Affordability

The national debate over the siting of subsidized housing has been further complicated by recent government initiatives in the area of sustainability. The Obama administration was the first to promulgate and pursue a set of policy principles directly related to sustainable urban development and "livability." The largest first-term initiative in this area was the Sustainable Communities Initiative (SCI), a partnership effort between HUD, the Department of Transportation, and the Environmental Protection Agency. Grants to local and regional governments were made in 2010 and 2011 to support regional planning and development efforts that would coordinate housing, urban development, and transportation investments to reduce energy consumption, environmental deterioration, and greenhouse gas emissions in major metropolitan areas. More than $230 million in grants were made to 143 recipients to coordinate local planning aimed at achieving six livability principles for metropolitan areas.[78] The principles emphasize transit and housing equity, coordinated local investment strategies, and growth that supports existing infrastructure investments.

At the center of SCI was the goal of coordinating housing and transportation policy. HUD took several additional steps in that direction, including development of a Location Affordability Index (LAI) in 2014 as a new way of measuring housing affordability. The LAI measures the combined housing and transportation costs in a neighborhood, providing a more nearly complete understanding of the true cost of living in any given area than is provided by traditional housing affordability measures. Whether it is used to determine how housing programs impact the transportation costs of assisted families or where to place assisted housing in order to minimize transportation costs, the LAI highlights the advantages of locating affordable housing in core areas that are well served by transit.

The Obama administration also provided support to local governments for transit-oriented development as a way of maximizing both housing and transit investments. Transit-oriented development was seen by the administration as a more efficient form of land use in metropolitan areas, ensuring greater job accessibility for lower-income residents, and ensuring a greater ridership base for the transit systems the administration supported. Also providing a rationale for the co-location of transit and affordable housing is the fact that transit invest-ments frequently drive up housing values nearby.[79] Some observers refer to this as "transit-induced gentrification" and recommend subsidized housing as a way of mitigating displacement that might result from rising housing prices.[80]

The spatial location of most subsidized housing means that it generally ranks high on various sustainability measures. In Chicago, for example, subsidized housing projects are located, on average, in more sustainable neighborhoods than those inhabited by housing choice voucher households.[81] Public housing high-rises for seniors and LIHTC units scored the highest in terms of neighbor-hood sustainability.

The challenge, of course, is to reconcile policy initiatives designed to enhance sustainability policy with the fair housing directive to disperse subsidized hous-ing. The sustainability imperative for the Obama administration was transit connectivity—that is, the co-location of assisted housing and transit to reduce the transportation costs of assisted households, and the more intensive use of existing infrastructure. Such strategies imply greater investment in affordable housing in core areas of metropolitan regions that are well-served by transit and other infrastructure. The spatial strategy of fair housing, in contrast, is to dis-perse and deconcentrate assisted households to "opportunity neighborhoods," many of which are ill-served or entirely unserved by transit.[82] While location-efficiency goals prioritize development in the core, the spatial objectives of fair housing emphasize the decentralization of low-income households of color.

The tension between the two goals is clearly recognized by fair housing advo-cates. A leading national advocacy organization for fair housing, the Poverty & Race Research Action Council, for example, called the LAI an "inappropriate tool for siting new low-income housing," and fair housing advocates have opposed transit-oriented development plans that call for affordable housing along transit lines because of fears that to locate assisted housing by transit would perpetuate segregation.[83] In fact, fair housing activists worry that HUD and the Department of Transportation overemphasize the importance of housing cost and transit access, and urge policy makers instead to "recognize the additional variables greatly impacting household costs and quality of life."[84]

Another response made to the sustainability challenge is to argue that the benefits of transit accessibility and even employment accessibility are not as important as the advantages of white, suburban neighborhoods. Pendall and Parilla, for example, write, "We suspect that the transportation and economic advantages, compared to lower poverty and lower crime areas . . . are probably modest."[85] Though some diminish the importance of the housing/transportation policy alignment, there is evidence that transportation is identified as a major impediment to employment for a significant number of very low-income families.[86] Very low-income people disproportionately lack automobiles, a pattern that is even more pronounced for welfare recipients.[87] Furthermore, even though jobs are suburbanizing, accessibility may be limited by poor transit coverage. In Chicago suburbs, for example, a ninety-minute commute provides poor residents access to only 14 percent of the region's jobs.[88] Ninety-five percent of households without a car and lacking transit service live in the suburbs.[89]

The availability of transit is one of the reasons why low-skilled workers have better job access in central cities compared to suburban residents.[90] In Los Angeles, for example, "poor inner-city job seekers have greater job accessibility than do most of their suburban counterparts. Moreover, poor inner-city job seekers do not have lesser job accessibility than the regional average."[91]

Fair Housing during the Obama Administration

Tensions between community development and the spatial goals of fair housing were intensified by several developments in fair housing policy during the Obama administration. One month after Obama's election in 2008, the National Commission on Fair Housing and Equal Opportunity, an independent group organized by fair housing advocates, issued a report expressing disappointment in the federal government's efforts to combat discrimination in housing.[92] Specifically, the report stated that "fair housing enforcement at HUD is failing" and pointed to a number of deficiencies in the agency's efforts in the years prior to 2008. The commission went so far as to recommend that fair housing enforcement be taken away from HUD and moved to a new and different agency. The federal government's disregard for effective enforcement of fair housing, according to the commission, had extended as well to the Department of Justice (DOJ), which under the law has the authority to initiate lawsuits against public and private actors engaging in "a pattern and practice of discrimination" in housing. The commission documented the small and declining number of housing discrimination cases filed by the DOJ through the first eight years of the new century.

In contrast to the indifferent enforcement of fair housing under his predecessors, Obama made fair housing a central objective, and his administration initiated several actions that fair housing advocates applauded.[93] The administration strengthened the administrative basis for fair housing enforcement and expanded the number and type of discrimination cases pursued. To the National Alliance for Fair Housing, these changes and others constituted a "sea change in the federal government's approach to fair housing."[94]

Westchester County

Early in Obama's first term, the DOJ settled a high-profile suit against Westchester County, a suburb of New York City, in which the county agreed to develop hundreds of subsidized units in predominantly white sections of the county and to prevent housing discrimination. The legal strategy behind the case was to tie the county's status as a recipient of HUD funds to the obligation to use HUD funds to further fair housing. The plaintiffs argued that the county should forfeit those federal funds because they were not being used to further fair housing objectives. The administration promised, furthermore, to hold hundreds of other cities and counties to the same standard.[95] Though the settlement has been plagued by the county's lack of progress in making good on its promises, the suit itself was an early and high-profile statement that the administration would take its fair housing responsibilities very seriously.

Disparate Impact

The distinction between discriminatory intent and discriminatory effect has been important in fair housing enforcement from the outset. Establishing disparate impact in housing discrimination cases is an easier standard to meet than showing discriminatory intent, and thus it widens the potential application of fair housing requirements. The decision to pursue cases using a disparate-impact claim has been an important point of variation in fair housing enforcement, with Republican and Democratic administrations choosing different standards. For years the courts have acknowledged the validity of fair housing claims based on the discriminatory effects of practices in question, as well as cases in which discriminatory intent can be shown. Aiming to standardize the interpretation of the disparate-impact rules, the Obama administration issued regulations in 2013 that define the conditions under which disparate-impact claims can be made.[96] The regulations were long awaited by fair housing advocates who hoped to formalize the government's recognition of a legal standard that would prohibit seemingly neutral policies and practices that have the effect of denying housing opportunities to members of protected classes.

Texas DHCA v. ICP

Despite overwhelming support for the notion of disparate impact by lower courts (the nine U.S. appellate courts that have considered the issue have confirmed disparate-impact claims), until 2015 the U.S. Supreme Court had never considered the issue in the context of housing discrimination. The Roberts court, however, seemed anxious to weigh in with a definitive statement. In 2013 the court agreed to review *Gallagher v. Magner*, a case in which the housing code enforcement of the city of Saint Paul, Minnesota, was argued to be driving up rents in low-income areas, producing a disparate and negative impact on people of color.[97] Fair housing advocates were not confident, given the makeup of the Supreme Court, that disparate impact would survive a direct legal challenge. At the eleventh hour, the parties in *Gallagher* were persuaded to settle out of court, depriving the court of its chance to settle the issue. Not to be denied, the court sought another case that would give it this opportunity. The justices settled on *Township of Mount Holly v. Mount Holly Gardens Citizens in Action, Inc.*[98] In this case, residents of Mount Holly Gardens sued to stop the township from pursuing a redevelopment plan that would displace them. Because the community was largely people of color, the legal argument was that the redevelopment would have a negative and disparate impact on members of a protected class. The Supreme Court agreed to hear this case in July 2013. Five months later the *Mount Holly* case, too, settled out of court, and fair housing advocates once again avoided a direct Supreme Court ruling on disparate impact.

In 2014, the Supreme Court tried yet a third time to address the issue of disparate impact in housing discrimination and agreed to hear the Texas Low Income Housing Tax Credit case, *Texas Department of Housing and Community Affairs et al. v. The Inclusive Communities Project, Inc., et al.* In the spring of 2015 the court heard arguments, and in July it issued a surprise ruling: in a 5–4 decision the court held that disparate impact claims are allowable under the Fair Housing Act. This represented an unexpected but significant victory for fair housing.

The potential for disparate impact to essentially "resolve" the debate over dispersal versus community development decisively in favor of dispersal is clear enough. If the fair housing argument concerning the perpetuation of segregation were to be accepted by the court, community development activities could be interpreted as having a negative and disparate impact on members of protected classes living in core neighborhoods. This issue was, of course, the substantive question at stake in *Texas DHCA v. ICP*. Such an outcome would make community development and affordable housing efforts in core neighborhoods subject to disparate-impact claims, essentially leaving them valid only where fair housing advocates approved. This would emphatically place community development in a subordinate position compared to the spatial objectives of fair housing. Importantly, however, the Supreme Court ruled only on the procedural question of whether disparate impact is an actionable claim under the Fair Housing Act. The court's ruling, however, did not reassess the substantive findings of the earlier ICP decision that the Texas Department of Housing and Community Affair's allocation of tax credits violated the Fair Housing Act. As the majority opinion clarified in the opening paragraph, "the question presented for the Court's determination is whether disparate-impact claims are cognizable under the Fair Housing Act."[99]

As to the fair housing / community development debate, the court reaffirmed the validity of multiple policy objectives in the operation of housing policy. The court reasoned that "from the standpoint of determining advantage or disadvantage to racial minorities, it seems difficult to say as a general matter that a decision to build low-income housing in a blighted inner-city neighborhood instead of a suburb is discriminatory, or vice versa."[100] Furthermore, noted the court, "If the specter of disparate-impact litigation causes private developers to no longer construct or renovate housing units for low-income individuals, then the FHA would have undermined its own purpose. . . . And as to governmental entities, they must not be prevented from achieving legitimate objectives."[101] The decision clearly acknowledges community development and puts it on equal footing with dispersal. The majority opinion holds that "disparate-impact liability mandates the 'removal of artificial, arbitrary, and unnecessary barriers,' not the displacement of valid governmental policies. . . . The FHA is not an instrument to force housing authorities to reorder their priorities."[102] The court continues, "It would be paradoxical to construe the FHA to impose onerous costs on actors who encourage revitalizing dilapidated housing in our Nation's cities merely because some other priority might seem preferable."[103] Thus, the Supreme Court decision in *Texas DHCA v. ICP* affirms the legitimacy of disparate impact claims but leaves intact the central debate between the competing policy objectives of integration and community development.

The decision relies on the 2013 HUD rule laying out the procedure for disparate-impact claims. According to the rule (and quoted by the court in its decision), disparate impact "does not mandate that affordable housing be located in neighborhoods with any particular characteristic."[104] The rule allows public agencies to demonstrate that the patterns producing disparate impact have been created in the pursuit of valid and alternative policy objectives. Disparate-impact claims prevail according to the court (relying on the 2013 rules) only if the plaintiffs can *then* demonstrate that the alternative policy objectives can be met without producing disparate impacts.

The interpretation of the ruling, however, by practitioners is what will actually determine its impact. One policy blog written shortly after the ruling maintains that "it is highly likely that developers and advocates of traditional community development will need to meet much higher standards for showing how current and future minority residents would benefit from revitalization."[105] The writers, both affiliated with the Urban Land Institute, go on to aver that "community developers may face more concerted legal opposition to their housing activities as well."[106] There is some evidence that governmental officials, too, see the court's ruling as a directive to shift strategies away from investment in the core. Two months after the decision, for example, an official with the Georgia Department of Community Affairs said, "If the end result [of the agency's practices] is that we are primarily building in high minority areas with no access to community resources, then we need to make changes in the Qualified Allocation Plan [of the tax credit program]."[107] If this interpretation prevails, the early net effect of *Texas DHCA v. ICP* will be a victory for the spatial strategy of fair housing advocates at the expense of community development.

Affirmatively Furthering Fair Housing

Obama's HUD also took action to codify the affirmatively furthering fair housing (AFFH) provision of the 1968 act. The AFFH provision thus requires that in addition to regulating the actions of the private sector in housing, the federal government ensure that its own programs and its own actions further fair housing goals. The AFFH clause has been interpreted to directly apply to federal actions implementing housing programs (for example, governing the siting of federally subsidized housing to ensure that the placement of subsidized units does not maintain or enhance patterns of segregation) and, more indirectly, to apply to the use of federal housing and community development funds by state and local governments.

AFFH establishes the obligation on the part of the federal government to ensure that local governments spend federal housing and community development funds in accordance with fair housing goals. Thus, local jurisdictions receiving federal Community Development Block Grant or HOME funds, for example, must certify that they are affirmatively furthering fair housing in their use of these federal funds. The suit against Westchester County described earlier was based on an assessment that the county had been spending federal grant funds in ways that reinforced patterns of racial segregation and furthermore had made false claims to the federal government about its programs.

Fair housing advocates have long complained that the AFFH goals have typically been subordinated within HUD, taking a backseat to concerns about program implementation and housing production goals. In addition, activists have criticized the weak nature of federal oversight of local governments' compliance with AFFH obligations. As a result, the Obama administration issued a set of rules for AFFH in 2015. Specifically, the rules strengthen the requirements for local governments to assess local fair housing issues and to incorporate fair housing goals into a local plan of action by laying out steps for analysis of local housing conditions.

The new AFFH regulations have been hailed by fair housing advocates as an important step in extending the effectiveness of the Fair Housing Act. Whether they lead to a generalized shift in local policy away from meeting housing needs in central neighborhoods and toward greater emphasis on dispersal and integration is yet to be determined.

The Widening Debate

The dispute related to affordable housing and fair housing has widened and deepened in recent years. The controversy occurs not only in the context of housing policy, but now also with respect to sustainability and transportation policy. In the housing policy arena, the recent HUD rules related to disparate impact and AFFH, and the Supreme Court ruling in *Texas DHCA v. ICP* have accentuated the dispute but not resolved it. Thomas Edsall's 2015 piece in the *New York Times* sums up the argument well. He cites HUD's AFFH regulations, the re-analysis of MTO outcomes demonstrating positive effects for young children, and the Supreme Court decision in *Texas DCHA v. ICP* as each challenging the community development approach to affordable housing.[108] The current policy environment, one that orbits so closely around the concept of opportunity and relies so heavily on ideas of dispersal and mobility, is likely to nurture the friction between integration and community development into the foreseeable future.

Conclusion

EVERYONE DESERVES TO LIVE IN AN OPPORTUNITY NEIGHBORHOOD

Assisted housing for the poor was barely ten years old in the United States before community members and policy makers began to weigh the issues of housing need and desegregation against each other. More than sixty years later, the debate endures, and may be as contentious as it ever has been. Increasingly, the debate focuses on the role of community development and affordable housing in communities of color. There is, in fact, an active conversation occurring about what community development should mean in a policy era dominated by the opportunity paradigm, and amid narratives about the inadequacy of local initiatives in the face of regional and global dynamics that produce patterns of neighborhood decline.[1]

Allies?

I have argued from the outset that the debate examined in this book is an argument among allies. Using King and Smith's analysis of racial politics in the United States, there are two overriding approaches to racial policy: a color-blind approach and a color-conscious strategy.[2] The logic of color-blind policy is that an absence of racial considerations in policy making and implementation will mean an absence of racism, discrimination, and differential treatment. The race-conscious coalition contests this as naïve at best and disingenuous at worst. Race consciousness begins with the proposition that past discrimination has created a social, political, and economic order that contains a multitude of processes and dynamics that favor whites over people of color. Color-blind policy leaves intact those advantages and in fact leaves them completely unquestioned.

But this debate is not one between these two coalitions at all. Fair housing advocacy and community development have both evolved as race-conscious movements aimed at producing greater racial equity. They both acknowledge past discrimination and the enduring inequalities produced by the methods of American racism. There is agreement that the discrimination that produces residential segregation is a denial of rights and that enforced segregation has been accompanied by tremendous differences in quality of public services, economic opportunity, and political influence that have greatly reduced the life chances of people of color.

There is agreement between the two movements that some conditions in core neighborhoods of American urban areas, neighborhoods that have been the areas of settlement for communities of color, are problematic—that these areas are characterized by highly problematic levels of crime, poor housing, inadequate schools, and declining public and private infrastructure. Furthermore, there is agreement that these conditions are the result not of inherent qualities of the residents themselves, but of public and private investment decisions that routinely advantage white areas and disadvantage communities of color. The processes of racial advantage and disadvantage, moreover, are cumulative and self-perpetuating, and they are individual as well as systemic. Residents of America's disadvantaged neighborhoods must confront conditions that many white Americans do not face: poor-performing and under-resourced schools that fail to provide adequate learning environments for children, exposure to toxic environmental hazards that produce adverse health outcomes, employment and "address" discrimination that denies them access to living-wage jobs, and housing discrimination that consigns them to poor-quality housing but also extracts rents out of proportion to the size and quality of accommodations. These are the daily insults to body and mind endured by victims of racial domination, fully acknowledged by fair housing advocates of integration as well as by advocates of affordable housing and community development.

There is agreement that in American metropolitan areas, some communities have effectively isolated themselves from others and created themselves as exclusive enclaves of white privilege and wealth. This dynamic is most often considered to be a problem of suburban exclusionism. Fifty years of legal history reflect the tendency of some communities to erect barriers to affordable housing in an attempt to limit the number of poor people and the number of people of color who can enter their communities as residents. Most metropolitan areas in the

United States, despite the greater diversity among suburbs in terms of race and class, retain areas of white racial exclusivity. This pattern is more intense in older urban areas of the Northeast and Midwest, but it nevertheless exists across the country.[3] These communities have been allowed by the vagaries of U.S. law and customs of home rule to define and maintain themselves as bastions of white affluence.

An implication of the above is that both traditions of community development and integration understand that there is a geography to racism and a geography to racial privilege. Certainly the landscape of advantage and well-being is uneven in American metropolitan areas, and regional equity is a goal of both movements. Recent work in equity mapping suggests, however, that opportunity comes in many forms and that these forms of opportunity have different and sometime contradictory geographies. Thus, neighborhoods vary by the type of opportunities they provide as much as by the quantity. The geography of opportunity is, in short, more complex than a simple black/white or city/suburb dichotomy.

Finally, as implied earlier, there is agreement between these movements that race-conscious policies are necessary to address the issue of racial inequality and its urban manifestation. Both integrationists and affordable housing activists agree that public policies must be instituted to address unequal systems and embedded institutional inequities. Thus, both sides agree that fair housing is necessary and needs to consciously attack systems that produce housing inequality along racial lines. Just as necessary is a community development movement that addresses the deficits of housing provision experienced in communities disproportionately inhabited by people of color.

Evolution of the Dispute

Why, then, given such extensive agreement, is there continued dispute between fair housing integrationists and affordable housing / community development advocates? The two movements act very little like allies. As Mara Sidney notes, even when not in outright conflict with each other, the two movements operate largely in independence from each other. Fair housing advocates, she argues, tend not to collaborate with affordable housing advocates, and "national fair housing policy has produced a population of local fair housing groups that have trouble developing allies and do little to mobilize the public behind their cause." Similarly, affordable housing advocates rarely engage fair housers in their work or in their policy advocacy.[4] Thus, lack of collaboration is a clear problem. However, the contemporary problems between the two movements go well beyond this.

The historical perspective offered in this book suggests that the dispute has evolved considerably over time. Some level of tension between the two movements is inherent in the fact that they represent alternative policy objectives in an environment of resource scarcity. Trade-offs exist between devoting resources to meet integration goals and resources that could be allocated to meeting community development and affordable housing goals in core neighborhoods. This tension could be resolved with adequate resources, though few envision that in the near future. Trade-offs will continue to exist. Such low-level debate about competing objectives is what characterized the integration / community development dispute in the early years (pre-1960s).

Subsequent events, however, have introduced deeper divisions between the two movements that constitute a heightening of the disagreement. The articulation of alternative visions of racial equity within the black civil rights movement of the 1950s and 1960s, for example, revealed fundamental philosophical differences between the integration and community development approaches. These two approaches articulate different visions of racial and urban equity. Integrationists invoke the need to reduce walls between groups to undo racial injustices, while community development advocates point to the need to develop internal capacity for self-determination as a precondition for racial equality and spatial equity. This philosophical divide moved the dispute beyond the idea of zero-sum competition for scarce resources.

The evolution of fair housing advocacy has also deepened the dispute. I have argued that it is possible to identify three stations of fair housing spatial strategy. The first station of fair housing, opening up exclusionary communities, is not incompatible with community development and affordable housing practices, except as competition for scarce resources. But the fair housing movement moved beyond the open communities strategy to advocate limiting the work of community developers by imposing constraints on the placement of subsidized housing, or by placing conditions upon community development work (the second station of fair housing spatial strategy). These strategies shifted the attention of fair housing away from the exclusionary community and toward practices within communities of color. Doing so led to a series of positions related to how much affordable housing and community development activity was warranted in communities of color. This, as I have argued, took the dispute to a new level. Implicit in this strategy is a criticism of community development and an argument that affordable housing and community development actually contribute to patterns of racial inequality and regional inequities. Siting guidelines and restrictions on affordable housing in areas that fair housing advocates feel have too many people of color, or have too much affordable housing, not only undermine the work and legitimacy of community development, but also have the effect of privileging integrationist objectives over those of affordable housing and community development. It is here that the integrationists say, in effect, that the work of affordable housing and community development should either serve integrationist goals or wait until integrationist goals are met.

Also problematic at this stage is the tendency for the burden of integrationist goals to be shifted from exclusionary white communities (the policy target in the first station) onto the shoulders of people of color. This was most apparent in integration maintenance programs that actively managed and constrained the choices of people of color in order to maintain a racial mix that was palatable to whites. But even as that approach was nullified by the courts as being discriminatory, fair housers were working to limit affordable housing in communities of color through siting guidelines.

The impulse to limit and guide the housing decisions of people of color rather than addressing the behaviors of exclusionary white communities is repeated and expanded in the third station of fair housing spatial advocacy. The third station, it will be recalled, is the dissolution of existing communities of color. These initiatives work by dismantling existing communities through redevelopment or demolition. These initiatives displace low-income people of color but leave exclusive white communities intact.[5]

Efforts to enforce a specific spatial arrangement of people within metropolitan areas, coupled with the reluctance to bother whites in the process, have unfortunately and frequently led to a range of initiatives that place the burden of pursuing integration on people of color. It is *their* forced displacement that fuels deconcentration and dispersal efforts. It is the restriction of public-sector investment in *their* communities that characterizes current fair housing advocacy. It was the negation of *their* housing choices that defined integration maintenance programs. And when quotas were overturned by the courts, integration management programs were designed to work through discouraging *their* mobility choices, while incentives were offered to whites. These strategies are pursued in deference to the low tolerance of whites for neighbors who are not white. But, as John Calmore writes, "in supporting fair housing, we must oppose racism."[6] Courts that order the restriction of choices for blacks in order to achieve the "greater good" of integration have not yet conceived of imposing such restrictions on whites. As a result, the pursuit of integration has too often taken on a negative aspect, stigmatizing people of color, and idealizing neighborhoods that retain high percentages of white people.[7] Not only do integration initiatives unfairly burden people of color, but, as Tommie Shelby argues, "policies that seek to end unjust racial inequality by pushing, or even nudging, blacks into residential integration or that make needed resources available only on condition that blacks are willing to integrate show a lack of respect for those they aim to assist."[8]

The second and third stations of fair housing spatial advocacy have deepened the dispute between community development and integration, in large part because they attempt to limit community development efforts and because they implicate community development and affordable housing in producing and reproducing patterns of racial and regional injustice. At its worst, the fair housing argument interprets community developers as a "poverty housing industry"—a phrase calculated to conjure images of a large-scale, impersonal constellation of actors who profit from the provision of housing to poor people.[9] In addition to being a cynical misrepresentation of the efforts of mostly neighborhood-based nonprofit organizations to increase standards of living and quality of life in disadvantaged neighborhoods, the use of the phrase is obviously divisive.

Prospects for Resolution

The prospects for *fully* resolving the tensions between community development and integration are dim, given continued resource deficits, budget limitations, and current policy trends toward privatization. The lack of sufficient resources will always put distinct objectives in a position of competition. These tensions have existed since the beginning of large-scale subsidized housing efforts in part because those efforts have always been underfunded relative to need. Tension between community development and fair housing that results from competition for resources, thus, is highly likely to persist.

What might be accomplished in the future, however, is to eliminate the deeper conflicts between the movements, conflicts that extend beyond ever-present competition for resources. The way forward depends on a common commitment across the two movements on the issues of choice and burden. The two movements need not be "converted" to the objectives of the other. Instead, the pursuit of objectives that increase the housing choice of members of the protected classes, as they themselves express them, without placing the burden for those outcomes on the shoulders of those same classes, allows community development and fair housing to coexist and to produce complementary benefits.

Resolution of the deeper conflicts between community development and integration, however, are quite unlikely as long as community development efforts are characterized as contributing to patterns of regional and racial inequality, and as long as integration goals are pursued in ways that impose restrictions and constraints on community development—that is, as long as efforts are made to privilege one set of goals over the other.

Our approach to issues of housing, neighborhoods, and racial equity should be fourfold. First, there is a need to ensure that all communities are inclusive and do not erect barriers to entry that systematically exclude lower-income people and people of color. This was the original fight of the open housing movement. Nor should communities systematically limit low-cost housing through the manipulation of local regulations with the aim or effect of depriving lower-income families of housing opportunities. We need to continue the seventy-year struggle to ensure equal access to housing for all. Renewed efforts need to be directed at and focused on opening up exclusionary communities. The Fair Housing Act should be used to sue the communities that deny opportunities, not the agencies or nonprofits that create them. The fight should target exclusionism and discrimination, not affordable housing and community development.

Second, people of color and low-income people who wish to move to racially and income-integrated neighborhoods should be supported in doing so. Voluntary mobility programs are a means of achieving this, and these programs should be continued. These efforts serve the objective of expanding choice in housing, a goal shared by fair housers and community developers.

Third, for people of color and low-income households who wish to stay in place and also to live in more secure, economically vibrant, well-serviced neighborhoods, there should be support for the community development efforts that can make this happen. In addition, there should be protection against the forces of gentrification present in so many cities that would produce neighborhood changes but simultaneously displace low-income people of color from such neighborhoods.[10]

Fourth, research shows that segregation rates are greater in metropolitan areas with greater inequality.[11] Thus, efforts to reduce secular inequality have a chance to reduce social divisions that produce and maintain high levels of residential segregation. These approaches elevate choice and shared burden as the guideposts for efforts to address racial and regional equity.

Enthusiasm in the media and in policy circles for the first two of these strategies (opening up exclusionary communities and voluntary mobility) has the potential to crowd out consideration of the third (community development). This must be avoided. Moving forward on these objectives requires that we not privilege any one over the others. Some have recommended privileging mobility and integration efforts by making reference to research showing how neighborhoods impact life chances. Yet the awareness that "place matters" for outcomes of racial justice does not, by itself, justify a dispersal approach any more than it justifies community development.[12] Moreover, there is no legal justification, despite the arguments of fair housing advocates, to privilege the pursuit of integration over other reasonable public policy objectives related to housing for poor families and the revitalization of disadvantaged communities. The opening up of exclusionary communities can and should occur in such a way as to not limit the pursuit of community development objectives.

Racial and Regional Equity

Integration efforts can be criticized for reifying white dominance through reference to "acceptable" levels and rates of mixing, and can be criticized for substituting the spatial arrangement of people for the pursuit of more fundamental goals of racial justice and equality. These criticisms suggest that integration efforts displace more fundamental questions of equity and power with lower-level concerns about residential mixing.

If these criticisms can be applied to fair housing, however, so too can affordable housing and community development be faulted if they are not connected to the larger pursuit of racial justice and regional equity. For community development efforts to improve upon integrationist initiatives they must confront issues of power and the power differentials experienced by communities of color. That is, community development needs always to be connected to issues of regional equity and racial justice.

The community development movement began with just such a self-consciously political objective of self-determination and resource-building within the black community. Some have since criticized the community development movement for losing that perspective and slipping into an apolitical service-delivery mode that does little or nothing to challenge political dynamics that produce and reproduce spatial and racial disadvantage.[13] To truly realize the original intent of the movement, however, community developers need to reconnect with the political. Social justice efforts like the Black Lives Matter movement should be as important to community development as are the shifting implementation guidelines related to the LIHTC program or the AFFH obligations of local governments. Post-Ferguson America requires a community development movement that is engaged on issues of regional and racial equity.

The conversation around the proper role for community development often focuses on strategic issues such as the "comprehensiveness" of projects and plans, and on the appropriate scale at which community development should operate. While these issues are important, ultimately the great promise of community development, and its great advantage over integration as a path toward racial justice, are in its potential political content. In this book I have argued that community development efforts in communities of color can be justified on their own terms related to the benefits that they produce. But in the pursuit of regional equity and racial justice, causes that both sides of the integration / community development dispute claim as important, it is the community development movement that has the greatest potential for connecting to social change and social justice efforts.

Everyone deserves to live in an opportunity neighborhood, not just those fortunate enough to get a mobility certificate, or those fortunate enough to "be accepted" into a white, middle-class community, or even those willing to move into a white middle-class community. Racial justice and regional equity demand a focus on what Mary Patillo calls the "stuff of equality" and not merely the spatial arrangement of people.

Notes

INTRODUCTION

1. Political scientist Mara Sidney, one of the few scholars to study the two movements side by side, points out that despite baseline agreements on issues of social justice, there is very little collaboration between advocates in the two camps. She writes, "Fair housing groups do not typically partner with the affordable housing movement in local movements for regional justice," and that "national fair housing policy has produced a population of local fair housing groups that have trouble developing allies and do little to mobilize the public behind their cause. . . . At the same time, for a variety of reasons, affordable housing advocates may not perceive fair housing or civil rights advocates as natural allies." Mara S. Sidney, "Fair Housing and Affordable Housing Advocacy: Reconciling the Dual Agenda," in *The Geography of Opportunity: Race and Housing Choice in Metropolitan America*, ed. Xavier de Souza Briggs (Washington, DC: Brookings Institution Press, 2005), 267.

2. Sheila Crowley and Danilo Pelletiere, *Affordable Housing Dilemma: The Preservation vs. Mobility Debate* (Washington, DC: National Low Income Housing Coalition, 2012).

3. Ibid., 5.

4. "Combined Principles—Intersection of Community Development and Fair Housing," revised draft, November 16, 2012, p. 1.

5. Ibid.

6. The relevance of the debate is also reflected in the ongoing "conversation" between fair housing and community development advocates on this issue. The National Housing Institute's *Shelterforce* (the "voice of community development") has been host to a prolonged discussion about the merits of mobility and community development strategies over the past several years. See, e.g., Bill Bynum, "To Move or to Improve?," *Rooflines*, 2016; "Shelterforce Exclusive: Interview with HUD Secretary Julian Castro," February 4, 2016; Staci Berger and Adam Gordon, "Fair Housing and Community Developers Can Work Together," *Shelterforce*, October 15, 2015; Peter Dreier, "The Revitalization Trap," *Shelterforce*, October 1, 2015; Brentin Mock, "The Failures and Merits of Place-Based Initiatives," *Atlantic Citylab*, May 25, 2015; Miriam Axel-Lute, "Seeking Solidarity between Place-Based and Economic Justice Work," *Rooflines*, June 1, 2015; Josh Ishimatsu, "The False Choice between Mobility and Community Development," *Rooflines*, August 4, 2014; and Philip Tegeler, "In Pursuit of a 'Both/and' Housing Policy—the Case of Housing Choice Vouchers," *Rooflines*, April 7, 2014.

7. My use of labels for different racial/ethnic groups requires some explanation. The phrase "people of color" is meant to refer to racial and ethnic groups other than "white, non-Hispanic." Thus, people of color include African Americans, Hispanic Americans, Native Americans, and Asian Americans. In this book I use the term interchangeably with "minority." The term "white" is used as shorthand for "white, non-Hispanic." The substance of most of the public policy issues examined in this book are most relevant for African Americans (a term I use interchangeably with "blacks"). Indeed, much of the history of fair housing and civil rights discussed in the book relates specifically to

African Americans. Further, the evidence shows that African Americans are subject to higher and more enduring levels of racial segregation than other racial/ethnic groups; see Lee Sigelman and Susan Welch, "The Contact Hypothesis Revisited: Black-White Interaction and Positive Racial Attitudes," *Social Forces* 71.3 (1993). All these labels are used purposefully. If a phenomenon applies to only African Americans, or if the historical issue concerned only (or overwhelmingly) African Americans, then the language used will be similarly specific. For more general statements I refer to people of color, acknowledging that although blacks may suffer the deepest forms of discrimination and housing deprivation in the country, other groups such as Hispanic Americans and Native Americans share a subordinate position in the political economy of American urban areas. For the most part, all the groups that make up "people of color" experience many of the housing deprivations examined in this book at a rate greater than do whites. The exception to this is Asian Americans, though this is not uniformly the case across all subgroups within Asian Americans. Certainly race is a social construction, but it is no less relevant or important for being so. The issues addressed in this book centrally involve the reality that access to adequate housing (however defined) is differentially distributed along racial/ethnic lines. The broadest divide is between whites and people of color, yet the starkest disparities are between whites and blacks. The terminology used in the following pages will shift according to the precise argument being made.

8. Desmond S. King and Rogers M. Smith, *Still a House Divided: Race and Politics in Obama's America* (Princeton, NJ: Princeton University Press, 2011).

9. Ibid., 17. These alliances manifest themselves in the housing field, according to King and Smith, much as they do in other fields such as employment policy, where racial inequalities are problematic.

10. Ibid., 7.

11. Elizabeth Anderson, *The Imperative of Integration* (Princeton, NJ: Princeton University Press, 2010).

12. King and Smith, *House Divided*, 24.

13. See, e.g., Alexander Polikoff, "Sustainable Integration or Inevitable Resegregation: The Troubling Questions," in *Housing Desegregation and Federal Policy*, ed. John Goering (Chapel Hill: University of North Carolina Press, 1986); Robert Lake and Jessica Winslow, "Integration Management: Municipal Constraints on Residential Mobility," *Urban Geography* 2.4 (1981); Leonard S. Rubinowitz and Elizabeth Trosman, "Affirmative Action and the American Dream: Implementing Fair Housing Policies in Federal Homeownership Programs," *Northwestern University Law Review* 74 (1979).

14. "Protected classes" is a reference to the population groups identified in the U.S. Fair Housing Act of 1968 that are specifically protected by the nondiscrimination mandates provided for in the act.

15. See, e.g., Lake and Winslow, "Integration Management."

16. Rubinowitz and Trosman, "Affirmative Action." See also Charles E. Daye, "Whither Fair Housing: Meditations on Wrong Paradigms, Ambivalent Answers, and a Legislative Proposal," *Washington University Journal of Law and Policy* 3 (2000): 241.

17. David Imbroscio, "'United and Actuated by Some Common Impulse of Passion': Challenging the Dispersal Consensus in American Housing Policy Research," *Journal of Urban Affairs* 30 (2008).

18. Alexander Polikoff, *Waiting for Gautreaux: A Story of Segregation, Housing, and the Black Ghetto* (Evanston, IL: Northwestern University Press, 2006). See also the ruling in Otero v. New York City Housing Authority, 354 F. Supp.941 (U.S. District Court, S.D. New York, 1973), and the examples provided by Lake and Winslow, "Integration Management."

19. See, as examples, the decision in Otero v. NYCHA; and Michael H. Schill, "Deconcentrating the Inner City Poor," *Chicago-Kent Law Review* 67 (1991).

20. The temporality of these stations is not strict. In fact, some of the efforts that are categorized in the second station evolved contemporaneously with those in the first. The temporal ordering is most prominent in the emergence of the third station, in which efforts are made at breaking up existing concentrations of people of color.

21. See, e.g., Justin D. Cummins, "Recasting Fair Share: Toward Effective Housing Law and Principled Social Policy," *Law & Inequality* 14 (1995).

22. Sharon Perlman Krefetz, "The Impact and Evolution of the Massachusetts Comprehensive Permit and Zoning Appeals Act: Thirty Years of Experience with a State Legislative Effort to Overcome Exclusionary Zoning," *Western New England Law Review* 22 (2000): 381; and Spencer M. Cowan, "Anti-Snob Land Use Laws, Suburban Exclusion, and Housing Opportunity," *Journal of Urban Affairs* 28 (2006).

23. Nico Calavita, Kenneth Grimes, and Alan Mallach, "Inclusionary Housing in California and New Jersey: A Comparative Analysis," *Housing Policy Debate* 8.1 (1997).

24. The use of the term "ghetto" is contentious and thus requires some explanation. The word carries a negative connotation and is a somewhat dated usage, being most widely used in the United States in the 1950s and '60s. The term was earlier used, of course, in reference to Jewish quarters in European cities. The usage migrated to the United States as social scientists and advocates compared the conditions of blacks in America to the Jews in Nazi-era ghettos. See Mitchell Duneier, *Ghetto: The Invention of a Place, the History of an Idea* (New York: Farrar, Straus and Giroux, 2016). As Peter Marcuse argues, the term is meant to signal a community that is segregated by force rather than by choice; see Marcuse, "The Ghetto of Exclusion and the Fortified Enclave: New Patterns in the United States," *American Behavioral Scientist* 41.3 (1997). In some cases the degree of volition that produces a segregated or racially/ethnically defined community is difficult to assess. Indeed within any segregated community there are undoubtedly families who are there by choice and others who are trapped there because of lack of alternatives. Middle-class black or Hispanic neighborhoods are generally not considered "ghettos" by those who reside there. Increasingly, even low-income minority neighborhood residents chafe at the use of the term "ghetto." In this book I use the term in two ways. The first is as a historical reference. Thus, when referring to the civil rights era, I adopt the usage of the times, referring to black neighborhoods the way that the principals did. I also use the term to signal neighborhoods that are the target of fair housing advocacy, neighborhoods that integrationists desire to desegregate. This is done to reflect the sense among integrationists that these communities are traps and that they do reflect forced segregation.

25. This point is not universally acknowledged. Political scientist David Imbroscio argues that the narrow concern with exclusionary zoning channels a great deal of political capital and effort that could have the effect of diverting resources from affordable housing efforts in the core. See Imbroscio, "Beyond Mobility: The Limits of Liberal Urban Policy," *Journal of Urban Affairs* 34.1 (2012). The strength of Imbroscio's claim here is tied to the issue of scarcity and opportunity costs raised earlier.

26. Though the most well-known case, Shannon v. HUD (436 F. 2d 809, 3d Cir. 1970) is by no means the first example of fair housing advocacy aimed at restricting the placement of subsidized housing in core neighborhoods. See the discussion in chapter 2.

27. See, e.g., Antonio Raciti, Katherine A. Lambert-Pennington, and Kenneth M. Reardon, "The Struggle for the Future of Public Housing in Memphis, Tennessee: Reflections on HUD's Choice Neighborhoods Planning Program," *Cities* 57 (2016); and Amy L. Howard and Thad Williamson, "Reframing Public Housing in Richmond, Virginia: Segregation, Resident Resistance and the Future of Redevelopment," *Cities* 57 (2016).

28. David Imbroscio's response to the regionalist argument in *Urban America Reconsidered* may be a notable exception, although his argument there goes far beyond the community development field; see Imbroscio, *Urban America Reconsidered: Alternatives for Governance and Policy* (Ithaca, NY: Cornell University Press, 2010).

1. THE INTEGRATION IMPERATIVE

1. See, e.g., Sandra J. Newman and Ann B. Schnare, "'. . . And a Suitable Living Environment': The Failure of Housing Programs to Deliver on Neighborhood Quality," *Housing Policy Debate* 8 (1997); Michael H. Schill and Susan M. Wachter, "The Spatial Bias of Federal Housing Law and Policy: Concentrated Poverty in Urban America," *University of Pennsylvania Law Review* 143 (1995); Robert Gray and Steven Tursky, "Local and Racial/Ethnic Occupancy for HUD Subsidized Family Housing in Ten Metropolitan Areas," in *Housing Desegregation and Federal Policy*, ed. John M. Goering (Chapel Hill: University of North Carolina Press, 1986); Ira Goldstein and William L. Yancey, "Public Housing Projects, Blacks, and Public Policy: The Historical Ecology of Public Housing in Philadelphia," in *Housing Desegregation and Federal Policy*, ed. John M. Goering (Chapel Hill: University of North Carolina Press, 1986); Douglas Massey and Shawn Kanaiaupuni, "Public Housing and the Concentration of Poverty," *Social Science Quarterly* 74.1 (1993).

2. Stacey Seicshnaydre, "How Government Housing Perpetuates Racial Segregation: Lessons from Post-Katrina New Orleans," *Catholic University Law Review* 60 (2010). See also Stacey Seicshnaydre, "The Fair Housing Choice Myth," *Cardozo Law Review* 33.3 (2012).

3. Several studies have shown a link between assisted housing and growth in concentrated poverty. See Goldstein and Yancey, "Public Housing," Massey and Kanaiaupuni, "Public Housing," and Lance Freeman, "The Impact of Assisted Housing Developments on Concentrated Poverty," *Housing Policy Debate* 14.1–2 (2003). See also Arnold R. Hirsch, *Making the Second Ghetto: Race and Housing in Chicago, 1940–1960*, 2nd ed. (New York: Cambridge University Press, 1996), for the argument about subsidized housing creating and reinforcing racial segregation.

4. See Robert J. Sampson and Jeffrey D. Morenoff, "Durable Inequality," in *Poverty Traps*, ed. Samuel Bowles, Steven N. Durlauf, and Karla Hoff (Princeton, NJ: Princeton University Press, 2006). Their study of Chicago over a twenty-year period showed a rigid hierarchy in which neighborhoods tended to remain in place relative to one another over time.

5. Ibid., 176.

6. Patrick Sharkey, *Stuck in Place: Urban Neighborhoods and the End of Progress toward Racial Equality* (Chicago: University of Chicago Press, 2013), 176.

7. Statement of Edward L. Holmgren, executive director of the National Committee against Discrimination in Housing, *The* Gautreaux *Decision and Its Effect on Subsidized Housing—Hearing before a Subcommittee of the Committee on Government Operations, United States House of Representatives, 95th Congress, 2nd Session* (Washington, DC: Government Printing Office, 1977), 85.

8. Statement of Alexander Polikoff, executive director of Business and Professional People in the Public Interest, *The* Gautreaux *Decision and Its Effect on Subsidized Housing—Hearing before a Subcommittee of the Committee on Government Operations, United States House of Representatives, 95th Congress, 2nd Session* (Washington, DC: Government Printing Office, 1977), 139.

9. Seicshnaydre, "How Government Housing," 687.

10. Gary Orfield, "The Movement for Housing Integration: Rationale and the Nature of the Challenge," in *Housing Desegregation and Federal Policy*, ed. John Goering (Chapel Hill: University of North Carolina Press, 1986), 26.

11. Explicitly race-based zoning was ruled unconstitutional by the U.S. Supreme Court in Buchanan v. Warley, 245 U.S. 60 (1917).

12. See, e.g., Maria Krysan, "Prejudice, Politics, and Public Opinion: Understanding the Sources of Racial Policy Attitudes," *Annual Review of Sociology* 26 (2000).

13. John Goering, "Political Origins and Opposition," in *Choosing a Better Life? Evaluating the Moving to Opportunity Social Experiment*, ed. John Goering and Judith D. Feins (Washington, DC: Urban Institute Press, 2003).

14. As examples of regionalist writing see Bruce Katz, ed., *Reflections on Regionalism* (Washington, DC: Brookings Institution Press, 2000); Peter Dreier, John H. Mollenkopf, and Todd Swanstrom, *Place Matters: Metropolitics for the Twenty-First Century*, 3rd ed. (Lawrence: University Press of Kansas, 2014); Manuel Pastor, Chris Benner, and Martha Matsuoka, *This Could be the Start of Something Big: How Social Movements for Regional Equity Are Reshaping Metropolitan America* (Ithaca, NY: Cornell University Press, 2009); David Rusk, *Inside Game, Outside Game: Winning Strategies for Saving Urban America* (Washington, DC: Brookings Institution Press, 1999).

15. Support for the demolition and redevelopment of public housing is a good example of this common approach. The movement to demolish and redevelop public housing was importantly abetted by fair housing desegregation lawsuits in the 1980s and 1990s targeting public housing authorities in cities across the country. The dismantling of public housing was also strongly supported by regionalists such as Bruce Katz and Peter Calthorpe, who saw the effort in terms of addressing debilitating patterns of place-based inequities within metropolitan areas. See Edward G. Goetz, "The Audacity of HOPE VI: Discourse and the Dismantling of Public Housing," *Cities* 35 (2013); Edward G. Goetz, *New Deal Ruins: Race, Economic Justice, and Public Housing Policy* (Ithaca, NY: Cornell University Press, 2013).

16. Rusk, *Inside Game*.

17. Chester Hartman and Gregory D. Squires, eds. *The Integration Debate: Competing Futures for American Cities* (New York: Routledge, 2010). See Susan Popkin et al., *The Hidden War: The Battle to Control Crime in Chicago's Public Housing* (Washington, DC: Abt Associates, 1996), on the exposure to crime of public housing residents in Chicago. Jonathan Kozol provides a memorable description of the biohazards confronting the ghetto of East Saint Louis, Missouri, in *Savage Inequalities: Children in America's Schools* (New York: Broadway Books, 2012).

18. Sharon Jackson et al., "The Relation of Residential Segregation to All-Cause Mortality: A Study in Black and White," *American Journal of Public Health* 90.4 (2000); and Angus Deaton and Darrne Lubotsky, "Mortality, Inequality and Race in American Cities and States," *Social Science and Medicine* 56 (2003).

19. Dolores Acevedo-Garcia, Theresa L. Osypuk, and Nancy McArdle, "Racial/Ethnic Integration and Child Health Disparities," in *The Integration Debate: Competing Futures for American Cities*, ed. Chester Hartman and Gregory D. Squires (New York: Routledge, 2010).

20. Hartman and Squires, *Integration Debate*.

21. Anderson, *Imperative*; Renee E. Walker, Christopher R. Keane, and Jessica G. Burke, "Disparities and Access to Healthy Food in the United States: A Review of the Food Deserts Literature," *Health and Place* 16.5 (2010).

22. Keith R. Ihlandfeldt and David L. Sjoquist, "The Spatial Mismatch Hypothesis: A Review of Recent Studies and Their Implications for Welfare Reform," *Housing Policy Debate* 9 (1998).

23. Melvin L. Oliver and Thomas M. Shapiro, "Race and Wealth," *Review of Black Political Economy* 17.4 (1989).

24. See Katrin Anacker, "Shaky Palaces? Analyzing Property Values and Their Appreciation Rates in Minority First Suburbs," *International Journal of Urban and Regional Research* 36.4 (2012); Katrin Anacker, "Still Paying the Race Tax? Analyzing Property Values in Homogeneous and Mixed-Race Suburbs," *Journal of Urban Affairs* 32.1 (2010); Lauren J. Krivo and Robert L. Kaufman, "Housing and Wealth Inequality: Racial-Ethnic Differences in Home Equity in the United States," *Demography* 41.3 (2004).

25. Rusk, *Inside Game*.

26. Hartman and Squires, *Integration Debate*; Xavier Briggs, "Brown Kids in White Suburbs: Housing Mobility and the Many Faces of Social Capital," *Housing Policy Debate* 9.1 (1998). This type of social capital is to be distinguished from a different type of social capital, what Briggs calls "bonding" social capital, which provides more day-to-day material benefits to low-income individuals from members of their support networks. Bonding social capital seems to be in abundance in very low-income neighborhoods—see, for example, Sudhir Venkatesh, *American Project: The Rise and Fall of a Modern Ghetto* (Cambridge, MA: Harvard University Press, 2000), or Rhonda Williams, *The Politics of Public Housing: Black Women's Struggles against Urban Inequality* (New York: Oxford University Press, 2004)—but it is less useful for generating economic opportunities that might support upward mobility.

27. See Briggs, "Brown Kids"; and Silvia Domínguez and Celeste Watkins, "Creating Networks for Survival and Mobility: Social Capital among African-American and Latin-American Low-Income Mothers," *Social Problems* 50.1 (2003).

28. A corollary to ghetto disadvantage is the evidence of the adverse effects of concentrated poverty. Concentrated poverty, it should be noted, did not emerge as a public policy problem until the late 1980s. The problem was simply not formally labeled and conceptualized during the years in which the fair housing movement emerged and grew. Nevertheless, the intense spatial concentration of poor households in American cities has become a central target of the fair housing movement since the 1990s. Concentrated poverty mirrors racial segregation in many ways, especially as it has been argued to damage the life chances of those living in such conditions. Furthermore, there is a heavy racial overlap to poverty concentrations. Most areas of concentrated poverty are also racially segregated neighborhoods, and poor African Americans, for example, are several times more likely to live in neighborhoods of concentrated poverty than are poor white households; see Paul Jargowsky, *Concentration of Poverty in the New Millennium: Changes in Prevalence, Composition and Location of High Poverty Neighborhoods* (Camden, NJ: Rutgers Center for Urban Research and Education, 2013).

29. Douglas Massey and Nancy A. Denton, *American Apartheid: Segregation and the Making of the Underclass* (Cambridge, MA: Harvard University Press, 1993); john powell, "Reflections on the Past, Looking to the Future: The Fair Housing Act at 40," *Journal of Affordable Housing and Community Development* 18.2 (2009); Anderson, *Imperative*.

30. Lawrence Bobo, "Keeping the Linchpin in Place: Testing the Multiple Sources of Opposition to Residential Integration," *International Review of Social Psychology* 2.3 (1989).

31. Sharkey, *Stuck in Place*.

32. Florence Roisman, "Affirmatively Furthering Fair Housing in Regional Housing Markets: The Baltimore Public Housing Desegregation Litigation," *Wake Forest Law Review* 42.2: 351. This is a more radical statement than it might appear, as many careful social scientists would aver that the correlation between segregation and social outcomes such as crime and drug abuse, though high and easily demonstrable, fall short of actual causation.

33. Anderson, *Imperative*, 64.

34. See, e.g., Camille Zubrinsky Charles, "The Dynamics of Racial Residential Segregation," *Annual Review of Sociology* 29 (2003).

35. Reynolds Farley, Elaine L. Fielding, and Maria Krysan, "The Residential Preferences of Blacks and Whites: A Four-Metropolis Analysis," *Housing Policy Debate* 8.4 (1997).

36. See, e.g., Stephen Grant Meyer, *As Long as They Don't Move Next Door: Segregation and Racial Conflict in American Neighborhoods* (Lanham, MD: Rowman & Littlefield, 2000).

37. Oliver and Shapiro call this the "racialization of state policy." Melvin Oliver and Thomas Shapiro, *Black Wealth / White Wealth* (New York: Routledge, 1995).

38. Meyer, *Next Door*.

39. Charles E. Connerly, "From Racial Zoning to Community Empowerment: The Interstate Highway System and the African American Community in Birmingham, Alabama," *Journal of Planning Education and Research* 22.2 (2002).

40. Michael Danielson, *The Politics of Exclusion* (New York: Columbia University Press, 1976).

41. Kenneth T. Jackson, *Crabgrass Frontier: The Suburbanization of the United States* (New York: Oxford University Press, 1985).

42. See Dreier, Mollenkopf, and Swanstrom, *Place Matters*; Schill and Wachter, "Spatial Bias"; and Christopher Bonastia, *Knocking on the Door: The Federal Government's Attempt to Desegregate the Suburbs* (Princeton, NJ: Princeton University Press, 2006).

43. Oliver and Shapiro, *Black Wealth*; Kevin Fox Gotham, "Separate and Unequal: The Housing Act of 1968 and the Section 235 Program," *Sociological Forum* 15.1 (2000); George Lipsitz and Melvin L. Oliver, "Integration, Segregation, and the Racial Wealth Gap," in *The Integration Debate: Competing Futures for American Cities*, ed. Chester Hartman and Gregory D. Squires (New York: Routledge, 2010).

44. See, e.g., Thomas J. Sugrue, *Sweet Land of Liberty: The Forgotten Struggle for Civil Rights in the North* (New York: Random House, 2009).

45. See, e.g., Peter Medoff and Holly Sklar, *Streets of Hope: The Fall and Rise of an Urban Neighborhood* (Boston: South End, 1994), for a graphic example of blockbusting.

46. See, e.g., Margery A. Turner et al., *Discrimination in Metropolitan Housing Markets: National Results from Phase 1 of the Housing Discrimination Study* (Washington, DC: Urban Institute, 2002); and Stephen L. Ross and Margery Austin Turner, "Housing Discrimination in Metropolitan America: Explaining Changes between 1989 and 2000," *Social Problems* 52.2 (2005).

47. Population Studies Center, Institute for Social Research, University of Michigan, "Race Segregation for Largest Metro Areas," http://www.psc.isr.umich.edu/dis/census/segregation2010.html. These figures are based on census block groups and thus differ slightly from indices calculated at the census tract level.

48. Rima Wilkes and John Iceland, "Hypersegregation in the Twenty-First Century," *Demography* 41.1 (2004).

49. John R. Logan, Brian J. Stults, and Reynolds Farley, "Segregation of Minorities in the Metropolis: Two Decades of Change," *Demography* 41.1 (2004).

50. Kori J. Stroub and Meredith P. Richards, "From Resegregation to Reintegration: Trends in the Racial/Ethnic Segregation of Metropolitan Public School," *American Educational Research Journal* 3 (2013).

51. Elizabeth Kneebone and Natalie Holmes, *U.S. Concentrated Poverty in the Wake of the Great Recession* (Washington, DC: Brookings Institution, 2016).

52. Ibid.

53. See the arguments in Schill, "Deconcentrating"; Florence Roisman, "Constitutional and Statutory Mandates for Residential Racial Integration and the Validity of

Race-Conscious, Affirmative Action to Achieve It," in *The Integration Debate: Competing Futures for American Cities*, ed. Chester Hartman and Gregory D. Squires (New York: Routledge, 2010); Anthony Downs, *Opening Up the Suburbs: An Urban Strategy for America* (New Haven, CT: Yale University Press, 1973).

54. For a suburban perspective see Scott W. Allard and Benjamin Roth, *Strained Suburbs: The Social Service Challenges of Rising Suburban Poverty*, Metropolitan Opportunity Series Report (Washington, DC: Brookings Institution, 2010).

55. See Schill, "Deconcentrating," and Edwin S. Mills, "Open Housing Laws as Stimulus to Central City Employment," *Journal of Urban Economics* 17 (1985).

56. National Conference on Fair Housing and Equal Opportunity, *The Future of Fair Housing: Report of the National Commission on Fair Housing and Equal Opportunity* (NCFHEO, 2008), 3.

57. Susan Clampet-Lundquist and Douglas S. Massey, "Neighborhood Effects on Economic Self-Sufficiency: A Reconsideration of the Moving to Opportunity Experiment," *American Journal of Sociology* 114.1 (2008).

58. Raj Chetty, Nathaniel Hendren, and Lawrence F. Katz, "The Effects of Exposure to Better Neighborhoods on Children: New Evidence from the Moving to Opportunity Experiment," working paper no. w21156 (Cambridge, MA: National Bureau of Economic Research, 2015). The findings of this paper are examined more fully in chapter 2.

59. Gordon W. Allport, *The Nature of Prejudice* (Cambridge, MA: Perseus, 1954).

60. See, e.g., Sigelman and Welch, "Contact Hypothesis"; and the review in Thomas F. Pettigrew and Linda R. Tropp, "A Meta-Analytic Test of Intergroup Contact," *Journal of Personality and Social Psychology* 90.5 (2006).

61. National Advisory Commission on Civil Disorders, Report of the National Advisory Commission on Civil Disorders (New York: Bantam, 1968), 480.

62. Anderson's argument in *The Imperative of Integration* includes this assertion on page 84. See also Gary Orfield's use of the expression as well; Orfield, "Movement for Housing," 20.

63. Anderson, *Imperative*, 102.

64. Ibid., 99.

65. Ibid., 134.

66. See the discussion in chap. 2.

67. Anderson, *Imperative*, 110.

68. See, e.g., John Charles Boger, "Toward Ending Residential Segregation: A Fair Share Proposal for the Next Reconstruction," *North Carolina Law Review* 71 (1992).

69. Orfield, "Movement for Housing."

70. Anderson, *Imperative*.

71. Rusk, *Inside Game*.

72. Pastor, Benner, and Matsuoka, *Something Big*, 9.

73. Rusk, *Inside Game*, 59.

74. Ibid.

75. Joseph Gibbons, "Does Racial Segregation Make Community-Based Organizations More Territorial? Evidence from Newark, NJ, and Jersey City, NJ," *Journal of Urban Affairs* 37.5 (2014).

76. Robert J. Sampson, *Great American City: Chicago and the Enduring Neighborhood Effect* (Chicago: University of Chicago Press, 2012).

77. This position is exemplified by the congressional testimony of Michael Meyers, the assistant director of the National Association for the Advancement of Colored People in 1978 that "the effect of gilding the ghetto [i.e., community development] is to deprive blacks of favorable, equal opportunities in housing." See Michael Meyers, "Prepared Statement," *The* Gautreaux *Decision and Its Effect on Subsidized Housing—Hearing before*

a Subcommittee of the Committee on Government Operations, House of Representatives, 95th Congress, 2nd Session, September 22, 1978. Claims such as these about community development efforts contradict the plea made by some for a "both/and" strategy that urges both community development and integration efforts.

2. AFFIRMATIVELY FURTHERING COMMUNITY DEVELOPMENT

1. Karen Chapple argues that "when we support integration, we often confuse the end with the means. Even if diversity is an important goal among urban planners, it is equality that matters from a civil rights perspective." See Chapple, *Planning Sustainable Cities and Regions: Towards More Equitable Development* (London: Routledge, 2015), 115. See also Imbroscio's argument about the thread of urban policy he calls "urban expansionism" in *Urban America Reconsidered*, p. 141. The argument is also made in the context of income and social mix policies; see, e.g., Loretta Lees, Tim Butler, and Gary Bridge, "Introduction: Gentrification, Social Mix/ing and Mixed Communities," in *Mixed Communities: Gentrification by Stealth?*, ed. Gary Bridge, Tim Butler, and Loretta Lees (Bristol, UK: Policy Press, 2012).

2. See Bridge, Butler, and Lees, *Mixed Communities*.

3. Barry Steffan et al., *Worst Case Housing Needs: A 2015 Report to Congress* (Washington, DC: U.S. Department of Housing and Urban Development, 2015).

4. Diane Yentel et al., *Out of Reach, 2016* (Washington, DC: National Low Income Housing Coalition, 2016). FMRs are rent estimates derived from market studies of metropolitan areas conducted annually by HUD. FMRs are set at the 40th percentile of rents of recent movers (households who moved within fifteen months of the rent survey). FMRs are adjusted for number of bedrooms and are used to determine payment standards for the federal housing choice voucher program.

5. The "housing wage" is the hourly wage necessary to afford a two-bedroom apartment at the fair market rent at 30 percent of the housing income. Yentel et al., *Out of Reach, 2016*.

6. Steffen et al., *Worst Case Housing*.

7. John O. Calmore, "Fair Housing v. Fair Housing: The Problems with Providing Increased Housing Opportunities through Spatial Deconcentration," *Clearinghouse Review* 14 (1980).

8. Frances Fox Piven and Richard Cloward, writing in 1967, observed that given the poor housing conditions of the urban core, "it seems clear . . . that if the poor are to obtain decent housing, massive subsidies must be granted for new and rehabilitated housing in the ghettos and slums." See Piven and Cloward, "The Case against Urban Desegregation," *Social Work* 12.1 (1967): 102.

9. William Wilen and Wendy Stasell, "*Gautreaux* and Chicago's Public Housing Crisis: The Conflict between Achieving Integration and Providing Decent Housing for Very Low-Income African Americans," *Clearinghouse Review* 34.3–4 (2000): 140.

10. See Preston H. Smith III, *Racial Democracy and the Black Metropolis: Housing Policy in Postwar Chicago* (Minneapolis: University of Minnesota Press, 2012).

11. Calmore, "Fair Housing," 8.

12. Shannon v. HUD, 436, F.2d 809 (3rd Cir. 1970).

13. Calmore, "Fair Housing," 18.

14. Ibid., 8. Calmore and many others agree with Tein that "subsidized housing tenants . . . should be able to choose better housing over integration." See Michael R. Tein, "The Devaluation of Nonwhite Community in Remedies for Subsidized Housing Discrimination," *University of Pennsylvania Law Review* 140.4 (1992): 1494.

15. Calmore, "Fair Housing." See also Roy L. Brooks, *Integration or Separation? A Strategy for Racial Equality* (Cambridge, MA: Harvard University Press, 1996).

16. See, e.g., Maria Krysan and Reynolds Farley, "The Residential Preferences of Blacks: Do They Explain Persistent Segregation?," *Social Forces* 80.3 (2002).

17. Daye, "Whither Fair Housing?"

18. Wilhelmina A. Leigh and James D. McGee, "A Minority Perspective on Residential Racial Integration," in *Housing Desegregation and Federal Policy*, ed. John Goering (Chapel Hill: University of North Carolina Press, 1986), 34.

19. John Calmore asked these very questions four decades ago; see Calmore, "Fair Housing."

20. This is certainly the case among many residents of public housing who have seen their communities demolished over the past twenty years. See Goetz, *New Deal Ruins*.

21. P. H. Smith III, *Racial Democracy*; King and Smith, *House Divided*.

22. The Kerner Commission in 1968 noted that housing conditions were one of the most important causes of the urban unrest of the 1960s. National Advisory Commission on Civil Disorders, *Report*.

23. Leigh and McGhee, "Minority Perspective," 39. See also Ceri Peach, "Good Segregation, Bad Segregation," *Planning Perspectives* 11.4 (1996): 395. Peach writes, "A clear distinction should be drawn between eliminating poor housing conditions and eliminating areas of ethnic concentration."

24. Alexander Von Hoffman, "Like Fleas on a Tiger? A Brief History of the Open Housing Movement," Harvard University, Joint Center for Housing Studies, 1998, 32.

25. Chester Hartman and Gary Squires, "Integration Exhaustion, Race Fatigue, and the American Dream," in *The Integration Debate: Competing Futures for American Cities*, ed. Chester Hartman and Gregory D. Squires (New York: Routledge, 2010); Sheryll Cashin, *The Failures of Integration: How Race and Class Are Undermining the American Dream* (New York: Public Affairs, 2004). The "integration exhaustion" may be more a case of shifting ideas about policy priorities. Cashin suggests that integration is not the goal it was a generation ago, quoting a resident of Washington, DC, writing in the *Washington Post*, "It's time to reverse an earlier generation's hopeful migration into white communities and attend to some unfinished business in the 'hood,'" p. 341.

26. Orlando Patterson, *The Ordeal of Integration: Progress and Resentment in America's "Racial" Crisis* (New York: Basic Civitas, 1998). On the history of violence and intimidation that met black families who led the way in housing integration see Meyer, *Next Door*.

27. Anderson, *Imperative*, 70.

28. Gregory Squires and Charles E. Kubrin, *Privileged Places: Race, Residence, and the Structure of Opportunity* (Boulder, CO: Lynne Rienner, 2006). The full quote is, "'By the time I come home I don't want to have to deal with white people anymore,'" 204–205.

29. Of course it might be argued that the contact hypothesis refers primarily to the enhanced tolerance of whites toward people of color as a result of increased exposure. Such an interpretation would, of necessity then, assume that people of color already find the behavior and attitudes of whites to be acceptable. But, here again, we must conclude that the phenomenon of integration fatigue provides evidence to the contrary.

30. Tommie Shelby, *Dark Ghettos: Injustice, Dissent, and Reform* (Cambridge, MA: Belknap Press of Harvard University Press, 2006).

31. Tein, "Devaluation," 1470. Tein remarked simply that "judicial remedies that force integration in subsidized housing fail to account for the right of minority tenants to choose not to integrate." As Wilen and Stasell note, "To the extent that integration policies require African-Americans to leave their neighborhoods against their will, they are deprived of freedom of choice to decide where to live, just as they were under former segregation policies." Wilen and Stasell, "*Gautreaux*," 140.

32. Tein, "Devaluation."

33. See Polikoff, *Waiting*, 214–216.

34. Goering, "Political Origins."

35. See Piven and Cloward, "Case against"; and Calmore, "Fair Housing."

36. Danielson, *Politics of Exclusion*.

37. See, e.g., Robert Neelly Bellah et al., *Habits of the Heart: Individualism and Commitment in American Life* (Berkeley: University of California Press, 1985); Danielson, *Politics of Exclusion*; and Goering, "Political Origins."

38. Whites continue to move away from communities in which people of color locate. See Daniel T. Lichter, Domenico Parisi, and Michael C. Taquino, "Toward a New Macro-Segregation? Decomposing Segregation within and between Metropolitan Cities and Suburbs," *American Sociological Review* 80.4 (2015).

39. J. Rosie Tighe, "Public Opinion and Affordable Housing: A Review of the Literature," *Journal of Planning Literature* 25.1 (2010).

40. Paul M. Sniderman and Edward G. Carmines, "Reaching beyond Race," *PS: Political Science & Politics* 30.3 (1997).

41. Goering, "Political Origins."

42. Patterns of white resistance to low-cost housing continue to prevail in all parts of the country, including liberal and progressive regions such as the San Francisco Bay area and the Twin Cities region of Minneapolis–Saint Paul. See, e.g., Megan Hansen, "Marin Residents Stand in Rain to Protest High-Density Housing Developments," *Marin Journal*, February 7, 2014; and Iris Perez, "Workforce Housing Project Bitterly Contested in Carver," Fox 9, March 2, 2015.

43. Megan Cottrell, "Did the Public Housing Transformation Destroy Chicago's Black Voter Base?," *Chicago Muckrakers*, January 4, 2011. The decline in the size of Chicago's black population was astounding in the 2000s—a loss of more than 175,000, or close to 17 percent of the black population (U.S. Census, author's calculations).

44. Seicshnaydre, "Government Housing," 708.

45. See the review in Edward G. Goetz and Karen Chapple, "You Gotta Move: Advancing the Debate on the Record of Dispersal," *Housing Policy Debate* 20.2 (2010).

46. Elvin Wyly and Daniel Hammel, "Islands of Decay in Seas of Renewal: Housing Policy and the Resurgence of Gentrification," *Housing Policy Debate* 10.4 (1999); Goetz, *New Deal Ruins*.

47. In 2014 the annual aggregate amount of residential mortgage lending in the United States was $1.39 trillion (http://www.consumerfinance.gov/hmda/explore#!/as_of_year=2014&section=summary). Most of this represented investment flows out of declining neighborhoods and into higher-income and more profitable places. The entire HUD budget for that same year was $41.5 billion. That is to say, the entire HUD budget, not all of which goes to real estate investment, is less than 3 percent of the annual amount of private-sector residential real estate investment. If one were to add commercial real estate investment, the percentage would shrink much further. To expect that this level of public-sector effort will offset private-market trends is to expect a great deal.

48. Iris Marion Young argues that integration efforts tend to focus on the movement of individuals into excluded areas, focusing on individual households and therefore not on the large systems that produce racial inequalities. See Young, *Inclusion and Democracy* (New York: Oxford University Press, 2002), 227.

49. Elizabeth Kneebone and Emily Garr, *The Suburbanization of Poverty: Trends in Metropolitan America, 2000 to 2008* (Washington, DC: Brookings Institution, 2010). See also Elizabeth Kneebone and Alan Berube, *Confronting Suburban Poverty in America* (Washington, DC: Brookings Institution Press, 2013).

50. Cited in Family Housing Fund, "The Need for Affordable Housing in the Twin Cities," Minneapolis, 1998.

51. To use the Twin Cities as an example again, in October 2012, the Metropolitan Housing and Redevelopment Agency reported close to three thousand names on its waiting list. Carver County reported a public housing waiting list of one to five years, depending on unit size. Scott County had not opened its Section 8 waiting list for five years after gathering over one thousand names in 2007; it estimated eight to nine hundred names on its public housing waiting list for two-, four-, and five-bedroom units. The demand for such housing is increasing rapidly. The Metropolitan Council estimated that 44,467 more units of affordable housing would be needed in suburban areas of the metropolitan area just to meet the increased demand generated by population growth in the suburbs between 2011 and 2020. Metropolitan Council of the Twin Cities, *Summary Report: Determining Affordable Housing Need in the Twin Cities, 2011–2020*," Saint Paul, MN, 2006.

52. Imbroscio, "Beyond Mobility." Imbroscio points to studies showing broad swaths of decline in suburban areas, including areas far beyond the inner-ring suburbs, and the shrinking number of places with safe housing close to work and with good public schools, citing Jerome M. Segal, *Graceful Simplicity: The Philosophy and Politics of the Alternative American Dream* (Berkeley: University of California Press, 2003), as well as Dreier, Mollenkopf, and Swanstrom, *Place Matters*.

53. John Goering, "Introduction to Section IV," in *Housing Desegregation and Federal Policy*, ed. John M. Goering (Chapel Hill: University of North Carolina Press, 1986), 202.

54. Edward G. Goetz, *Clearing the Way: Deconcentrating the Poor in Urban America* (Washington, DC: Urban Institute Press, 2003).

55. Jennifer Comey, Xavier Briggs, and Gretchen Weismann, "Struggling to Stay out of High-Poverty Neighborhoods: Lessons from the Moving to Opportunity Experiment," Urban Institute Policy Brief No. 6, March 2008. In another study, this one of the Twin Cities metropolitan area, the most common type of move by Section 8 voucher holders who were given the opportunity to "port" their vouchers to any community in the region was to take a voucher from a suburban community and move to one of the central cities (Minneapolis or Saint Paul). See Elizabeth G. D. Malaby and Barbara Lukermann, "Given Choice: The Effects of Portability in Section 8 Rental Housing Assistance," *CURA Reporter* 26.2 (1996).

56. Calmore, "Fair Housing."

57. The only systematic analysis of this question is twenty years old. See Naomi Baillin Wish and Stephen Eisdorfer, "The Impact of Mount Laurel Initiatives: An Analysis of the Characteristics of Applicants and Occupants," *Seton Hall Law Review* 27 (1997).

58. Alan Berube, Elizabeth Kneebone, and Carey Nadeau, *The Re-emergence of Concentrated Poverty: Metropolitan Trends in the 2000s* (Washington, DC: Brookings Institution, 2011).

59. Lake and Winslow reasonably ask, "What is the acceptable black/white ratio to serve public interests?" Lake and Winslow, "Integration Management." See also Chapple, *Planning Sustainable Cities*.

60. Indeed, one of the claims made on behalf of the Gautreaux program—wrongly, it turned out—was that such a mobility program could address the "spatial mismatch" problem in which new jobs were located far from lower-income communities, making it difficult for residents of those communities to access employment opportunities. The widely cited positive employment benefits of moving to suburbs among Gautreaux families was actually the absence of a negative effect of moving. Suburban families were no more likely to be employed after moving than they were before moving, while those who moved within the city experienced a more than 10 percentage point decline in employment. See Susan J. Popkin, James E. Rosenbaum, and Patricia M. Meaden, "Labor Market Experiences of Low-Income Black Women in Middle-Class Suburbs: Evidence from a Survey of Gautreaux Program Participants," *Journal of Policy Analysis and Management* 12.3 (1993).

61. See, for example, Goetz and Chapple, "You Gotta Move," for a review.

62. Young, *Inclusion and Democracy*.

63. Chetty, Hendren, and Katz, "Effects of Exposure."

64. The authors also suggest there is evidence that the thirteen-and-under treatment group enrolled in "better" schools than did those in the control group. To accept this, one would have to accept the authors' notion that the average earnings of graduates is an accurate measure of school quality, an idea that seems problematic at best.

65. Thomas B. Edsall, "Where Should a Poor Family Live?," *New York Times*, August 5, 2015.

66. Chetty, Hendren, and Katz, "Effects of Exposure," 3, italics in the original.

67. Larry Orr et al., *Moving to Opportunity for Fair Housing Demonstration Program: Interim Impacts Evaluation* (Washington, DC: U.S. Department of Housing and Urban Development, 2003).

68. Comey, Briggs, and Weismann, "Struggling," 3.

69. Robert J. Chaskin and Mark L. Joseph, *Integrating the Inner City: The Promise and Perils of Mixed-Income Public Housing Transformation* (Chicago: University of Chicago Press, 2015).

70. Ibid., 190–191.

71. Ibid., 134. See also Laura Tach, "More Than Bricks and Mortar: Neighborhood Frames, Social Processes, and the Mixed-Income Redevelopment of a Public Housing Project," *City & Community* 8 (2009); and James Fraser and Edward Kick, "The Role of Public, Private, Nonprofit and Community Sectors in Shaping Mixed-Income Housing Outcomes in the U.S.," *Urban Studies* 44.12 (2007).

72. Chaskin and Joseph, *Integrating*, 216.

73. Much of the literature referenced in this section is reviewed and summarized in Rebecca Cohen, *The Impacts of Affordable Housing on Health: A Research Summary* (Washington, DC: Center for Housing Policy, 2011); and Rebecca Cohen and Keith Wardrip, *Should I Stay or Should I Go? Exploring the Effects of Housing Instability and Mobility on Children* (Washington, DC: Center for Housing Policy, 2011).

74. Joseph Harkness and Sandra J. Newman, "Housing Affordability and Children's Well-Being: Evidence from the National Survey of America's Families," *Housing Policy Debate* 16.2 (2005).

75. Elizabeth L. March et al., *Rx for Hunger: Affordable Housing* (Boston: Children's HealthWatch and Medical-Legal Partnership, 2009).

76. Deborah A. Frank et al., "Heat or Eat: The Low Income Home Energy Assistance Program and Nutritional and Health Risks among Children Less Than 3 Years of Age," *Pediatrics* 118.5 (2006); Alan Meyers, Diane B. Cutts, et al., "Subsidized Housing and Children's Nutritional Status: Data from a Multisite Surveillance Study," *Archives of Pediatrics and Adolescent Medicine* 159 (2005); Alan Meyers, D. Rubin, et al., "Public Housing Subsidies May Improve Poor Children's Nutrition," *American Journal of Public Health* 83.1 (1993).

77. Fredrik Andersson et al., "Childhood Housing and Adult Earnings: Between-Siblings Analysis of Housing Vouchers and Public Housing," National Bureau of Economic Research, Cambridge, MA, Working Paper 22721 (2016).

78. Craig E. Pollack and Julia Lynch, "Health Status of People Undergoing Foreclosure in the Philadelphia Region," *American Journal of Public Health* 99.10 (2009).

79. Susan J. Smith et al., "Housing as Health Capital: How Health Trajectories and Housing Paths Are Linked," *Journal of Social Issues* 59.3 (2003); Sarah Nettleton and Roger Burrows, "Mortgage Debt, Insecure Home Ownership and Health: An Exploratory Analysis," *Sociology of Health and Illness* 20.5 (1998); Scott Weich and Glyn Lewis, "Poverty, Unemployment, and Common Mental Disorders: Population Based Cohort Study," *British Medical Journal* 317 (1998).

80. Carolina Guzman, Rajiv Bhatia, and Chris Durazo, *Anticipated Effects of Residential Displacement on Health: Results from Qualitative Research*, San Francisco Department of Public Health and South of Market Community Action Network, 2005; Sheridan Bartlett, "The Significance of Relocation for Chronically Poor Families in the USA," *Environment and Urbanization* 9.1 (1997).

81. See, e.g., Bonnie T. Zima, K. B. Wells, and H. E. Freeman, "Emotional Behavioral Problems and Severe Academic Delays among Sheltered Homeless Children in Los Angeles County," *American Journal of Public Health* 84.2 (1994); Lisa A. Goodman, Leonard Saxe, and Mary Harvey, "Homelessness as Psychological Trauma," *American Psychologist* 46.11 (1991); Ellen L. Bassuk and Lynn Rosenberg, "Psychosocial Characteristics of Homeless Children and Children with Homes," *Pediatrics* 85.3 (1990); David L. Wood et al., "Health of Homeless Children and Housed, Poor Children," *Pediatrics* 86.6 (1990).

82. See Richard D. Cohn et al., "National Prevalence and Exposure Risk for Cockroach Allergen in U.S. Households," *Environmental Health Perspectives* 114.4 (2006); Rick Nevin and David E. Jacobs, "Windows of Opportunity: Lead Poisoning Prevention, Housing Affordability, and Energy Conservation," *Housing Policy Debate* 17.1 (2006); Patrick Breysse et al., "The Relationship between Housing and Health: Children at Risk," *Environmental Health Perspectives* 112.15 (2004); G. R. Istre et al., "Deaths and Injuries from House Fires," *New England Journal of Medicine* 344.25 (2001).

83. Maria R. A. Cardoso et al., "Crowding: Risk Factor or Protective Factor for Lower Respiratory Disease in Young Children?," *BMC Public Health* 4.1 (2004); M. A. Baker et al., "Household Crowding: A Major Risk Factor for Epidemic Meningococcal Disease in Auckland Children," *Pediatric Infectious Disease Journal* 19.10 (2000); Gary W. Evans et al., "Chronic Residential Crowding and Children's Well-Being: An Ecological Perspective," *Child Development* 69.6 (1998); S. J. Lepore, G. W. Evans, and M. N. Palsane, "Social Hassles and Psychological Health in the Context of Chronic Crowding," *Journal of Health and Social Behavior* 32.4 (1991); Walter R. Gove, Michael Hughes, and Omer R. Galle, "Overcrowding in the Home: An Empirical Investigation of Its Possible Pathological Consequences," *American Sociological Review* 44.1 (1979).

84. Arthur J. Reynolds, Chin-Chih Chen, and Janette E. Herbers, "School Mobility and Education Success: A Research Synthesis and Evidence on Prevention," paper prepared for the Workshop on the Impact of Mobility and Change on the Lives of Young Children, Schools, and Neighborhoods, June 29–30, 2009, National Academies, Washington, DC; Edward Scanlon and Kevin Devine, "Residential Mobility and Youth Well-Being: Research, Policy, and Practice Issues," *Journal of Sociology and Social Welfare* 28.1 (2001); Will Craig, *The Kids Mobility Project* (Minneapolis: Center for Urban and Regional Affairs, University of Minnesota, 1998); David Kerbow, *Patterns of Urban Student Mobility and Local School Reform*, Technical Report No. 5 (Chicago: University of Chicago Center for Research on the Education of Students Placed at Risk, 1996).

85. Maya Brennan, Patrick Reed, and Lisa Sturtevant, *The Impacts of Affordable Housing on Education: A Research Summary* (Washington, DC: Center for Housing Policy, 2011).

86. Kerbow, *Patterns*.

87. Sandra J. Newman and C. Scott Holupka, "Housing Affordability and Children's Well-Being," working paper, Center on Housing, Neighborhoods, and Communities, Institute for Health and Social Policy, Johns Hopkins University, 2013; and Sandra J. Newman and C. Scott Holupka, "Housing Affordability and Investments in Children," *Journal of Housing Economics* 24 (2014).

88. Keith Wardrip, Laura Williams, and Suzanne Hague, *The Role of Affordable Housing in Creating Jobs and Stimulating Local Economic Development: A Review of the Literature* (Washington, DC: Center for Housing Policy, 2011).

89. National Association of Home Builders, *The Local Economic Impact of Typical Housing Tax Credit Developments* (Washington, DC, 2010).

90. Chris Walker, *Affordable Housing for Families and Neighborhoods: The Value of Low-Income Housing Tax Credits in New York City* (Columbia, MD, and Washington, DC: Enterprise Community Partners Inc. and Local Initiatives Support Corporation, 2010). See also Wardrip et al., *Affordable Housing*.

91. Sean Zielenbach, Richard Voith, and M. Mariano, "Estimating the Local Economic Impacts of HOPE VI," *Housing Policy Debate* 20.3 (2010).

92. Wardrip et al., *Affordable Housing*.

93. Lei Deng, Roberto G. Quercia, Wei Li, and Janekke Ratcliffe, "Risky Borrowers or Risky Mortgages: Disaggregating Effects Using Property Score Models," *Journal of Real Estate Research* 33.2 (2011).

94. Wardrip et al., *Affordable Housing*.

95. Alex E. Schwartz, Scott Susin, and Ionu Voicu, "Has Falling Crime Driven New York City's Real Estate Boom?," *Journal of Housing Research* 14.1 (2003). One study showed that increased property values would allow New York City to recapture a $2.4 billion investment in subsidized housing over a twenty-year period; Alex E. Schwartz et al., "The External Effects of Place-Based Subsidized Housing," *Regional Science and Urban Economics* 36.6 (2006).

96. Wardrip, *Affordable Housing*.

97. Kitashree Chakrabarti and Junfu Zhang, "Unaffordable Housing and Local Employment Growth," working paper no. 10–3, New England Public Policy Center at the Federal Reserve Bank of Boston, 2010.

98. Schwartz et al., "External Effects." One direct study of the crime-reduction question indicates that targeted housing rehabilitation by CDCs does indeed reduce crime problems. A study of fourteen multifamily, low-income housing developments purchased and rehabilitated by community development corporations in Minneapolis from 1986 to 1994 showed that in the aggregate there was a significantly lower level of crime calls (both total and violent crimes) from these properties after their conversion to subsidized housing. See Edward G. Goetz, Hin Kin Lam, and Anne Heitlinger, *There Goes the Neighborhood? The Impact of Subsidized Multi-Family Housing on Urban Neighborhoods* (Minneapolis: Center for Urban and Regional Affairs, University of Minnesota, 1996).

99. Studies of New York City, Portland, Seattle, Dallas, Cleveland, and Santa Clara found that projects have resulted in an increase in market prices of nearby homes in surrounding neighborhoods. The Santa Clara study found greater benefits in low-income neighborhoods than in other areas. A national study of tax credit projects found a similar effect—that increases in property values occurred in declining neighborhoods. The national study also found that tax credit projects "reduce incomes in gentrifying areas in neighborhoods near the 30th percentile of the income distribution" and have no impact on the construction of other new multifamily housing in stable or declining neighborhoods. Properties in suburban Minneapolis–Saint Paul neighborhoods with tax credit properties performed as well or better after construction of tax credit projects and in comparison to control neighborhoods. A study of Polk County, Iowa (Des Moines), found a lower rate of appreciation for property near tax credit projects, though no effects were found for projects with an income mix or "high quality" design. Tax credit projects for the elderly were associated with a higher-than-market rate of appreciation. A study focusing on more suburban neighborhoods in Wisconsin indicates that LIHTC projects there had no significant effect on neighborhood home values, and a study in suburban New Jersey found no negative effects of tax credit projects on property values. A study of tax credit properties in Philadelphia showed that surrounding properties experienced a slight decline in property values. See Ingrid Gould Ellen et al., "Does Federally Subsidized

Rental Housing Depress Neighborhood Property Values?," *Journal of Policy Analysis and Management* 26.2 (2007); Jennifer Johnson and Beata Bednarz, *Neighborhood Effects of the Low Income Housing Tax Credit Program: Final Report* (Washington, DC: U.S. Department of Housing and Urban Development, 2002); Roxanne Ezzet-Lofstrom and James Murdoch, "The Effect of Low Income Housing Tax Credit Units on Residential Property Values in Dallas County," *Williams Review* 1.1 (2006); Lan Deng, "The External Neighborhood Effects of Low-Income Housing Tax Credit Projects Built by Three Sectors," *Journal of Urban Affairs* 33.2 (2011); Nathaniel Baum-Snow and Justin Marion, "The Effects of Low Income Housing Tax Credit Developments on Neighborhoods," *Journal of Public Economics* 93 (2009); Maxfield Research, *A Study of the Relationship between Affordable Family Rental Housing and Home Values in the Twin Cities* (Minneapolis, MN: Family Housing Fund, 2000); Richard Funderburg and Heather MacDonald, "Neighbourhood Valuation Effects from New Construction of Low-Income Housing Tax Credit Projects in Iowa: A Natural Experiment," *Urban Studies* 47.8 (2010); Richard K. Green, Stephen Malpezzi, and Kiat-Ying Seah, "Low Income Housing Tax Credit Housing Developments and Property Values," Center for Urban Land Economics Research, University of Wisconsin, 2002; Len Albright, Elizabeth S. Derickson, and Douglas Massey, "Do Affordable Housing Projects Harm Suburban Communities? Crime, Property Values, and Property Taxes in Mt. Laurel, New Jersey," SSRN, 2011; Chang-Moo Lee, Dennis P. Culhane, and Susan M. Wachter, "The Differential Impacts of Federally Assisted Housing Programs on Nearby Property Values: A Philadelphia Case Study," *Housing Policy Debate* 10 (1999).

100. Ingrid Gould Ellen and Ionu Voicu, "Nonprofit Housing and Neighborhood Spillovers," *Journal of Policy Analysis and Management* 25.1 (2005). Nonprofit housing projects in Minneapolis were also found to have a positive impact on nearby property values; see Goetz, Lam, and Heitlinger, *There Goes the Neighborhood*. Both for-profit and nonprofit-owned developments produced benefits in Santa Clara, California; see Deng, "External Neighborhood Effects."

101. William A. Rabiega, Ta-win Lin, and Linda M. Robinson, "The Property Value Effects of Public Housing Projects in Low and Moderate Density Residential Neighborhoods," *Land Economics* 6.2 (1984); Lee et al., "Differential Impacts"; Robert F. Lyons and Scott Loveridge, "An Hedonic Estimation of the Effect of Federally Subsidized Housing on Nearby Residential Property Values," Staff Paper P93–6, Department of Agriculture and Applied Economics, University of Minnesota, Saint Paul, 1993). A study of New York City's local effort to invest in subsidized housing revealed "significant and sustained" benefits for surrounding neighborhoods that increased with project size; see Schwartz et al., "Eternal Effects."

102. Ellen et al., "Federally Subsidized Rental"; George C. Galster, Anna Santiago, and Peter Tatian, "Assessing the Property Value Impacts of the Dispersed Subsidized Housing Program in Denver," *Journal of Policy Analysis and Management* 20 (2001).

103. Ellen et al., "Federally Subsidized Rental."

104. Robert A. Simons, A. J. Magner, and Esmail Baku, "Do Housing Rehabs Pay Their Way? A National Case Study," *Journal of Real Estate Research* 25.4 (2003); Chengri Ding, Robert Simons, and Esmail Baku, "The Effect of Residential Investment on Nearby Property Values: Evidence from Cleveland, Ohio," *Journal of Real Estate Research* 19.1 (2000); Kelly D. Edmiston, "Nonprofit Housing Investment and Local Area Home Values," *Economic Review*, First Quarter 2012; Schwartz, Susin, and Voicu, "Falling Crime."

105. See Daniel Trudeau, "The Persistence of Segregation in Buffalo, New York: *Comer vs. Cisneros* and Geographies of Relocation Decisions among Low-Income Black Households," *Urban Geography* 27.1 (2006) on the reluctance to make an initial outward move; and Comey, Briggs, and Weismann, "Struggling," for the tendency of families to move back to lower-income neighborhoods.

106. See, e.g., Goetz, *Clearing the Way*, on lack of demand for mobility. The literature on the resistance to forced removal is growing: see, e.g., John Arena, *Driven from New Orleans: How Nonprofits Betray Public Housing and Promote Privatization* (Minneapolis: University of Minnesota Press, 2012); Jason Hackworth, "Destroyed by HOPE: Public Housing, Neoliberalism, and Progressive Housing Activism in the US," in *Where the Other Half Lives: Lower Income Housing in a Neoliberal World*, ed. Sarah Glynn (London: Pluto, 2009); Amy Howard, *More Than Shelter: Activism and Community in San Francisco Public Housing* (Minneapolis: University of Minnesota Press, 2014); Patricia Wright, "Community Resistance to CHA Transformation: The History, Evolution, Struggles, and Accomplishments of the Coalition to Protect Public Housing," in *Where Are Poor People to Live? Transforming Public Housing Communities*, ed. Larry Bennett, Janet L. Smith, and Patricia Wright (Armonk, NY: M. E. Sharpe, 2006); Goetz, *New Deal Ruins*; Melissa Arrigiota Fernández, "Constructing 'the Other,' Practicing Resistance: Public Housing and Community Politics in Puerto Rico" (PhD thesis, London School of Economics and Political Science, 2010).

107. Jeff Spinner-Halev, "The Trouble with Diversity," in *Critical Urban Studies: New Directions*, ed. Jonathan S. Davies and David L. Imbroscio (Albany: SUNY Press, 2010). Spinner-Halev specifically argues that "the problem of choice also haunts many of the proposed solutions to the problem of segregation," 115.

108. Thomas C. Schelling, "A Process of Residential Segregation: Neighborhood Tipping," in *Racial Discrimination in Economic Life*, ed. Anthony H. Pascal (Lexington, MA: Lexington Books, 1972), 157.

109. These preferences have been fairly stable over time. See Krysan and Farley, "Residential Preferences"; Lawrence Bobo and Camille L. Zubrinsky, "Attitudes on Residential Integration: Perceived Status Differences, Mere In-Group Preference, or Racial Prejudice?," *Social Forces* 74.3 (1996); Reynolds Farley et al., "'Chocolate City, Vanilla Suburbs': Will the Trend toward Racially Separate Communities Continue?," *Social Science Research* 7.4 (1978).

110. Rubinowitz and Trosman, "Affirmative Action."

111. Shelby, *Dark Ghettos*.

112. Spinner-Halev, "Trouble," 115–116. Spinner-Halev was referring specifically to Dreier, Mollenkopf, and Swanstrom's *Place Matters*.

113. Schill, "Deconcentrating," 839.

114. This has been pointed out by Calmore, "Fair Housing," Tein, "Devaluation," and by Lake and Winslow, "Integration Management." As Calmore argues, the rigid pursuit of equal opportunity goals may actually restrict choice rather than enhance it; "in the name of expanding choice and opportunities, the fair housing imperative actually restricts housing for poor, inner-city neighborhoods" (p. 8).

115. Henry Cisneros, "A New Moment for People and Cities," in *From Despair to Hope: HOPE VI and the New Promise of Public Housing in America's Cities*, ed. Henry G. Cisneros and Lora Engdahl (Washington, DC: Brookings Institution Press, 2009), 13.

116. Lake and Winslow, "Integration Management," 323. In the Netherlands, pro-integrative policy was abandoned because of protests over the "way it limited choices for the migrant minorities it was supposed to help." See Young, *Inclusion and Democracy*, 220.

117. William A. V. Clark, "Race, Class, and Space: Outcomes of Suburban Access for Asians and Hispanics," *Urban Geography* 27.6 (2006); and von Hoffman, "Fleas on a Tiger."

118. See Kimberly Skobba and Edward G. Goetz, "Mobility Decisions of Very Low-Income Households," *Cityscape* 15.2 (2013).

119. Casey J. Dawkins, "Are Social Networks the Ties That Bind Families to Neighborhoods?," *Housing Studies* 21.6 (2006).

120. Rolf Pendall and Joe Parilla, "Comment on Emily Talen and Julia Koschinsky's 'Is Subsidized Housing in Sustainable Neighborhoods? Evidence from Chicago': 'Sustainable' Urban Form and Opportunity; Frames and Expectations for Low-Income Households," *Housing Policy Debate* 21.1 (2011).

121. Squires and Kubrin, *Privileged Places*, 19.

122. Peach, "Good Segregation"; Peter Marcuse, "The Enclave, the Citadel, and the Ghetto: What Has Changed in the Post-Fordist US City," *Urban Affairs Review* 33.2 (1997).

123. See, e.g., Young, *Inclusion and Democracy*, 218; Shelby, *Dark Ghettos*, 39.

124. Young condemns segregation for how it limits choice and reproduces structural inequality, and she lays out ways of distinguishing between forced segregation and clustering. Segregation, she argues, occurs when spatial concentration of social groups is accompanied by systemic power differential and stigma.

125. Young, *Inclusion and Democracy*, 216.

126. Ibid.

127. Ibid., 197.

128. Ibid., 216.

129. Iris Marion Young, *Justice and the Politics of Difference* (Princeton, NJ: Princeton University Press, 1990), 47.

130. Shelby, *Dark Ghettos*, 39.

131. Susan S. Fainstein, *The Just City* (Ithaca, NY: Cornell University Press, 2010). Karen Chapple argues that this "means reconceptualizing policy and planning to provide more security to families in need across the region, regardless of where we think opportunity lies. Housing policy should continue to work to provide housing options across the region, but with the goal of integration at the scale of the district or place, rather than the neighborhood." Chapple, *Planning Sustainable Cities*, 291.

132. See Imbroscio, *Urban America*; David Imbroscio, "Shaming the Inside Game: A Critique of the Liberal Expansionist Approach to Addressing Urban Problems," *Urban Affairs Review* 42.2 (2006); David Imbroscio, "'United and Actuated by Some Common Impulse of Passion': Challenging the Dispersal Consensus in American Housing Policy Research," *Journal of Urban Affairs* 30.2 (2008).

133. This is the "obligatory caveat" I mentioned in the introduction.

134. Imbroscio, "Shaming," 224.

135. Imbroscio, *Urban America*, 5.

136. In his critique of regionalism, Imbroscio parts ways with Young. Where Young argues for policy making at a scale that matches the problem, Imbroscio sees greater benefit in retaining the autonomy of central cities in ways that will be described below.

137. Janet L. Smith, "Integration: Solving the Wrong Problem," in *The Integration Debate: Competing Futures for American Cities*, ed. Chester Hartman and Gregory D. Squires (New York: Routledge, 2010).

138. Mary Patillo, "The Problem of Integration," New York University, Furman Center, January 20, 2014.

139. Ibid. See also Mary Patillo, "Investing in Poor Black Neighborhoods 'As Is,'" in *Public Housing and the Legacy of Segregation*, ed. Margery Austin Turner, Susan J. Popkin, and Lynette Rawlings (Washington, DC: Urban Institute Press, 2009).

140. Young, *Inclusion and Democracy*, 219.

141. Ibid., 221.

142. Ibid., 227.

143. Ibid.

144. Imbroscio, *Urban America*, 144.

145. Patillo, "Problem."

146. Ibid.

147. Beverly Tatum, quoted in Anderson, *Imperative*, 134.

148. Young, *Inclusion and Democracy*, 217.

149. Shelby, *Dark Ghettos*, 60.

150. There is a considerable social science literature documenting the ways in which lower-income families depend on informal sources of support to make ends meet. These "personal safety nets" are reciprocal arrangements between similarly situated people. Support networks are typically made up of neighbors and family members living nearby. See, e.g., Carole Stack, *All Our Kin: Strategies for Survival in a Black Community* (New York: Harper & Row, 1975); Kathryn Edin and Laura Lein, *Making Ends Meet: How Single Mothers Survive Welfare and Low-Wage Work* (New York: Russell Sage Foundation, 1997); and Domínguez and Watkins, "Mobility."

151. Dawkins, "Ties That Bind."

152. Shelby, *Dark Ghettos*, 70.

153. Sudhir Venkatesh, *Off the Books: The Underground Economy of the Urban Poor* (Cambridge, MA: Harvard University Press, 2006).

154. See, e.g., Hank V. Savitch and Ronald K. Vogel, "Suburbs without a City: Power and City-County Consolidation," *Urban Affairs Review* 39.6 (2004).

155. See Imbroscio, *Urban America*, 142; J. Philip Thompson, "Review of *Place Matters*," *Urban Affairs Review* 37.3 (2002).

156. Imbroscio also points out that central cities are the location of a "legacy of organizations dedicated to serving the poor" and people of color, and organizations dedicated to empowering disadvantaged groups. Imbroscio, *Urban America*, 144. See also Dan Clawson, *The Next Upsurge: Labor and the New Social Movements* (Ithaca, NY: Cornell University Press, 2003).

157. Leigh and McGhee, "Minority Perspective"; Tein, "Devaluation"; Calmore, "Fair Housing"; Stephen Steinberg, "The Myth of Concentrated Poverty," in *The Integration Debate: Competing Futures for American Cities*, ed. Chester Hartman and Gregory Squires (New York: Routledge, 2010); and Wilen and Stasell, "*Gautreaux*."

158. Young, *Inclusion and Democracy*, 209 for the first quote and 225 for the second.

159. Anderson, *Imperative*, 133. Imbroscio argues that the dynamic of political mobilization seen in disadvantaged communities would likely disappear through integration; Imbroscio, *Urban America*.

160. Young, *Inclusion and Democracy*.

161. A point Downs made early on; Downs, *Opening Up*.

162. Fraser and Kick, "Shaping Mixed-Income"; James C. Fraser, "Beyond Gentrification: Mobilizing Communities and Claiming Space," *Urban Geography* 25.5 (2004); Calmore, "Fair Housing."

163. See, e.g., Polikoff, *Waiting*, on the need for radical surgery in segregated neighborhoods to completely change the socioeconomic dynamics.

164. Wilen and Stasell, "*Gautreaux*."

165. Ibid.; Deirdre Oakley and Keri Burchfeld, "Out of the Projects, Still in the Hood: The Spatial Constraints on Public Housing Residents' Relocation in Chicago," *Journal of Urban Affairs* 31.5 (2009).

166. Mindy Fullilove, *Root Shock: How Tearing Up City Neighborhoods Hurts America, and What We Can Do about It* (New York: One World / Ballantine, 2009); Karen J. Gibson, "The Relocation of the Columbia Villa Community: Views from Residents," *Journal of Planning Education and Research* 27.1 (2007); Lynne C. Manzo, Rachel G. Kleit, and Dawn Couch, "Moving Three Times Is Like Having Your House on Fire Once: The Experience of Place and Impending Displacement among Public Housing Residents," *Urban Studies* 45.9 (2008); Susan Greenbaum et al., "Deconcentration and Social Capital: Contradictions of a Poverty Alleviation Policy," *Journal of Poverty* 12.2 (2008).

167. See Douglas S. Massey et al., *Climbing Mount Laurel: The Struggle for Affordable Housing and Social Mobility in an American Suburb* (Princeton, NJ: Princeton University Press, 2013).

168. Young, *Inclusion and Democracy*, 226. See also Shelby, *Dark Ghettos*.

3. THE "HOLLOW PROSPECT" OF INTEGRATION

1. Jackson, *Crabgrass Frontier*.

2. See Hirsch, *Second Ghetto*; and Dreier, Mollenkopf, and Swanstrom, *Place Matters*.

3. See, e.g., P. H. Smith, *Racial Democracy*; James Q. Wilson, *Negro Politics: The Search for Leadership* (Glencoe, IL: Free Press, 1960); and Horace R. Cayton, *Black Metropolis: A Study of Negro Life in a Northern City* (Chicago: University of Chicago Press, 1970).

4. P. H. Smith, *Racial Democracy*, 96.

5. Ibid., 70.

6. Ibid.

7. See Lawrence J. Vale, *From the Puritans to the Projects: Public Housing and Public Neighbors* (Cambridge, MA: Harvard University Press, 2009); Bradford D. Hunt, *Blueprint for Disaster: The Unraveling of Chicago Public Housing* (Chicago: University of Chicago Press, 2009).

8. Hunt, *Blueprint*; Martin Meyerson and Edward C. Banfield, *Politics, Planning and the Public Interest: The Case of Public Housing in Chicago* (New York: Free Press, 1955); and Hirsch, *Second Ghetto*.

9. Wilson, *Negro Politics*, 188.

10. Bonastia, *Knocking on the Door*, 67.

11. See Newman and Schnare, "Suitable Living Environment," for national figures.

12. Wilson, *Negro Politics*, 188.

13. Ibid.

14. Juliet Saltman, *Open Housing as a Social Movement: Challenge, Conflict and Change* (Lexington, MA: Heath Lexington Books, 1971).

15. Paul E. King, "Exclusionary Zoning and Open Housing: A Brief Judicial History," *Geographical Review* 1 (1978).

16. Saltman, *Open Housing as a Social Movement*.

17. P. H. Smith, *Racial Democracy*, 121.

18. The ban on discrimination in the operation of publicly assisted housing was made national by President John F. Kennedy in 1962, via executive order. The idea of conditioning federal funds on progress made in desegregation resurfaced in the first Nixon administration, though not adopted then. Currently, HUD is authorized by Congress to withhold certain block grant funds from communities that are flouting their fair housing obligations. The threat of withholding federal funds is an explicit part of HUD's new rule on affirmatively furthering fair housing.

19. Von Hoffman, "Fleas on a Tiger," 20. See also Charles Abrams, *Forbidden Neighbors: A Study of Prejudice in Housing* (New York: Harper, 1955), 273.

20. This phrase came from the NCDH national newsletter, *Trends*, October 1959. See Saltman, *Open Housing as a Social Movement*, 38, fn. 37.

21. Karl E. Taeuber, "Residential Segregation," *Scientific American* 213.2 (1965).

22. Saltman, *Open Housing as a Social Movement*.

23. Ibid.

24. Ibid.

25. Ibid.

26. Preston Smith III argues that prior to the Second World War there was a strong social democratic strain in black politics. Especially in the area of housing, black leaders defined the interests of the community in terms of the need for the working class

and lower-income households to be adequately housed. Support for public housing, for example, was class-based advocacy in favor of expanding welfare state responsibilities. Indeed, there was significant support for Catherine Bauer's notion of public housing as mass housing for workers, modeled on European approaches. Smith juxtaposes this orientation with what he terms "racial democracy," which is defined by race-based claims to equality that simultaneously relegate class issues. Smith argues that racial democracy came to dominate during the postwar civil rights period. See P. H. Smith, *Racial Democracy*.

27. Flora Bryant Brown, "The NAACP Sponsored Sit-Ins by Howard University Students in Washington, D.C., 1943–1944," *Journal of Negro Education* 4 (2000). See also Mark Newman, *The Civil Rights Movement* (Westport, CT: Praeger, 2004).

28. The organization would later change its name to the Congress of Racial Equality.

29. See the history in Meyer, *Next Door*.

30. Janet Abu-Lughod, *Race, Space, and Riots in Chicago, New York, and Los Angeles* (Oxford: Oxford University Press, 2007); and Newman, *Civil Rights Movement*. See also Thomas J. Sugrue, *The Origins of the Urban Crisis: Race and Inequality in Postwar Detroit* (Princeton, NJ: Princeton University Press, 1996).

31. Peniel E. Joseph, ed., *The Black Power Movement: Rethinking the Civil Rights–Black Power Era* (New York: Routledge, 2006), 2.

32. James Tyner, *The Geography of Malcolm X: Black Radicalism and the Remaking of American Space* (New York: Routledge, 2006), 79.

33. Ibid., 79.

34. Ibid., 87.

35. Ibid., 86.

36. Ibid., 83. This is from the address that came to be known as the "Ballot or the Bullet" speech.

37. Manning Marable, *Race, Reform, and Rebellion: The Second Reconstruction in Black America, 1945–1990* (Oxford: University Press of Mississippi, 1991).

38. Newman, *Civil Rights Movement*; Marable, *Race, Reform and Rebellion*; August Meier and Elliott Rudwick, *CORE: A Study in the Civil Rights Movement, 1942–1968* (New York: Oxford University Press, 1973).

39. Akynyele O. Umoja, "1964: The Beginning of the End of Nonviolence in the Mississippi Freedom Movement," *Radical History Review* 85 (2003).

40. Marable, *Race, Reform and Rebellion*, 73.

41. Roy Innes, the chair of CORE at the time, maintains that whites voluntarily left the organization and while doing so took important resources, such as the donor contact list, with them. Others argue that CORE forced whites out of the organization in the name of black self-determination. See Marcus D. Pohlmann, ed., *African American Political Thought*, vol. 1 (New York: Taylor & Francis, 2003), esp. "Truth, Lies and Consequences," 381–404.

42. See Robert Weisbrot and G. Calvin Mackenzie, *The Liberal Hour: Washington and the Politics of Change in the 1960s* (New York: Penguin, 2009), on the means by which Democratic Party leaders responded to the Freedom Party challenge.

43. Joseph, *Black Power*.

44. Ibid.

45. Robert L. Allen, *Black Awakening in Capitalist America: An Analytic History* (New York: Doubleday, 1970), 19.

46. See Amy Abugo Ongiri, *Spectacular Blackness: The Cultural Politics of the Black Power Movement and the Search for a Black Aesthetic* (Charlottesville, VA: University of Virginia Press, 2010); William L. Van DeBurg, *New Day in Babylon: The Black Power Movement and American Culture, 1965–1975* (Chicago: University of Chicago Press, 1992).

47. Juliet Saltman, *Open Housing: Dynamics of a Social Movement* (New York: Praeger, 1978). The integrationist leaders of the civil rights movement argued that increased aggression in word and action were, in fact, threats to the racial justice movement rather than its next stage. See Marable, *Race, Reform, and Rebellion.*

48. Robert O. Self, *American Babylon: Race and the Struggle for Postwar Oakland* (Princeton, NJ: Princeton University Press, 2003).

49. Joseph, *Black Power*, 174.

50. Joe R. Feagin and Harlan Hahn, *Ghetto Riots: The Politics of Violence in American Cities* (New York: Macmillan, 1973).

51. In 1967, FBI director J. Edgar Hoover ordered operatives "to expose, disrupt, misdirect, discredit, or otherwise neutralize the activities of black nationalist, hate-type organizations and groupings, their leadership, spokesmen, membership and supporters." See Clayborne Carson, *In Struggle: SNCC and the Black Awakening of the 1960s* (Cambridge, MA: Harvard University Press, 1981). The effort, called the Counterintelligence Program (COINTELPRO), particularly targeted the Black Panthers. Marable reports that within two years of its formation, "the Panthers had been targeted by 233 separate actions. . . . In 1969 alone, 27 Black Panthers were killed by the police, and 749 were jailed or arrested." Marable, *Race, Reform, and Rebellion*, 125.

52. Joseph, *Black Power*. See also Kenneth S. Jolly, *Black Liberation in the Midwest: The Struggle in St. Louis, Missouri, 1964–1970* (New York: Routledge, 2006); Charles E. Jones, "The Political Repression of the Black Panther Party, 1966–1971: The Case of the Oakland Bay Area," *Journal of Black Studies* 18.4 (1988); David Cunningham, "The Patterning of Repression: FBI Counterintelligence and the New Left," *Social Forces* 82.1 (2003).

53. See Kevin M. Kruse, *White Flight: Atlanta and the Making of Modern Conservatism* (Princeton, NJ: Princeton University Press, 2005); Kyle Crowder, "The Racial Context of White Mobility: An Individual-Level Assessment of the White Flight Hypothesis," *Social Science Research* 29.2 (2000).

54. Larry H. Long, "How the Racial Composition of Cities Change," *Land Economics* 51.3 (1975).

55. Farley et al., "'Chocolate City.'"

56. This pattern of urban development had established itself years earlier. The U.S. Commission on Civil Rights used the term "white noose" to describe American urban development as early as 1961. U.S. Commission on Civil Rights, *Housing: 1961 Commission on Civil Rights Report* (Washington, DC: Government Printing Office, 1961).

57. Allen, *Black Awakening*, 166.

58. Ibid., 19.

59. Alice O'Connor, *Poverty Knowledge: Social Science, Social Policy, and the Poor in Twentieth-Century US History* (Princeton, NJ: Princeton University Press, 2009).

60. Ibid.

61. James Defilippis, *Unmaking Goliath: Community Control in the Face of Global Capital* (New York: Routledge, 2004).

62. O'Connor, *Poverty Knowledge*.

63. Ibid.

64. John T. Baker, "Community Development Corporations: A Legal Analysis," *Valparaiso University Law Review* 13 (1978).

65. Stokely Carmichael and Charles V. Hamilton, *Black Power: The Politics of Liberation in America* (New York: Vintage, 1966), 46.

66. Ibid., 46.

67. Kenneth B. Clark, *Dark Ghetto: Dilemmas of Social Power* (Hanover, NH: Wesleyan University Press, 1965), 28, quoted in Carmichael and Hamilton, *Black Power*, 18.

68. Allen, *Black Awakening*, 64. The black capitalism movement received a significant boost from Richard Nixon, campaigning for the presidency in 1968. As evidence of how widely adopted the concept of black power had become in two short years, Nixon offered *his* support for the idea in March 1968. He defined it as "the power the people should have over their own destinies, the power to affect their own communities, the power that comes from participation in the political and economic processes of society." While this language comes very close to that used by black nationalists, Nixon's operationalization of the concept was a set of initiatives such as Small Business Administration loans for black enterprises, tax incentives for business development in disadvantaged neighborhoods, and the expansion of black homeownership. At the time Nixon laid out his first ideas about black capitalism, he distinguished his proposal from the War on Poverty approach of the Johnson administration, noting that "what we do not need now is another round of unachievable promises of unavailable federal funds." Allen, *Black Awakening*, 192.

69. Newman, *Civil Rights Movement*. In addition to these economic debates, contested ideas about the political orientation of the civil rights movement were swirling. While the mainstream civil rights movement had long advocated integration and participation within broadly accepted political venues, i.e., working with liberals and allies within the Democratic Party, other ideas, such as community control, were circulating widely.

70. Nishani Frazier, "A McDonald's That Reflects the Soul of a People: Hough Area Development Corporation and Community Development in Cleveland," in *The Business of Black Power: Community Development, Capitalism, and Corporate Responsibility in Postwar America*, ed. Laura Warren Hill and Julia Rabig (Rochester, NY: University of Rochester Press, 2012), 70.

71. Brian Purnell, "'What We Need Is Brick and Mortar': Race, Gender, and Early Leadership of the Bedford-Stuyvesant Restoration Corporation," in Hill and Rabig, *Business of Black Power*.

72. Julia Rabig, "'A Fight and a Question': Community Development Corporations, Machine Politics, and Corporate Philanthropy in the Long Urban Crisis," in Hill and Rabig, *Business of Black Power*.

73. Ibid.

74. Ibid.

75. Laura Warren Hill and Julia Rabig, introduction to Hill and Rabig, *Business of Black Power*, 9.

76. National Advisory Commission on Civil Disorders, *Report*, 1.

77. Bonastia, *Knocking on the Door*, 101.

78. See Meyer, *Next Door*, for a complete description.

79. Jill S. Quadagno, *The Color of Welfare: How Racism Undermined the War on Poverty* (New York: Oxford University Press, 1994).

80. Bonastia, *Knocking on the Door*.

81. Carmichael and Hamilton, *Black Power*, 17.

82. Ibid., 41.

83. Ibid., 53.

84. Ibid., 46.

85. Ibid., 54.

86. Allen, *Black Awakening*.

87. Quoted in Saltman, *Open Housing as a Social Movement*, 43.

88. Ibid.

89. Sidney Fine, "Michigan and Housing Discrimination, 1949–1969," *Michigan Historical Review* 23.2 (1997) 102.

90. Saltman, *Open Housing: Dynamics*, 66.

91. Bonastia, *Knocking on the Door*, 78.

92. Saltman, *Open Housing as a Social Movement*, 155.

93. David Goldberg, "From Landless to Landlords: Black Power, Black Capitalism, and the Co-optation of Detroit's Tenants' Rights Movement, 1964–69," in Hill and Rabig, *Business of Black Power*, 161.

94. Danielson, *Politics of Exclusion*, 149.

95. Saltman, *Open Housing: Dynamics*.

96. Ibid., 310–311.

97. Danielson, *Politics of Exclusion*, 150.

98. Saltman, *Open Housing as a Social Movement*.

99. Ibid., 125.

100. Saltman, *Open Housing: Dynamics*.

101. Bonastia, *Knocking on the Door*, 67.

4. THE THREE STATIONS OF FAIR HOUSING SPATIAL STRATEGY

1. Carmichael and Hamilton, *Black Power*, 155.

2. See Frederick Siegel, *Troubled Journey: From Pearl Harbor to Ronald Reagan* (New York: Hill & Wang, 1984). This argument that white flight was a response to the urban riots of the 1960s is contested by many, including Heather Ann Thompson, "Rethinking the Politics of White Flight in the Postwar City: Detroit, 1945–1980," *Journal of Urban History* 25 (1999).

3. Von Hoffman, "Fleas on a Tiger."

4. George Metcalf, *Fair Housing Comes of Age* (New York: Greenwood, 1988); Massey and Denton, *American Apartheid*.

5. Massey and Denton, *American Apartheid*.

6. Michael J. Vernarelli, "Where Should HUD Locate Assisted Housing? The Evolution of Fair Housing Policy," in *Housing Desegregation and Federal Policy*, ed. John Goering (Chapel Hill: University of North Carolina Press, 1986).

7. Polikoff, "Sustainable Integration"; Daye, "Whither 'Fair' Housing."

8. Robert Lake, "Postscript: Unresolved Themes in the Evolution of Fair Housing," in *Housing Desegregation and Federal Policy*, ed. John Goering (Chapel Hill: University of North Carolina Press, 1986); and others.

9. Jean Eberhart Dubofsky, "Fair Housing: A Legislative History and a Perspective," *Washburn Law Journal* 8 (1968).

10. Lake and Winslow, "Integration Management"; Rubinowitz and Trosman, "Affirmative Action."

11. Lake and Winslow, "Integration Management," 318.

12. See, e.g., Robert G. Schwemm, "Overcoming Structural Barriers to Integrated Housing: A Back-to-the-Future Reflection on the Fair Housing Act's 'Affirmatively Further' Mandate," *Kentucky Law Journal* 100 (2011).

13. Roisman, "Affirmatively Furthering," 385. Roisman also tells the story of Nixon and Romney, arguing that they knew affirmatively furthering fair housing meant moving blacks to suburbs.

14. Ibid., 373–374.

15. Lake and Winslow, "Integration Management," 316.

16. Roisman, "Affirmatively Furthering"; and Roisman, "Constitutional and Statutory Mandates."

17. Mara S. Sidney, *Unfair Housing: How National Policy Shapes Community Action* (Lawrence: University Press of Kansas, 2003).

18. Ibid.

19. Lake and Winslow, "Integration Management," 318.

20. Tein, "Devaluation," 1467, n. 23.

21. Sidney, *Unfair Housing.*

22. Ibid., 32.

23. Ibid., 33.

24. Michael P. Seng and F. Willis Caruso, "Achieving Integration through Private Litigation," in *The Integration Debate: Competing Futures for American Cities,* ed. Chester Hartman and Gregory D. Squires (New York: Routledge, 2010).

25. "Shelterforce Exclusive: Interview with HUD Secretary Julian Castro," *Shelterforce,* February 4, 2016. Castro said similar things in late 2015 on MSNBC. "This idea that we ought to get folks into, at their choice, areas of higher opportunity makes a lot of sense. Just a couple months ago there was very powerful research from a group out of Harvard led by Raj Chetty that said when you get families into higher opportunity areas, that has great outcomes in terms of educational achievement, in terms of income. At the same time, you can't forget about the distressed areas and investing in the older urban core neighborhoods. . . . In these distressed urban neighborhoods, it's not enough just to focus on housing, or just improving the education or transportation, you have to focus on all of these things." He went on the say that the government cannot "forget about folks who also want to live [in central neighborhoods], where they have lived forever. That's their home, that's where they want to be. If you gave them a choice to go somewhere else they wouldn't because they want to live there." Interview with Melissa Harris Perry, August 30, 2015.

26. Roisman, "Constitutional and Statutory Mandates."

27. NAACP, Boston Chapter v. Secretary of Housing and Urban Development, 817 F.2d (1st Cir. 1987); Roisman, "Affirmatively Furthering"; Roisman, "Constitutional and Statutory Mandates."

28. Lake and Winslow, "Integration Management."

29. Saltman, *Open Housing: Dynamics.*

30. See, e.g., King, "Exclusionary Zoning." A range of state courts, in cases like Appeal of Kit-Mar Builders, 439 Pa. 466, 268 A.2d 765 (1970), striking down lot size requirements; Bristow v. City of Woodhaven, 35 Mich App. 205, 192 N.W.2d 322 (1971), striking down restrictions on mobile home parks; and most famously, Southern Burlington County NAACP v. Township of Mt. Laurel, 336 A.2d 713, 731–33 (N.J. 1975), invalidating the use of restrictions on multifamily housing to exclude lower-cost housing, ruled in these early years to reduce regulatory barriers to opening up the suburbs.

31. See, e.g., Kennedy Park Homes Association v. City of Lackawanna, N.Y., 436 F.2d 108 (1971); and United States v. City of Black Jack Missouri, 508 F. 2d 1179 (1974).

32. Bonastia, *Knocking on the Door,* 99.

33. Ibid., 103.

34. Danielson, *Politics of Exclusion.*

35. Bonastia, *Knocking on the Door*; Danielson, *Politics of Exclusion.*

36. Bonastia, *Knocking on the Door,* 107.

37. Ibid., 109.

38. Danielson, *Politics of Exclusion.*

39. Ibid., 154.

40. Ibid., 153.

41. Ibid., 148–156.

42. Ibid., 154.

43. Ibid., 149–155.

44. Ibid., *Politics of Exclusion.*

45. David Listokin, *Fair Share Housing Allocation* (New Brunswick, NJ: Center for Urban Policy Research, 1976).

46. See Newman and Schnare, "Suitable Living Environment."

47. Saltman, *Open Housing: Dynamics*, 99.

48. See, e.g., Rolf Pendall, "Why Voucher and Certificate Users Live in Distressed Neighborhoods," *Housing Policy Debate* 11.4 (2000).

49. Edward G. Goetz, "Housing Dispersal Programs," *Journal of Planning Literature* 18.1 (2003).

50. See, for example, Malaby and Lukermann, "Given Choice Choice: The Effects of Portability in Section 8 Rental Housing Assistance." The effort to enhance the dispersion of voucher holders continued in 2016 with the creation of "Small Area FMRs" that expand the number of neighborhoods in which Housing Choice Vouchers can be used. It is expected that the Small Area FMRs will provide voucher holders with better access to high-opportunity neighborhoods.

51. Recall Seicshnaydre's impassioned plea for greater subsidized housing in "opportunity" areas, noting that as long as the politically easy decision to continue concentrating it in core areas is taken, little to no progress in outlying areas will be made.

52. Roisman, "Affirmatively Furthering."

53. Saltman, *Open Housing as a Social Movement*.

54. Shannon v. HUD.

55. Vernarelli, "Where Should HUD Locate," 219, quoting from Shannon v. HUD at 822. See also Bonastia, *Knocking on the Door*, 128, on the limited nature of the Shannon decision.

56. Vernarelli, "Where Should HUD Locate," 219–220.

57. Danielson, *Politics of Exclusion*, 154.

58. Vernarelli, "Where Should HUD Locate."

59. Ibid., 223.

60. Goering, "Introduction."

61. Ibid., 201.

62. My brief history here is based largely on chapters 2 and 3 of Leonard S. Rubinowitz and James E. Rosenbaum, *Crossing the Class and Color Lines: From Public Housing to White Suburbia* (Chicago: University of Chicago Press, 2000).

63. Rubinowitz and Rosenbaum, *Crossing*, chap. 2. Because the CHA would not cooperate with the plaintiff's counsel, the two "parties proceeded largely independently" in proposing remedies. The CHA's proposal consisted of merely not considering race in siting future public housing. The judge adopted the remedy offered by the plaintiffs.

64. Rubinowitz and Rosenbaum, *Crossing*, 36.

65. Andrea Gill, "'Gilding the Ghetto' and Debates over Chicago's *Gautreaux* Program," in Hill and Rabig, *Business of Black Power*, 184–214.

66. Ibid., 190.

67. Ibid., 194.

68. Ibid., 199.

69. Cardiss Collins, "Introductory Remarks," in *The* Gautreaux *Decision and Its Effect on Subsidized Housing—Hearing before a Subcommittee of the Committee on Government Operations, United States House of Representatives, 95th Congress, 2nd Session* (Washington, DC: Government Printing Office, 1977), 2.

70. Ibid., 2.

71. Statement of Ronald Laurent, senior vice president, McElvain Reynolds Co., in *The* Gautreaux *Decision and Its Effect on Subsidized Housing—Hearing before a Subcommittee of the Committee on Government Operations, United States House of Representatives, 95th Congress, 2nd Session* (Washington, DC: Government Printing Office, 1977), 64.

72. Collins, "Introductory Remarks," 3.

73. "Statement of Alexander Polikoff, Executive Director, Business and Professional People in the Public Interest; Accompanied by Milton Shader, Cocounsel," in *The*

Gautreaux *Decision and Its Effect on Subsidized Housing—Hearing before a Subcommittee of the Committee on Government Operations, United States House of Representatives, 95th Congress, 2nd Session* (Washington, DC: Government Printing Office, 1977), 138.

74. Quoted in Gill, "'Gilding the Ghetto,'" 200.

75. Polikoff, *Waiting for* Gautreaux, 241.

76. Ibid., 289.

77. See Goetz, *Clearing the Way*.

78. Harvey Luskin Molotch, *Managed Integration: Dilemmas of Doing Good in the City* (Berkeley: University of California Press, 1972), 111.

79. Ibid., 82. See also W. Dennis Keating, *The Suburban Racial Dilemma: Housing and Neighborhoods* (Philadelphia: Temple University Press, 1994), on how integration maintenance programs are perceived by many to operate in ways that favor white families and cater specifically to their neighborhood preferences.

80. Molotch, *Managed Integration*, 101.

81. William J. Wilson and Richard Taub, *There Goes the Neighborhood: Racial, Ethnic and Class Tensions in Four Chicago Neighborhoods and Their Meaning for America* (New York: Knopf Doubleday, 2011), 179.

82. Lake and Winslow, "Integration Management."

83. See, e.g., Daye, "Whither 'Fair' Housing."

84. Lake and Winslow, "Integration Management," 322.

85. Ibid.

86. The most famous case on this issue is United States v. Starrett City Associates, 488 U.S. 946; 109 S. Ct. 376; 102 L. Ed. 2d 365; 1988 U.S. 5023, which struck down a strict quota system of tenant assignment in a New York apartment development. Decisions in Williamsburg Fair Housing Committee v. New York City Housing Authority, 493 F. Supp. 1225 (S.D.N.Y. 1980); Burney v. Housing Authority of the County of Beaver, 551 F. Supp. 746 (W.D. Pa. 1982); and U.S. v. Charlottesville Redevelopment and Housing Authority, 718 F. Supp. 461 (W.D. Va. 1989) also invalidated race-conscious tenant selection schemes. See Keating, *Suburban Racial Dilemma*.

87. Otero et al. v. New York City Housing Authority et al., 484 F.2d 1122 (1973).

88. Though the defendants disputed the figures, they never offered any alternatives of their own.

89. Otero et al. v. New York City Housing Authority et al., 484 F.2d 1122 (1973), 2.

90. Rubinowitz and Trosman, "Affirmative Action."

91. Ibid.

92. Otero et al. v. New York City Housing Authority et al., 484 F.2d 1122 (1973), 28.

93. Ibid.

94. Ibid., 29.

95. Ibid., 30.

96. Lake and Winslow, "Integration Management," 322.

97. John Relman, Glenn Schlactus, and Shalini Goel, "Creating and Protecting Pro-integration Programs under the Fair Housing Act," in *The Integration Debate: Competing Futures for American Cities*, ed. Chester Hartman and Gregory D. Squires (New York: Routledge, 2010).

98. Ibid.

99. Ibid., 45.

100. Goetz, *New Deal Ruins*.

101. Joe R. Feagin, *Racist America: Roots, Current Realities, and Future Reparations*, 3rd ed. (New York: Routledge, 2014). In a similar fashion, the evidence shows that affluent households are more segregated than households below the poverty level, yet our efforts to desegregate focus on poor families and on households of color, largely leaving

affluent and white communities free from policy initiatives that might alter their residential patterns. See Sean F. Reardon and Kendra Bischoff, "No Neighborhood Is an Island," *Discussion 9: Residential Income Segregation*, New York University, Furman Center, 2014.

102. See, e.g., Oakley and Burchfeld, "Out of the Projects."

103. Goering, "Introduction."

104. Roisman, "Affirmatively Furthering."

105. Susan J. Popkin et al., *Baseline Assessment of Public Housing Desegregation Cases: Cross-Site Report*, vol. 1 (Washington, DC: U.S. Department of Housing and Urban Development, 2000); Susan J. Popkin et al., *Baseline Assessment of Public Housing Desegregation Cases: Case Studies*, vol. 2 (Washington, DC: U.S. Department of Housing and Urban Development, 2000).

106. See, e.g., Gibson, "Columbia Villa"; Goetz, *New Deal Ruins*.

107. See Goetz, *Clearing the Way*, describing the opposition of Southeast Asian immigrant residents in Minneapolis protesting their forced removal from public housing demolished as a result of the consent decree in Hollman v. Cisneros.

108. See Goetz, *New Deal Ruins*, for cases of de facto demolition across the country.

109. Polikoff, *Waiting for* Gautreaux, 301.

110. Wilen and Stasell, "*Gautreaux*."

111. Ibid.

112. Polikoff, *Waiting for* Gautreaux, 301.

113. Wilen and Stasell, "*Gautreaux*," 135.

114. Oakley and Burchfeld, "Out of the Projects."

115. Wilen and Stasell, "*Gautreaux*," 118.

116. Goetz, *New Deal Ruins*.

117. Goetz and Chapple, "You Gotta Move."

118. Alexander Polikoff, "HOPE VI and the Deconcentration of Poverty," in *From Despair to Hope: HOPE VI and the New Promise of Public Housing in America's Cities*, ed. Henry Cisneros and Lora Engdahl (Washington, DC: Brookings Institution Press, 2009).

119. Alexander Polikoff, "Public Housing Destruction: Is It Worth It?," *For the Public Interest: The BPI Newsletter*, February 2003. See also Wright, "Community Resistance."

5. NEW ISSUES, UNRESOLVED QUESTIONS, AND THE WIDENING DEBATE

1. See the work of Imbroscio, "'United and Actuated" and "Shaming the Inside Game," as well as Goetz, *Clearing the Way*.

2. Goetz, *New Deal Ruins*.

3. Part of the impetus for creating something like the housing-plus-transportation (H+T) index is acknowledgment that these two typically constitute the largest expense categories for low-income families, and that some families have been trading off between the two. In the context of homeownership, the phrase "drive to qualify" captures the notion of families locating in exurban areas, some distance from metropolitan cores, in order to find mortgages they can afford. They are then faced with high transportation expenses (both financially and in terms of time) associated with more remote locations.

4. See Edward G. Goetz, "The Fair Housing Tightrope in the Obama Administration: Balancing Competing Policy Objectives of Fair Housing and Locational Efficiency in Assisted Housing," *Journal of Urban Affairs* 37.1 (2015).

5. Marc Baldassare, *Trouble in Paradise: The Suburban Transformation of America* (New York: Columbia University Press, 1986); Scott A. Bollens, "Municipal Decline and Inequality in American Suburban Rings, 1960–1980," *Regional Studies* 22 (1988); William H. Lucy and David L. Phillips, *Confronting Suburban Decline: Strategic Planning for Metropolitan Renewal* ((Washington, DC: Island Press, 2000).

6. Becky M. Nicolaides, *My Blue Heaven: Life and Politics in the Working-Class Suburbs of Los Angeles, 1920–1965* (Chicago: University of Chicago Press, 2002); Andrew Wiese, *Places of Their Own: African American Suburbanization in the Twentieth Century* (Chicago: University of Chicago Press, 2004).

7. Chapple, *Planning Sustainable Cities*, 17.

8. See Nancy A. Denton and Joseph R. Gibbons, "Twenty-First-Century Suburban Demography: Increasing Diversity yet Lingering Exclusion," in *Social Justice in Diverse Suburbs: History, Politics, and Prospects*, ed. Christopher Niedt (Philadelphia: Temple University Press, 2013); Matthew Hall and Barrett Lee, "How Diverse Are US Suburbs?," *Urban Studies* 47.1 (2010); Alan Berube and William H. Frey, *A Decade of Mixed Blessing: Urban and Suburban Poverty in Census 2000* (Washington, DC: Brookings Institution, Center on Urban and Metropolitan Policy, 2002); john a. powell and Jason Reece, "The Future of Fair Housing and Fair Credit: From Crisis to Opportunity," *Cleveland State Law Review* 57 (2009).

9. Wiese, *Places of Their Own*, 5.

10. See, e.g., Brian A. Mikelbank, "A Typology of U.S. Suburban Places," *Housing Policy Debate* 15.4 (2004); Bernadette Hanlon, Thomas Vicino, and J. R. Short, "The New Metropolitan Reality in the US: Rethinking the Traditional Model," *Urban Studies* 43.12 (2006); and Bernadette Hanlon, "A Typology of Inner-Ring Suburbs: Class, Race, and Ethnicity in U.S. Suburbia," *City & Community* 8.3 (2009).

11. Joel Garreau, *Edge Cities: Life on the New Frontier* (New York: Doubleday, 1987); Robert E. Lang and Jennifer B. LeFurgy, *Boomburbs: The Rise of America's Accidental Cities* (Washington, DC: Brookings Institution Press, 2007); Robert Fishman, *Bourgeois Utopias: The Rise and Fall of Suburbia* (New York: Basic Books, 1987); Alan Berube et al., *Finding Exurbia: America's Fast-Growing Communities at the Metropolitan Fringe* (Washington, DC: Brookings Institution, 2006); Wei Li, "Los Angeles' Chinese Ethnoburb: Evolution of Ethnic Community and Economy," paper presented at the annual meeting of the Association of American Geographers, March 15, 1995; Wei Li, "Anatomy of a New Ethnic Settlement: The Chinese Ethnoburb in Los Angeles," *Urban Studies* 35.3 (1998).

12. See, e.g., Denton and Gibbons, "Twenty-First-Century," though this is a commonly held viewpoint by academics and journalists alike.

13. See Kevin Helliker, "U.S. News: Chicago Population Sinks to 1920 Level," *Wall Street Journal*, February 16, 2011; and Judy Keen, "Blacks' Exodus Reshapes Cities," *USA Today*, May 19, 2011.

14. See powell and Reece, "Future of Fair Housing," on the general point, and William J. Craig, "Minorities in the Twin Cities: What the 2010 U.S. Census Tells Us," *CURA Reporter* 41.2 (2011), for an example in one metropolitan area.

15. Douglas S. Massey and Nancy A. Denton, "Suburbanization and Segregation in US Metropolitan Areas," *American Journal of Sociology* 94.3 (1988).

16. Katrin B. Anacker, "Immigrating, Assimilating, Cashing In? Analyzing Property Values in Suburbs of Immigrant Gateways," *Housing Studies* 28.5 (2013).

17. William A. V. Clark, *Immigrants and the American Dream* (New York: Guilford, 2003); Audrey Singer, *New Geography of United States Immigration* (Washington, DC: Brookings Institution, 2009).

18. Kneebone and Berube, *Confronting Suburban Poverty*. Robert Suro, Jill Wilson, and Audrey Singer, "Immigration and Poverty in America's Suburbs," Brookings Institution, Paper No. 20, Metropolitan Opportunity Series, 2011.

19. Kneebone and Holmes, *Concentrated Poverty*. Kneebone and Holmes use American Community Survey data for the period of 2010–2014 to show that after the recession "the number of poor people living in concentrated poverty in suburbs grew nearly twice as fast as in cities."

20. Kneebone and Berube, *Confronting Suburban Poverty*, 29.

21. Kneebone and Berube, *Confronting Suburban Poverty*.

22. Wyly and Hammel, "Islands of Decay"; Goetz, *New Deal Ruins*.

23. See, e.g., the study by *Governing* showing high rates of gentrification even before the housing crash: Mike Maciag, "Gentrification in America Report," *Governing*, 2015. Though gentrification is measured in many different ways by researchers, there is overwhelming consistency in the findings pointing to clear patterns of gentrification in American cities.

24. For New York City see, e.g., D. W. Gibson, *The Edge Becomes the Center: An Oral History of Gentrification in the 21st Century* (New York: Overlook, 2015). For San Francisco see Richard Gonzalez, "As Rent Soars, Longtime San Francisco Tenants Fight to Stay," National Public Radio, December 3, 2013, and James Tracy, *Dispatches against Displacement: Field Notes from San Francisco's Housing Wars* (Oakland, CA: AK, 2014). For Washington, DC, see Chris Myers Asch and George Derek Musgrove, "'We Are Headed for Some Bad Trouble': Gentrification and Displacement in Washington, DC, 1920–2014," in *Capital Dilemma: Growth and Inequality in Washington, DC*, ed. Derek Hyra (New York: Routledge, 2016); and Derek Hyra, "The Back-to-the-City Movement: Neighborhood Redevelopment and Processes of Political and Cultural Displacement," *Urban Studies* 52.10 (2015). See also Daniel Hartley, "Gentrification and Financial Health," Federal Reserve Bank of Cleveland, November 6, 2013. Hartley's study indicates that fourteen American cities saw more than one in five of their lower-priced census tracts gentrify between 2000 and 2007.

25. Derek Hyra, *Making the Gilded Ghetto: Race, Class and Politics in the Cappucino City* (Chicago: University of Chicago Press, forthcoming).

26. See Perry Stein, "Is Pricey Shaw a Model for Retaining Affordability amid Regentrification?," *Washington Post*, May 21, 2015; and Aaron C. Davis and Abigail Hauslohner, "DC Council Passes $13 Billion Budget Focusing on Schools, Homelessness," *Washington Post*, May 27, 2015.

27. J. K. Dineen, "Feds Reject Housing Plan Meant to Help Minorities Stay in SF," *San Francisco Chronicle*, August 17, 2016.

28. Richard Gonzales, "Feds to Allow Preferences for Low-Income Applicants in S.F. Housing Complex," National Public Radio, September 23, 2016.

29. Henry Graba, "Obama Administration to San Francisco: Your Anti-gentrification Plan Promotes Segregation," *Moneybox*, August 17, 2016.

30. U.S. Department of Housing and Urban Development, "Rootedness," May 17, 2016.

31. I will occasionally retain quotation marks around the phrase to remind the reader of the discursive aspect of this term. Historically, many of the metrics used to designate such neighborhoods have had little to do with opportunity directly, and when they have, they have tended to focus on a subset of opportunities. The result is a phrase that generally reflects a political project more than an objective assessment of neighborhood conditions.

32. Rusk, *Inside Game*.

33. Goetz, *Clearing the Way*.

34. See Henry G. Cisneros and Lora Engdahl, eds., *From Despair to Hope: HOPE VI and the New Promise of Public Housing in America's Cities* (Washington, DC: Brookings Institution Press, 2009), especially chapters 2 and 3 for a full explication of the HOPE VI model.

35. The Gautreaux and MTO mobility programs utilize simple dichotomies. In Gautreaux the threshold between low-opportunity neighborhoods and high-opportunity neighborhoods was an African American population of 30 percent. In the MTO program it was a poverty population of 10 percent.

36. This is a dualism that long predates the emergence of the "opportunity" paradigm. As noted in chapters 3 and 4, a common analysis of American urban problems in the last half of the twentieth century referenced the "white noose" around American cities, in which poorer communities of color inside the central cities are contrasted with white, middle- and upper-income suburban communities outside. See Peter Marris, "The Social Implications of Urban Redevelopment," *Journal of the American Institute of Planners* 28.3 (1962); Self, *American Babylon*.

37. The Hollman desegregation lawsuit consent decree used both race and poverty to define opportunity neighborhoods. See Goetz, *Clearing the Way*.

38. Current initiatives to operationalize and measure "opportunity neighborhoods" typically utilize Geographic Information System (GIS) technologies to map opportunity. GIS has allowed analysts to engage in opportunity mapping, sometimes called equity mapping, focusing on the distribution of multiple opportunity characteristics across a metropolitan landscape.

39. See, e.g., Bill Sadler et al., *The Denver Regional Equity Atlas: Mapping Access to Opportunity at a Regional Scale* (Denver: Mile High Connects, 2012).

40. Dolores Acevedo-Garcia et al., "Neighborhood Opportunity and Location Afford-ability for Low-Income Renter Families," *Housing Policy Debate* 26.4–5 (2016).

41. See, e.g., Institute on Race and Poverty, *Access to Opportunity in the Twin Cities Metropolitan Area* (Minneapolis, 2007).

42. Kirwan Institute, *Equity, Opportunity, and Sustainability in the Central Puget Sound Region* (Seattle, WA: Puget Sound Regional Council, 2012). Neighborhoods can be arrayed, the authors contend, by a single composite measure of opportunity. The result is a somewhat willful disregard for the greater information that could be provided by a more nuanced definition of opportunity.

43. Sadler et al., *Denver Regional Equity*.

44. See, e.g., Sarah Treuhaft, *Community Mapping for Health Equity Advocacy*, 2009, which contains five case studies of mapping for regional health equity; and Coalition for a Livable Future, *Regional Equity Atlas: The Portland Metro Region's Geography of Opportunity*.

45. Popkin et al., *Baseline Assessment*, vol. 1.

46. The full list of selection criteria that QAPs must include is "project location, hous-ing needs characteristics, project characteristics, including whether the project includes the use of housing as part of a community revitalization plan, sponsor characteristics, tenant populations with special housing needs, public housing waiting lists, tenant popu-lations of individuals with children, projects intended for eventual tenant ownership, the energy efficiency of the project, and the historic nature of the project." Internal Revenue Code §42 (m)(1)(C).

47. Internal Revenue Code §42 (m)(1)(B)(ii). The QCT incentive was added to the program by amendment in 1989; see Michael Hollar and Kurt Usowsky, "Low Income Housing Tax Credit Qualified Census Tracts," *Cityscape: A Journal of Policy Development and Research* 9.3 (2007).

48. Elizabeth K. Julian, "Recent Advocacy Related to the Low Income Housing Tax Credit and Fair Housing," *Journal of Affordable Housing* 18.2 (2009): 186.

49. See, e.g., Jill Khadduri, *Creating Balance in the Locations of LIHTC Developments: The Role of Qualified Allocation Plans* (Washington, DC: Poverty and Race Research Action Council and Abt Associates, 2013); Casey Dawkins, "The Spatial Pattern of Low Income Housing Tax Credit Properties," *Journal of the American Planning Association* 79.3 (2013).

50. Khadduri, *Creating Balance*, 2.

51. Ibid.

52. See Florence Roisman, "Mandates Unsatisfied: The Low Income Housing Tax Credit Program and Civil Rights Laws," *University of Miami Law Review* 52 (1998); Lance Freeman, *Siting Affordable Housing: Location and Neighborhood Trends of Low Income Housing Tax Credit Developments in the 1990s* (Washington DC: Brookings Institution, 2004); Kirk McClure, "The Low-Income Housing Tax Credit Program Goes Mainstream and Moves to the Suburbs," *Housing Policy Debate* 17 (2006); Deirdre Oakley, "Locational Patterns of Low-Income Housing Tax Credit Developments: A Sociospatial Analysis of Four Metropolitan Areas," *Urban Affairs Review* 43 (2008); Keren M. Horn and Katherine M. O'Regan, *The Low Income Housing Tax Credit and Racial Segregation* (New York: Furman Center for Real Estate and Public Policy, NYU, 2011); Lan Deng, "Comparing the Effects of Housing Vouchers and Low-Income Housing Tax Credits on Neighborhood Integration and School Quality," *Journal of Planning Education and Research* 27 (2007); Casey J. Dawkins, *Exploring the Spatial Distribution of Low Income Housing Tax Credit Properties* (Washington, DC: U.S. Department of Housing and Urban Development, 2011); Dawkins, "Spatial Pattern"; Shannon Van Zandt and Pratik C. Mhatre, "Growing Pains: Perpetuating Inequality through the Production of Low-Income Housing in the Dallas / Fort Worth Metroplex," *Urban Geography* 30.5 (2009); Jill Khadduri, Larry Buron, and Carissa Climaco, *Are States Using the Low Income Housing Tax Credit to Enable Families with Children to Live in Low Poverty and Racially Integrated Neighborhoods?*, report prepared for the Poverty and Race Research Action Council and the National Fair Housing Alliance (Cambridge, MA: Abt Associates, 2006).

53. Horn and O'Regan, *Low Income Housing*.

54. Matthew Freedman and Tamara McGavock, "Low-Income Housing Development, Poverty Concentration, and Neighborhood Inequality," *Journal of Policy Analysis and Management* 34.4 (2015): 805–834. See also Baum-Snow and Marion, "Effects of Low-Income Housing."

55. Ingrid Gould Ellen, Keren M. Horn, and Katherine M. O'Regan, "Poverty Concentration and the Low Income Housing Tax Credit: Effects of Siting and Tenant Composition," *Journal of Housing Economics* 34 (2016); Ingrid Gould Ellen, Katherine M. O'Regan, and Ionu Voicu, "Siting, Spillovers, and Segregation: A Re-examination of the Low Income Housing Tax Credit Program," in *Housing Markets and the Economy: Risk, Regulation, Policy; Essays in Honor of Karl Case*, ed. Edward Glaeser and John Quigley (Cambridge, MA: Lincoln Institute for Land Policy, 2009); Rebecca Diamond and Timothy McQuade, "Who Wants Affordable Housing in Their Backyard? An Equilibrium Analysis of Low Income Property Development," NBER Working Paper No. 22204, April 2016.

56. Freeman, *Siting Affordable Housing*, and Oakley, "Locational Patterns."

57. Van Zandt and Mhatre, "Growing Pains"; Dawkins, "Spatial Pattern."

58. The definition of "low racial concentration" is census tracts with fewer than 25 percent of the population African American. Jill Khadduri and Carissa Climaco, *LIHTC Awards in Ohio, 2006–2015: Where Are They Providing Housing for Families with Children?* (Cambridge, MA: Abt Associates, 2016).

59. Dawkins, *Spatial Distribution*, 35.

60. Diamond and McQuade, "Who Wants Affordable Housing"; Ellen, O'Regan, and Voicu, "Siting, Spillovers, and Segregation"; and Ellen, Horn, and O'Regan, "Poverty Concentration," all use the first standard (does the program increase segregation or concentrations of poverty?) to assess the program, and Van Zandt and Mhatre, "Growing Pains"; and Khadduri and Climaco, *LIHTC Awards*, use the second standard (does the program achieve integration?).

61. Julian, "Recent Advocacy."

62. *In re Adoption of 2003 Low Income Housing Tax Credit Allocation Plan*, 848 A. 2d 1, 5 (N.J. Super. Ct. App. Div. 2004). Another suit was filed in 2002 by the Connecticut

Civil Liberties Union against the state allocating agency in Connecticut on the basis of the segregatory impact of LIHTC in the Hartford metropolitan area, *In Re Declaratory Ruling on Connecticut Low Income Housing Tax Credit Program*; see the brief description in Horn and O'Regan, "Low Income Housing."

63. James A. Long, "The Low-Income Housing Tax Credit in New Jersey: New Opportunities to Deconcentrate Poverty through the Duty to Affirmatively Further Fair Housing," *NYU Annual Survey of American Law* 66 (2010): 75.

64. Robert Neuwirth, "Renovation or Ruin," *Shelterforce Online* 137, September/October, 2004.

65. See also Khadduri's contention that she "has found no research showing that distressed neighborhoods with LIHTC investments improve as measured by other quality measures such as well-performing schools, responsive public services, or safety." Khadduri, *Creating Balance*, 2.

66. Neuwirth, "Renovation or Ruin."

67. Ingrid Gould Ellen, Keren M. Horn, et al., *Effect of QAP Incentives on the Location of LIHTC Properties* (Washington, DC: U.S. Department of Housing and Urban Development, 2015).

68. The Inclusive Communities Project, Inc., v. The Texas Department of Housing and Community Affairs, Complaint filed March 28, 2008, in the US. District Court, Northern District of Texas, Dallas Division. 3:08-CV-546-D, 12.

69. ICP v. TDHCA complaint, 7 and 10.

70. ICP v. TDHCA complaint.

71. Ibid.

72. The ICP case was appealed to the U.S. Supreme Court in 2015. The issue that the Supreme Court considered, however, was simply whether any party could make a legal claim on the basis of disparate impacts, or whether instead a litigant must prove discriminatory intent. The Supreme Court ruling in the summer of 2015, that disparate impact is indeed an actionable claim under the Fair Housing Act, was a major victory for ICP and for fair housing more generally. But the court did not rule on the substance of the case related to the location of tax credit housing. The Supreme Court sent the case back to the district court to resolve that issue. Using the Supreme Court's test, the district court decided in favor of the State of Texas, concluding that the ICP had not proven that the action of the Texas DHCA had caused the maldistribution of tax credit housing. See Julieta Chiquillo, "After Supreme Court Victory, Dallas Nonprofit Loses Racial Suit against Texas Agency," *Dallas Morning News*, August 31, 2016.

73. Housing Discrimination Complaint: Metropolitan Interfaith Council on Affordable Housing, et al. v. State of Minnesota, et al.

74. See Institute on Metropolitan Opportunity, *Reforming Subsidized Housing Policy in the Twin Cities to Cut Costs and Reduce Segregation* (Minneapolis, 2014), in which CDC salaries are published and alleged to contribute to a high cost of subsidized housing in the central cities. This report also contains a facile "analysis" of a single community development project on the south side of Minneapolis. The analysis covers a period during which the project in question was never more than half complete, is conducted at a scale much too large for a serious attempt to search for impacts, and, for the most part, focuses on outcomes of demographic change rather than benefits to existing populations and businesses (even though changing the demographic makeup of the neighborhood is not the intent of this project, or many other community development projects). Deficient in virtually every relevant aspect of research design, the study is nevertheless offered as evidence that community development efforts do not work. The "study" was later reproduced, unimproved, in an academic policy journal. For more see Edward G. Goetz, "Poverty Pimping the CDCs: The Search for Dispersal's Next Bogeyman," *Housing Policy*

Debate 25.3 (2015); and Alex E. Schwartz, "The Low-Income Housing Tax Credit, Community Development, and Fair Housing: A Response to Orfield et al.," *Housing Policy Debate* 26.2 (2015).

75. See the discussion later in this chapter.

76. See Housing Justice Center, *Preliminary Analysis of MICAH Fair Housing Complaint against State, MHFA, Met Council* (Saint Paul, MN, 2015); Metropolitan Council of the Twin Cities, "Response to Housing Discrimination Complaint," Saint Paul, MN, March 12, 2015; State of Minnesota, "Re: *MICAH et al. v. State of Minnesota et al.* Title VI Case Number 05-15-0003-6, Responses of State of Minnesota and Minnesota Housing Finance Agency," March 12, 2015; all available from the author.

77. Such "analyses of impediments to fair housing" have been required of all HUD subgrantees for years. The novel element of the settlement, therefore, seems to be the commitment to a more robust community engagement process. Jessie Van Berkel, "Minneapolis and St. Paul Settle Federal Housing Complaints, Agree to Further Review," *Minneapolis Star-Tribune*, May 17, 2016.

78. *Sustainable Communities Initiative Progress Report*, prepared by Summit Consulting for the U.S. Department of Housing and Urban Development, April 2014. The six principles are (1) provide more transportation choices; (2) promote equitable, affordable housing; (3) enhance economic competitiveness; (4) support existing communities; (5) coordinate policies and leverage investment; and (6) value communities and neighborhoods.

79. See, e.g., Daniel Immergluck, "Large Redevelopment Initiatives, Housing Values and Gentrification: The Case of the Atlanta Beltline," *Urban Studies* 46 (2009); and Daniel Baldwin Hess and Tangerine Maria Almeida, "Impact of Proximity to Light Rail Rapid Transit on Station-Area Property Values in Buffalo, New York," *Urban Studies* 44.5 (2007).

80. Casey Dawkins and Rolf Moeckel, "Transit-Induced Gentrification: Who Will Stay, and Who Will Go?," *Housing Policy Debate* 26.4-5 (2016); Matthew E. Kahn, "Gentrification Trends in New Transit-Oriented Communities: Evidence from 14 Cities That Expanded and Built Rail Transit Systems," *Real Estate Economics* 35.2 (2007) 2.

81. Emily Talen and Julia Koschinsky, "Is Subsidized Housing in Sustainable Neighborhoods? Evidence from Chicago," *Housing Policy Debate* 21.1 (2011).

82. See, e.g., Acevedo-Garcia et al., "Neighborhood Opportunity," on the tradeoffs between location affordability and some indices of opportunity.

83. Philip Tegeler and Hanna Chouest, "The 'Housing + Transportation Index' and Fair Housing," Poverty and Race Research Action Council, Policy Brief, 2011. See also Oak Park Regional Housing Center, "Affirmatively Furthering Fair Housing and the Center for Neighborhood Technology's H+T Affordability Index," February 2012, available from author.

84. Oak Park Regional Housing Center, "Affirmatively Furthering," 2.

85. Pendall and Parilla, "Comment," 35.

86. Sanchez et al. cite a State of Illinois study that found that 41 percent of former welfare recipients named transportation as a major barrier to their continued employment. Thomas W. Sanchez et al., *The Right to Transportation: Moving to Equity* (Chicago: Planners Press, APA, 2007).

87. Ibid.

88. Kneebone and Berube, *Confronting Suburban Poverty*.

89. Ibid.

90. See Lingqian Hu, "Job Accessibility of the Poor in Los Angeles: Has Suburbanization Affected Spatial Mismatch?," *Journal of the American Planning Association* 81.1 (2015); and Mizuki Kawabata, "Job Access and Employment among Low-Skilled Autoless Workers in US Metropolitan Areas," *Environment and Planning A* 35.9 (2003).

91. Hu, "Job Accessibility," 40. See also Shen's work on employment accessibility in central cities. Shen measures not just the location of jobs, but their availability through turnover and job growth. Qing Shen, "Location Characteristics of Inner-City Neighborhoods and Employment Accessibility of Low-Wage Workers," *Environment and Planning B: Planning and Design* 25 (1998); Qing Shen, "A Spatial Analysis of Job Openings and Access in a U.S. Metropolitan Area," *Journal of the American Planning Association* 67 (2001). Lens finds that residents of public housing had better access to employment than residents of other forms of subsidized housing because of the centrality of public housing in cities. See Michael Lens, "Employment Accessibility among Housing Subsidy Recipients," *Housing Policy Debate* 24.4 (2014). Pendall et al. reinforce the importance of transit for low-income households, though they argue the benefits of car ownership on employment and earnings exceed those of access to transit. See Rolf Pendall et al., *Driving to Opportunity: Understanding the Links among Transportation Access, Residential Outcomes, and Economic Opportunity for Housing Voucher Recipients* (Washington, DC: Urban Institute, 2014).

92. National Commission on Fair Housing and Equal Opportunity, *The Future of Fair Housing: Report of the National Commission on Fair Housing and Equal Opportunity*, 2008.

93. See, e.g., Poverty and Race Research Action Council, *Affirmatively Furthering Fair Housing at HUD: A First Term Report Card* (Washington, DC, 2013).

94. National Fair Housing Alliance, *Expanding Opportunity: Systemic Approaches to Fair Housing* (Washington, DC, 2014).

95. King and Smith, *House Divided*, 137–138.

96. 24 CFR Part 100 Implementation of the Fair Housing Act's Discriminatory Effects Standard; Final Rule, Fed. Reg. vol. 78, no. 32, February 15, 2013.

97. Gallagher v. Magner, 619 F. 3d 823 (2010).

98. Township of Mount Holly v. Mt. Holly Gardens Citizens in Action, Inc., 568 U.S. (2012).

99. Texas DHCA v. ICP, 571 US 1 (2015), 1.

100. Ibid., 20.

101. Ibid., 21.

102. Ibid., 18.

103. Ibid., 19.

104. 78 Fed. Reg. 11476, and quoted in Texas DHCA v. ICP, 571 US 1 (2015), 19.

105. Stockton Williams and Maya Brennan, "A New Landscape of Housing Access and Opportunity," *Urban Land: The Magazine of the Urban Land Institute*, November 30, 2015.

106. Ibid.

107. *Atlanta Progressive News*, "What a Fair Housing Victory in the U.S. Supreme Court Means for Atlanta," September 19, 2015.

108. Edsall, "Where?"

CONCLUSION

1. See Chapple, *Planning Sustainable Cities*; Jim Capraro, "Can Successful Community Development Be Anything but Comprehensive?," *Shelterforce*, July 17, 2013; Axel-Lute, "Seeking Solidarity"; Mtamanik Youngblood and Harold Barnette, "Community Development Corporations at a Crossroads," *Shelterforce*, July 17, 2013; Kathe Newman and Edward Goetz, "Reclaiming Neighborhood from the Inside Out: Regionalism, Globalization, and Critical Community Development," *Urban Geography* 37.5 (2015); Josh Ishimatsu, "Can Organizing Resuscitate Community Development?," *Shelterforce*, November 22, 2013; Josh Ishimatsu, "Neighborhoods or Regions? A Trick Question," *Shelterforce*, July 17, 2013.

2. King and Smith, *House Divided*.

3. Edward G. Goetz, Tony Damiano, and Jason Hicks, "Racially Concentrated Areas of Affluence: A Preliminary Investigation" (unpublished paper, Humphrey School of Public Affairs, Minneapolis, 2015).

4. Sidney, "Fair Housing," 267.

5. This technique was most pronounced in the federal HOPE VI program, which displaced tens of thousands of very low-income people of color to other largely segregated and high-poverty neighborhoods. Desegregation lawsuits were much more likely to combine the dismantling of a segregated community with efforts to integrate white communities, through mobility programs or scattered site development.

6. John O. Calmore, "Race/ism Lost and Found: The Fair Housing Act at Thirty," *University of Miami Law Review* 52 (1997).

7. The stigmatization of communities of color remains an inherent element of integrationist efforts if the objective of such efforts is a desired mix of people. Catering to white prejudices and preferences will always keep people of color in a subordinate position. If opening up exclusionary communities is instead pursued as a means of enhancing choice in the housing market and eliminating discriminatory barriers to housing, then the need to maintain an acceptable mix disappears along with the need to incorporate white preferences.

8. Shelby, *Dark Ghettos*, 75.

9. Myron Orfield et al., "High Costs and Segregation in Subsidized Housing Policy," *Housing Policy Debate* 25 (2015). The label was picked up and repeated, unquestioningly, by Thomas Edsall in the *New York Times*, "Where?"

10. Together, these three components are essentially what Michael Bodaken and Ellen Lurie Hoffman of the National Housing Trust call a "Mobility Plus" strategy. See Bodaken and Hoffman, "The Need for a Balanced Approach to Fair Housing" (NYU–Furman Center, September 28, 2015).

11. Sean F. Reardon and Kendra Bischoff, "Income Inequality and Income Segregation," *American Journal of Sociology* 116.4 (2011).

12. Patrick Sharkey, *Stuck in Place*.

13. Defilippis, *Unmaking Goliath*.

Sources

Abrams, Charles. *Forbidden Neighbors: A Study of Prejudice in Housing.* New York: Harper, 1955.

Abu-Lughod, Janet. *Race, Space, and Riots in Chicago, New York, and Los Angeles.* Oxford: Oxford University Press, 2007.

Acevedo-Garcia, Dolores, Nancy McArdle, Erin Hardy, Keri-Nicole Dillman, Jason Reece, Unda Ioana Crisan, David Norris, and Theresa L. Osypuk. "Neighborhood Opportunity and Location Affordability for Low-Income Renter Families." *Housing Policy Debate* 26.4–5 (2016): 607–645.

Acevedo-Garcia, Dolores, Theresa L. Osypuk, and Nancy McArdle. "Racial/Ethnic Integration and Child Health Disparities." In *The Integration Debate: Competing Futures for American Cities,* edited by Chester Hartman and Gregory D. Squires, 131–152. New York: Routledge, 2010.

Albright, Len, Elizabeth S. Derickson, and Douglas Massey. "Do Affordable Housing Projects Harm Suburban Communities? Crime, Property Values, and Property Taxes in Mt. Laurel, New Jersey." 2011. SSRN: http://ssrn.com/abstract=1865231 or http://dx.doi.org/10.2139/ssrn.1865231.

Allard, Scott W., and Benjamin Roth. *Strained Suburbs: The Social Service Challenges of Rising Suburban Poverty.* Metropolitan Opportunity Series Report. Washington, DC: Brookings Institution, 2010.

Allen, Robert L. *Black Awakening in Capitalist America: An Analytic History.* New York: Doubleday, 1970.

Allport, Gordon W. *The Nature of Prejudice.* Cambridge, MA: Perseus, 1954.

Anacker, Katrin. "Immigrating, Assimilating, Cashing In? Analyzing Property Values in Suburbs of Immigrant Gateways." *Housing Studies* 28.5 (2013): 720–745.

——. "Shaky Palaces? Analyzing Property Values and Their Appreciation Rates in Minority First Suburbs." *International Journal of Urban and Regional Research* 36.4 (2012): 791–816.

——. "Still Paying the Race Tax? Analyzing Property Values in Homogeneous and Mixed-Race Suburbs." *Journal of Urban Affairs* 32.1 (2010): 55–77.

Anderson, Elizabeth. *The Imperative of Integration.* Princeton, NJ: Princeton University Press, 2010.

Andersson, Fredrik, John C. Laltiwanger, Mark J. Kutzbach, Giordano E. Palloni, Henry O. Pollakowski, and Daniel H. Weinberg. "Childhood Housing and Adult Earnings: Between-Siblings Analysis of Housing Vouchers and Public Housing." National Bureau of Economic Research, Cambridge, MA. Working Paper 22721, 2016. http://www.nber.org/papers/w22721.

Arena, John. *Driven from New Orleans: How Nonprofits Betray Public Housing and Promote Privatization.* Minneapolis: University of Minnesota Press, 2012.

Asch, Chris Meyers, and George Derek Musgrove. "'We Are Headed for Some Bad Trouble': Gentrification in Washington, DC, 1920–2014." In *Capital Dilemma: Growth and Inequality in Washington, DC,* edited by Derek Hyra and Sabiyha Prince, 107–135. New York: Routledge, 2016.

Atlanta Progressive News. "What a Fair Housing Victory in the U.S. Supreme Court Means for Atlanta." September 19, 2015. http://atlantaprogressivenews.com/2015/09/19/what-a-fair-housing-victory-in-the-u-s-supreme-court-means-for-atlanta/.

Axel-Lute, Miriam. "Seeking Solidarity between Place-Based and Economic Justice Work." *Rooflines,* June 1, 2015. http://www.rooflines.org/4120/seeking_solidarity_between_place-based_and_economic_justice_work/.

Baker, John T. "Community Development Corporations: A Legal Analysis." *Valparaiso University Law Review* 13 (1978): 33.

Baker, M., A. McNicholas, N. Garrett, N. Jones, J. Stewart, C. Koberstein, and D. Lennon. "Household Crowding: A Major Risk Factor for Epidemic Meningococcal Disease in Auckland Children." *Pediatric Infectious Disease Journal* 19.10 (2000): 983–990.

Baldassare, Marc. *Trouble in Paradise: The Suburban Transformation of America.* New York: Columbia University Press, 1986.

Bartlett, Sheridan. "The Significance of Relocation for Chronically Poor Families in the USA." *Environment and Urbanization* 9.1 (1997): 121–132.

Bassuk, Ellen L., and Lynn Rosenberg. "Psychosocial Characteristics of Homeless Children and Children with Homes." *Pediatrics* 85.3 (1990): 257–261.

Baum-Snow, Nathaniel, and Justin Marion. "The Effects of Low-Income Housing Tax Credit Developments on Neighborhoods." *Journal of Public Economics* 93 (2009): 654–666.

Bellah, Robert Neelly, Steven M. Tipton, William M. Sullivan, Richard Madsen, and Ann Swidler. *Habits of the Heart: Individualism and Commitment in American Life.* Berkeley: University of California Press, 1985.

Berger, Staci, and Adam Gordon. "Fair Housing and Community Developers Can Work Together." *Shelterforce,* October 15, 2015. http://www.shelterforce.org/article/4278/fair_housing_and_community_developers_ican_i_work_together/.

Berube, Alan, and William H. Frey. *A Decade of Mixed Blessing: Urban and Suburban Poverty in Census 2000.* Washington, DC: Brookings Institution, Center on Urban and Metropolitan Policy, 2002.

Berube, Alan, Elizabeth Kneebone, and Carey Nadeau. *The Re-emergence of Concentrated Poverty: Metropolitan Trends in the 2000s.* Washington, DC: Brookings Institution, 2011. http://www.brookings.edu/research/papers/2011/11/03-poverty-kneebone-nadeau-berube.

Berube, Alan, Audrey Singer, Jill H. Wilson, and William H. Frey. *Finding Exurbia: America's Fast-Growing Communities at the Metropolitan Fringe.* Washington, DC: Brookings Institution, 2006.

Bobo, Lawrence. "Keeping the Linchpin in Place: Testing the Multiple Sources of Opposition to Residential Integration." *International Review of Social Psychology* 2.3 (1989): 305–323.

Bobo, Lawrence, and Camille L. Zubrinsky. "Attitudes on Residential Integration: Perceived Status Differences, Mere In-Group Preference, or Racial Prejudice?" *Social Forces* 74.3 (1996): 883–909.

Bodaken, Michael, and Ellen Lurie Hoffman. "The Need for a Balanced Approach to Fair Housing." NYU–Furman Center, September 28, 2015. http://furmancenter.org/research/iri/bodakenhoffman.

Boger, John Charles. "Toward Ending Residential Segregation: A Fair Share Proposal for the Next Reconstruction." *North Carolina Law Review* 71 (1992): 1573.

Bollens, Scott A. "Municipal Decline and Inequality in American Suburban Rings, 1960–1980." *Regional Studies* 22 (1988): 277–285.

Bonastia, Christopher. *Knocking on the Door: The Federal Government's Attempt to Desegregate the Suburbs.* Princeton, NJ: Princeton University Press, 2006.

Brennan, Maya, Patrick Reed, and Lisa Sturtevant. *The Impacts of Affordable Housing on Education: A Research Summary.* Washington, DC: Center for Housing Policy, 2011.

Breysse, Patrick, Nick Farr, Warren Galke, Bruce Lanphear, Rebecca Morley, and Linda Bergofsky. "The Relationship between Housing and Health: Children at Risk." *Environmental Health Perspectives* 112.15 (2004): 1583–1588.

Bridge, Gary, Tim Butler, and Loretta Lees. *Mixed Communities: Gentrification by Stealth?* Bristol, UK: Policy Press, 2012.

Briggs, Xavier. "Brown Kids in White Suburbs: Housing Mobility and the Many Faces of Social Capital." *Housing Policy Debate* 9.1 (1998): 177–221.

Brooks, Roy L. *Integration or Separation? A Strategy for Racial Equality.* Cambridge, MA: Harvard University Press, 1996.

Brown, Flora Bryant. "The NAACP Sponsored Sit-Ins by Howard University Students in Washington, D.C., 1943–1944." *Journal of Negro Education* 4 (2000): 274–286.

Bynum, Bill. "To Move or to Improve?" *Rooflines,* 2016. http://rooflines.org/4685/to_move_or_to_improve/?utm_source=Why+Your+Community+Should+Kick+the+Subsidy+Habit---&utm_campaign=Why+Your+Community+Should+Kick+the+Subsidy+Habit&utm_medium=email.

Calavita, Nico, Kenneth Grimes, and Alan Mallach. "Inclusionary Housing in California and New Jersey: A Comparative Analysis." *Housing Policy Debate* 8.1 (1997): 109–142.

Calmore, John O. "Race/ism Lost and Found: The Fair Housing Act at Thirty." *University of Miami Law Review* 52 (1997): 1067–1130.

——. "Fair Housing v. Fair Housing: The Problems with Providing Increased Housing Opportunities through Spatial Deconcentration." *Clearinghouse Review* 14 (May 1980).

Capraro, Jim. "Can Successful Community Development Be Anything but Comprehensive?" *Shelterforce,* July 17, 2013. http://www.shelterforce.org/article/3344/can_successful_community_development_be_anything_but_comprehensive/.

Cardoso, Maria R. A., Simon N. Cousens, Luiz F. de Góes Siqueira, Fatima M. Alves, and Luiz A. V. D'Angelo. "Crowding: Risk Factor or Protective Factor for Lower Respiratory Disease in Young Children?" *BMC Public Health* 4.1 (2004): 19–26.

Carmichael, Stokely, and Charles V. Hamilton. *Black Power: The Politics of Liberation in America.* New York: Vintage, 1966.

Carson, Clayborne. *In Struggle: SNCC and the Black Awakening of the 1960s.* Cambridge, MA: Harvard University Press, 1981.

Cashin, Sheryll. *The Failures of Integration: How Race and Class Are Undermining the American Dream.* New York: Perseus, 2005.

Cayton, Horace R. *Black Metropolis: A Study of Negro Life in a Northern City.* Chicago: University of Chicago Press, 1970.

Chakrabarti, Kitashree, and Junfu Zhang. "Unaffordable Housing and Local Employment Growth." Working paper no. 10–3. New England Public Policy Center at the Federal Reserve Bank of Boston, 2010.

Chapple, Karen. *Planning Sustainable Cities and Regions: Towards More Equitable Development.* London: Routledge, 2015.

Charles, Camille Zubrinsky. "The Dynamics of Racial Residential Segregation." *Annual Review of Sociology* 29 (2003): 167–207.

Chaskin, Robert J., and Mark L. Joseph. *Integrating the Inner City: The Promise and Perils of Mixed-Income Public Housing Transformation.* Chicago: University of Chicago Press, 2015.

Chetty, Raj, Nathaniel Hendren, and Lawrence F. Katz. "The Effects of Exposure to Better Neighborhoods on Children: New Evidence from the Moving to Opportunity Experiment." Working paper no. w21156. Cambridge, MA: National Bureau of Economic Research, 2015.

Chiquillo, Julieta. "After Supreme Court Victory, Dallas Nonprofit Loses Racial Suit against Texas Agency." *Dallas Morning News,* August 31, 2016. http://www. dallasnews.com/news/dallas/2016/08/31/supreme-court-victory-dallas-non profit-loses-racial-bias-suit-texas-agency.

Cisneros, Henry. "A New Moment for People and Cities." In Cisneros and Engdahl, *From Despair to Hope,* 3–14.

Cisneros, Henry, and Lora Engdahl, eds. *From Despair to Hope: HOPE VI and the New Promise of Public Housing in America's Cities.* Washington, DC: Brookings Institution Press, 2009.

Clampet-Lundquist, Susan, and Douglas S. Massey. "Neighborhood Effects on Economic Self-Sufficiency: A Reconsideration of the Moving to Opportunity Experiment." *American Journal of Sociology* 114.1 (2008): 107–143.

Clark, Kenneth B. *Dark Ghetto: Dilemmas of Social Power.* Hanover, NH: Wesleyan University Press, 1965.

Clark, William A. V. "Race, Class, and Space: Outcomes of Suburban Access for Asians and Hispanics." *Urban Geography* 27.6 (2006): 489–506.

——. *Immigrants and the American Dream: Remaking the Middle Class.* New York: Guilford, 2003.

Clawson, Dan. *The Next Upsurge: Labor and the New Social Movement.* Ithaca, NY: Cornell University Press, 2003.

Coalition for a Livable Future. *Regional Equity Atlas: The Portland Metro Region's Geography of Opportunity.* http://clfuture.org/equity-atlas.

Cohen, Rebecca. *The Impacts of Affordable Housing on Health: A Research Summary.* Washington, DC: Center for Housing Policy, 2011.

Cohen, Rebecca, and Keith Wardrip. *Should I Stay or Should I Go? Exploring the Effects of Housing Instability and Mobility on Children.* Washington, DC: Center for Housing Policy, 2011.

Cohn, Richard D., Samuel J. Arbes Jr., Renee Jaramillo, Laura H. Reid, and Darryl Zeldin. "National Prevalence and Exposure Risk for Cockroach Allergen in U.S. Households. *Environmental Health Perspectives* 114.4 (2006): 522–526.

Collins, Cardiss. "Introductory Remarks." In *The* Gautreaux *Decision and Its Effect on Subsidized Housing: Hearing before a Subcommittee of the Committee on Government Operations, House of Representatives, Ninety-Fifth Congress, Second Session, September 22, 1978.* Washington, DC: Government Printing Office, 1978.

"Combined Principles—Intersection of Community Development and Fair Housing." Revised draft, November 16, 2012. http://www.prrac.org/pdf/Shared_Principles_ 11-22-12.pdf.

Comey, Jennifer, Xavier Briggs, and Gretchen Weismann. "Struggling to Stay out of High-Poverty Neighborhoods: Lessons from the Moving to Opportunity Experiment." Urban Institute Policy Brief No. 6. Washington, DC, March 2008.

Connerly, Charles E. "From Racial Zoning to Community Empowerment: The Interstate Highway System and the African American Community in Birmingham, Alabama." *Journal of Planning Education and Research* 22.2 (2002): 99–114.

Cottrell, Megan. "Did the Public Housing Transformation Destroy Chicago's Black Voter Base?" *Chicago Muckrakers*, January 4, 2011. http://www.chicagonow.com/chicago-muckrakers/2011/01/did-the-public-housing-transformation-destroy-chicagos-black-voter-base/.

Cowan, Spencer M. "Anti-Snob Land Use Laws, Suburban Exclusion, and Housing Opportunity." *Journal of Urban Affairs* 28.3 (2006): 295–313.

Craig, William J. "Minorities in the Twin Cities: What the 2010 U.S. Census Tells Us." *CURA Reporter* 41.2 (2011): 27–30.

——. *The Kids Mobility Project*. Minneapolis: Center for Urban and Regional Affairs, University of Minnesota, 1998. http://www.cura.umn.edu/sites/cura.advantage labs.com/files/publications/D9800.pdf.

Crowder, Kyle. "The Racial Context of White Mobility: An Individual-Level Assessment of the White Flight Hypothesis." *Social Science Research* 29.2 (2000): 223–257.

Crowley, Sheila, and Danilo Pelletiere. *Affordable Housing Dilemma: The Preservation vs. Mobility Debate*. Washington, DC: National Low Income Housing Coalition, 2012.

Cummins, Justin D. "Recasting Fair Share: Toward Effective Housing Law and Principled Social Policy." *Law & Inequality* 14 (1995): 339.

Cunningham, David. "The Patterning of Repression: FBI Counterintelligence and the New Left." *Social Forces* 82.1 (2003): 209–240.

Danielson, Michael. *The Politics of Exclusion*. New York: Columbia University Press, 1976.

Davis, Aaron C., and Abigail Hauslohner. "DC Council Passes $13 Billion Budget Focusing on Schools, Homelessness." *Washington Post*, May 27, 2015. https://www.washingtonpost.com/local/dc-politics/dc-council-passes-13-billion-budget-focusing-on-schools-homelessness/2015/05/27/2631002e-03e5-11e5-a428-c984eb077d4e_story.html.

Dawkins, Casey J. "The Spatial Pattern of Low Income Housing Tax Credit Properties." *Journal of the American Planning Association* 79.3 (2013): 222–234.

——. *Exploring the Spatial Distribution of Low Income Housing Tax Credit Properties*. Washington, DC: U.S. Department of Housing and Urban Development, 2011.

——. "Are Social Networks the Ties That Bind Families to Neighborhoods?" *Housing Studies* 21.6 (2006): 867–881.

Dawkins, Casey, and Rolf Moeckel. "Transit-Induced Gentrification: Who Will Stay, and Who Will Go?" *Housing Policy Debate* 26.4–5 (2016): 801–818.

Daye, Charles E. "Whither 'Fair' Housing: Meditations on Wrong Paradigms, Ambivalent Answers, and a Legislative Proposal." *Washington University Journal of Law and Policy* 3 (2000): 241–284.

Deaton, Angus, and Darrne Lubotsky. "Mortality, Inequality and Race in American Cities and States." *Social Science and Medicine* 56 (2003): 1139–1153.

Defilippis, James. *Unmaking Goliath: Community Control in the Face of Global Capital*. New York: Routledge, 2004.

Deng, Lan. "The External Neighborhood Effects of Low-Income Housing Tax Credit Projects Built by Three Sectors." *Journal of Urban Affairs* 33.2 (2011): 143–166.

——. "Comparing the Effects of Housing Vouchers and Low-Income Housing Tax Credits on Neighborhood Integration and School Quality." *Journal of Planning Education and Research* 27 (2007): 20–35.

Deng, Lei, Roberto G. Quercia, Wei Li, and Janekke Ratcliffe. "Risky Borrowers or Risky Mortgages: Disaggregating Effects Using Property Score Models." *Journal of Real Estate Research* 33.2 (2011): 245–277.

Denton, Nancy A., and Joseph R. Gibbons. "Twenty-First-Century Suburban Demography: Increasing Diversity Yet Lingering Exclusion." In *Social Justice in Diverse Suburbs: History, Politics, and Prospects*, edited by Christopher Niedt, 13–30. Philadelphia: Temple University Press, 2013.

Diamond, Rebecca, and Timothy McQuade. "Who Wants Affordable Housing in Their Backyard? An Equilibrium Analysis of Low Income Property Development." National Bureau of Economic Research Working Paper No. 22204, April 2016. http://www.nber.org/papers/w22204.

Dineen, J. K. "Feds Reject Housing Plan Meant to Help Minorities Stay in SF." *San Francisco Chronicle*, August 17, 2016. http://www.sfchronicle.com/politics/article/Feds-reject-housing-plan-meant-to-help-minorities-9146987.php?t=b0de125679.

Ding, Chengri, Robert Simons, and Esmail Baku. "The Effect of Residential Investment on Nearby Property Values: Evidence from Cleveland, Ohio." *Journal of Real Estate Research* 19.1 (2000): 23–48.

Domínguez, Silvia, and Celeste Watkins. "Creating Networks for Survival and Mobility: Social Capital among African-American and Latin-American Low-Income Mothers." *Social Problems* 50.1 (2003): 111–135.

Downs, Anthony. *Opening Up the Suburbs: An Urban Strategy for America*. New Haven, CT: Yale University Press, 1973.

Dreier, Peter. "The Revitalization Trap." *Shelterforce*, October 1, 2015. http://www.shelterforce.org/article/4111/the_revitalization_trap/.

Dreier, Peter, John H. Mollenkopf, and Todd Swanstrom. *Place Matters: Metropolitics for the Twenty-First Century*. 3rd ed. Lawrence: University Press of Kansas, 2014.

Dubofsky, Jean Eberhart. "Fair Housing: A Legislative History and a Perspective." *Washburn Law Journal* 8 (1968): 149.

Duneier, Mitchell. *Ghetto: The Invention of a Place, the History of an Idea*. New York: Farrar, Straus and Giroux, 2016.

Edin, Kathryn, and Laura Lein. *Making Ends Meet: How Single Mothers Survive Welfare and Low-Wage Work*. New York: Russell Sage Foundation, 1997.

Edmiston, Kelly D. "Nonprofit Housing Investment and Local Area Home Values." *Economic Review*. First quarter 2012: 67–96. Federal Reserve Bank of Kansas City. http://www.kansascityfed.org/publicat/econrev/pdf/12q1Edmiston.pdf.

Edsall, Thomas B. "Where Should a Poor Family Live?" *New York Times*, August 5, 2015. http://www.nytimes.com/2015/08/05/opinion/where-should-a-poor-family-live.html?_r=0.

Ellen, Ingrid Gould, Keren M. Horn, Yiwen Kuai, Roman Pazuniak, and Michael David Williams. *Effect of QAP Incentives on the Location of LIHTC Properties*. Washington, DC: U.S. Department of Housing and Urban Development, 2015.

Ellen, Ingrid Gould, Keren M. Horn, and Katherine M. O'Regan. "Poverty Concentration and the Low Income Housing Tax Credit: Effects of Siting and Tenant Composition." *Journal of Housing Economics* 34 (2016): 49–59.

Ellen, Ingrid Gould, Katherine M. O'Regan, and Ionu Voicu. "Siting, Spillovers, and Segregation: A Re-examination of the Low Income Housing Tax Credit Program." In *Housing Markets and the Economy: Risk, Regulation, Policy; Essays in Honor of Karl Case*, edited by Edward Glaeser and John Quigley, 223–267. Cambridge, MA: Lincoln Institute for Land Policy, 2009.

Ellen, Ingrid Gould, Michael H. Schill, Alex E. Schwartz, and Ionu Voicu. "Does Federally Subsidized Rental Housing Depress Neighborhood Property Values?" *Journal of Policy Analysis and Management* 26.2 (2007): 257–280.

Ellen, Ingrid Gould, and Ionu Voicu. "Nonprofit Housing and Neighborhood Spillovers." *Journal of Policy Analysis and Management* 25.1 (2005): 31–52.

Evans, Gary W., Stephen J. Lepore, B. R. Shejwal, and M. N. Palsane. "Chronic Residential Crowding and Children's Well-Being: An Ecological Perspective." *Child Development* 69.6 (1998): 1514–1523.

Ezzet-Lofstrom, Roxanne, and James Murdoch. "The Effect of Low Income Housing Tax Credit Units on Residential Property Values in Dallas County." *Williams Review* 1.1 (2006): 107–124. SSRN: http://ssrn.com/abstract=976038.

Fainstein, Susan S. *The Just City*. Ithaca, NY: Cornell University Press, 2010.

Family Housing Fund. "The Need for Affordable Housing in the Twin Cities." Minneapolis, 1998. http://www.fhfund.org/educational_materials_fact_sheets.htm.

Farley, Reynolds, Elaine L. Fielding, and Maria Krysan. "The Residential Preferences of Blacks and Whites: A Four-Metropolis Analysis." *Housing Policy Debate* 8.4 (1997): 763–800.

Farley, Reynolds, Howard Schuman, Suzanne Bianchi, Diane Colasanto, and Shirley Hatchett. "'Chocolate City, Vanilla Suburbs': Will the Trend toward Racially Separate Communities Continue?" *Social Science Research* 7.4 (1978): 319–344.

Feagin, Joe R. *Racist America: Roots, Current Realities, and Future Reparations*. 3rd ed. New York: Routledge, 2014.

Feagin, Joe R., and Harlan Hahn. *Ghetto Revolts: The Politics of Violence in American Cities*. New York: Macmillan, 1973.

Fernández, Melissa Arrigiota. "Constructing 'The Other,' Practicing Resistance: Public Housing and Community Politics in Puerto Rico." PhD thesis, London School of Economics and Political Science, 2010.

Fine, Sidney. "Michigan and Housing Discrimination, 1949–1969." *Michigan Historical Review* 23.2 (1997): 81–114.

Fishman, Robert. *Bourgeois Utopias: The Rise and Fall of Suburbia*. New York: Basic Books, 1987.

Frank, Deborah A., Nicole B. Neault, Anne Skalicky, John T. Cook, Jacqueline D. Wilson, Suzette Levenson, Alan F. Meyers, Timothy Heeren, Diana B. Cutts, Patrick H. Casey, Maureen M. Black, and Carol Berkowitz. "Heat or Eat: The Low Income Home Energy Assistance Program and Nutritional and Health Risks among Children Less Than 3 Years of Age." *Pediatrics* 118.5 (2006): 1293–1302.

Fraser, James C. "Beyond Gentrification: Mobilizing Communities and Claiming Space." *Urban Geography* 25.5 (2004): 437–457.

Fraser, James, and Edward L. Kick. "The Role of Public, Private, Nonprofit and Community Sectors in Shaping Mixed-Income Housing Outcomes in the U.S." *Urban Studies* 44.12 (2007): 2357–2377.

Frazier, Nishani. "A McDonald's That Reflects the Soul of a People: Hough Area Development Corporation and Community Development in Cleveland." In Hill and Rabig, *Business of Black Power*, 68–94.

Freedman, Matthew, and Tamara McGavock. "Low-Income Housing Development, Poverty Concentration, and Neighborhood Inequality." *Journal of Policy Analysis and Management* 34.4 (2015): 805–834.

Freeman, Lance. *Siting Affordable Housing: Location and Neighborhood Trends of Low Income Housing Tax Credit Developments in the 1990s*. Washington DC: Brookings Institution, Census 2000 Survey Series, 2004.

——. "The Impact of Assisted Housing Developments on Concentrated Poverty." *Housing Policy Debate* 14.1–2 (2003): 103–141.

Fullilove, Mindy. *Root Shock: How Tearing Up City Neighborhoods Hurts America, and What We Can Do about It*. New York: One World / Ballantine, 2009.

Funderburg, Richard, and Heather MacDonald. "Neighbourhood Valuation Effects from New Construction of Low-Income Housing Tax Credit Projects in Iowa: A Natural Experiment." *Urban Studies* 47.8 (2010): 1745–1771.

Garreau, Joel. *Edge Cities: Life on the New Frontier*. New York: Doubleday, 1987.

Gibbons, Joseph. "Does Racial Segregation Make Community-Based Organizations More Territorial? Evidence from Newark, NJ, and Jersey City, NJ." *Journal of Urban Affairs* 37.5 (2014): 600–619.

Gibson, D. W. *The Edge Becomes the Center: An Oral History of Gentrification in the 21st Century*. New York: Overlook, 2015.

Gibson, Karen J. "The Relocation of the Columbia Villa Community: Views from Residents." *Journal of Planning Education and Research* 27.1 (2007): 5–19.

Gill, Andrea. "'Gilding the Ghetto' and Debates over Chicago's Gautreaux Program." In Hill and Rabig, *Business of Black Power*, 184–214.

Goering, John. "Political Origins and Opposition." In *Choosing a Better Life? Evaluating the Moving to Opportunity Social Experiment*, edited by John Goering and Judith D. Feins, 37–58. Washington, DC: Urban Institute Press, 2003.

——, ed. *Housing Desegregation and Federal Policy*. Chapel Hill: University of North Carolina Press, 1986.

——. Introduction to section 4 ("Racial Desegregation and Federal Housing Policies") in Goering, *Housing Desegregation and Federal Policy*, 197–213.

Goetz, Edward G. "The Fair Housing Tightrope in the Obama Administration: Balancing Competing Policy Objectives of Fair Housing and Locational Efficiency in Assisted Housing." *Journal of Urban Affairs* 37.1 (2015): 53–56.

——. "Poverty Pimping the CDCs: The Search for Fair Housing's New Bogeyman." *Housing Policy Debate* 25.3 (2015): 608–618.

——. "The Audacity of HOPE VI: Discourse and the Dismantling of Public Housing." *Cities* 35 (2013): 342–348.

——. *New Deal Ruins: Race, Economic Justice, and Public Housing Policy*. Ithaca, NY: Cornell University Press, 2013.

——. *Clearing the Way: Deconcentrating the Poor in Urban America*. Washington, DC: Urban Institute Press, 2003.

——. "Housing Dispersal Programs." *Journal of Planning Literature* 18.1 (2003): 3–16.

Goetz, Edward G., and Karen Chapple. "You Gotta Move: Advancing the Debate on the Record of Dispersal." *Housing Policy Debate* 20.2 (2010): 1–28.

Goetz, Edward G., Tony Damiano, and Jason Hicks, 2015. "Racially Concentrated Areas of Affluence: A Preliminary Investigation." Unpublished paper, Humphrey School of Public Affairs, Minneapolis. http://www.cura.umn.edu/: publications/catalog/niweb1.

Goetz, Edward G., Hin Kin Lam, and Anne Heitlinger. 1996. *There Goes the Neighborhood? The Impact of Subsidized Multi-family Housing on Urban Neighborhoods*. Minneapolis: Center for Urban and Regional Affairs, University of Minnesota.

Goldberg, David. "From Landless to Landlords: Black Power, Black Capitalism, and the Co-optation of Detroit's Tenants' Rights Movement, 1964–69." In Hill and Rabig, *Business of Black Power*, 157–183.

Goldstein, Ira, and William L. Yancey. "Public Housing Projects, Blacks, and Public Policy: The Historical Ecology of Public Housing in Philadelphia." In Goering, *Housing Desegregation and Federal Policy*, 262–289.

Gonzales, Richard. "Feds to Allow Preferences for Low-Income Applicants in S. F. Housing Complex." National Public Radio, September 23, 2016. http://www. kpbs.org/news/2016/sep/23/feds-to-allow-preferences-for-low-income/.

———. "As Rent Soars, Longtime San Francisco Tenants Fight to Stay." National Public Radio, December 3, 2013. http://www.npr.org/2013/12/03/247531636/ as-rent-soars-longtime-san-francisco-tenants-fight-to-stay.

Goodman, Lisa A., Leonard Saxe, and Mary Harvey. "Homelessness as Psychological Trauma." *American Psychologist* 46.11 (1991): 1170–1179.

Gotham, Kevin Fox. "Separate and Unequal: The Housing Act of 1968 and the Section 235 Program." *Sociological Forum* 15.1 (2000): 13–37.

Gove, Walter R., Michael Hughes, and Omer R. Galle. "Overcrowding in the Home: An Empirical Investigation of Its Possible Pathological Consequences." *American Sociological Review* 44.1 (1979): 59–80.

Graba, Henry. "Obama Administration to San Francisco: Your Anti-gentrification Plan Promotes Segregation." *Moneybox*, August 17, 2016. http://www.slate.com/ blogs/moneybox/2016/08/17/a_local_preference_affordable_housing_plan_in_ san_francisco_might_violate.html.

Gray, Robert, and Steven Tursky. "Local and Racial/Ethnic Occupancy for HUD Subsidized Family Housing in Ten Metropolitan Areas." In Goering, *Housing Desegregation and Federal Policy*, 235–252.

Green, Richard K., Stephen Malpezzi, and Kiat-Ying Seah. "Low Income Housing Tax Credit Housing Developments and Property Values." Center for Urban Land Economics Research, University of Wisconsin, 2002. http://medinamn.us/ wp-content/uploads/2014/04/Low-Income-Housing-Tax-Credit-Housing- Developments-and-Property-Values-UW-Study.pdf.

Greenbaum, Susan, Wendy Hathaway, Cheryl Rodriquez, Ashley Spalding, and Beverly Ward. "Deconcentration and Social Capital: Contradictions of a Poverty Alleviation Policy." *Journal of Poverty* 12.2 (2008): 201–228.

Guzman, Carolina, Rajiv Bhatia, and Chris Durazo. *Anticipated Effects of Residential Displacement on Health: Results from Qualitative Research*. San Francisco Department of Public Health and South of Market Community Action Network, 2005. http://www.pewtrusts.org/~/media/assets/2005/ hiareporttrinityplazahousingredevelopment.pdf.

Hackworth, Jason. "Destroyed by HOPE: Public Housing, Neoliberalism, and Progressive Housing Activism in the US." In *Where the Other Half Lives: Lower Income Housing in a Neoliberal World*, edited by Sarah Glynn, 232–256. London: Pluto, 2009.

Hall, Matthew, and Barrett Lee. "How Diverse Are US Suburbs?" *Urban Studies* 47.1 (2010): 3–28.

Hanlon, Bernadette. "A Typology of Inner-Ring Suburbs: Class, Race, and Ethnicity in U.S. Suburbia." *City & Community* 8.3 (2009): 221–246.

Hanlon, Bernadette, Thomas Vicino, and J. R. Short. "The New Metropolitan Reality in the US: Rethinking the Traditional Model." *Urban Studies* 43.12 (2006).

Hansen, Megan. "Marin Residents Stand in Rain to Protest High-Density Housing Developments." *Marin Journal*, February 7, 2014. http://www.marinij.com/ general-news/20140207/marin-residents-stand-in-rain-to-protest-high-density- housing-developments.

Harkness, Joseph, and Sandra Newman. "Housing Affordability and Children's Well- Being: Evidence from the National Survey of America's Families." *Housing Policy Debate* 16.2 (2005): 223–255.

Hartley, Daniel. "Gentrification and Financial Health." Federal Reserve Bank of
    Cleveland, November 6, 2013. https://www.clevelandfed.org/en/newsroom-
    and-events/publications/economic-trends/2013-economic-trends/et-20131106-
    gentrification-and-financial-health.aspx.
Hartman, Chester, and Gregory D. Squires, eds. *The Integration Debate: Competing
    Futures for American Cities.* New York: Routledge, 2010.
——. "Integration Exhaustion, Race Fatigue, and the American Dream." In Hartman
    and Squires, *Integration Debate*, 1–8.
Helliker, Kevin. "U.S. News: Chicago Population Sinks to 1920 Level." *Wall Street
    Journal*, February 16, 2011.
Hess, Daniel Baldwin, and Tangerine Maria Almeida. "Impact of Proximity to Light
    Rail Rapid Transit on Station-Area Property Values in Buffalo, New York."
    Urban Studies 44.5–6 (2007): 1041–1068.
Hill, Laura Warren, and Julia Rabig. Introduction to *The Business of Black Power:
    Community Development, Capitalism, and Corporate Responsibility in Postwar
    America*, edited by Laura Warren Hill and Julia Rabig, 1–14. Rochester, NY:
    University of Rochester Press, 2012.
Hirsch, Arnold R. *Making the Second Ghetto: Race and Housing in Chicago, 1940–1960.*
    Chicago: University of Chicago Press, 2009.
Hollar, Michael, and Kurt Usowsky. "Low Income Housing Tax Credit Qualified
    Census Tracts." *Cityscape: A Journal of Policy Development and Research*
    9.3 (2007): 153–159.
Holmgren, Edward L. "Statement of Edward L. Holmgren, Executive Director
    of the National Committee against Discrimination in Housing." In *The
    Gautreaux Decision and Its Effect on Subsidized Housing—Hearing before a
    Subcommittee of the Committee on Government Operations, United States
    House of Representatives, 95th Congress, 2nd Session*, 84–87. Washington, DC:
    Government Printing Office, 1977.
Horn, Keren M., and Katherine M. O'Regan. *The Low Income Housing Tax Credit and
    Racial Segregation.* New York: Furman Center for Real Estate and Public Policy,
    NYU, 2011.
Housing Justice Center. *Preliminary Analysis of MICAH Fair Housing Complaint
    against State, MHFA, Met Council.* Saint Paul, MN, 2015.
Howard, Amy L. *More Than Shelter: Activism and Community in San Francisco Public
    Housing.* Minneapolis: University of Minnesota Press, 2014.
Howard, Amy L., and Thad Williamson. "Reframing Public Housing in Richmond,
    Virginia: Segregation, Resident Resistance and the Future of Redevelopment."
    Cities 57 (2016): 33–39.
Hu, Lingqian. "Job Accessibility of the Poor in Los Angeles: Has Suburbanization
    Affected Spatial Mismatch?" *Journal of the American Planning Association*
    81.1 (2015): 30–45.
Hunt, D. Bradford. *Blueprint for Disaster: The Unraveling of Chicago Public Housing.*
    Chicago: University of Chicago Press, 2009.
Hyra, Derek. *Making the Gilded Ghetto: Race, Class and Politics in the Cappucino City.*
    Chicago: University of Chicago Press, forthcoming.
——. "The Back-to-the-City Movement: Neighbourhood Redevelopment and
    Processes of Political and Cultural Displacement." *Urban Studies* 52.10 (2015):
    1753–1773.
Ihlandfeldt, Keith R., and David L. Sjoquist. "The Spatial Mismatch Hypothesis: A
    Review of Recent Studies and Their Implications for Welfare Reform." *Housing
    Policy Debate* 9 (1998): 849–892.

Imbroscio, David. "Beyond Mobility: The Limits of Liberal Urban Policy." *Journal of Urban Affairs* 34.1 (2012): 1–20.

——. *Urban America Reconsidered: Alternatives for Governance and Policy.* Ithaca, NY: Cornell University Press, 2010.

——. "'United and Actuated by Some Common Impulse of Passion': Challenging the Dispersal Consensus in American Housing Policy Research." *Journal of Urban Affairs* 30.2 (2008): 111–130.

——. "Shaming the Inside Game: A Critique of the Liberal Expansionist Approach to Addressing Urban Problems." *Urban Affairs Review* 42.2 (2006): 224–248.

Immergluck, Daniel. "Large Redevelopment Initiatives, Housing Values and Gentrification: The Case of the Atlanta Beltline." *Urban Studies* 46 (2009): 1725–1747.

Institute on Metropolitan Opportunity. *Reforming Subsidized Housing Policy in the Twin Cities to Cut Costs and Reduce Segregation.* Minneapolis, 2014. http://www1.law.umn.edu/uploads/ee/52/ee52be92915228d3a453e5428ea40c07/Subsidized-Housing-in-the-Twin-Cities-1-7-14.pdf.

Institute on Race and Poverty. *Access to Opportunity in the Twin Cities Metropolitan Area,* Minneapolis, 2007.

Ishimatsu, Josh. "Can Organizing Resuscitate Community Development?" *Shelterforce,* November 22, 2013. http://www.rooflines.org/3521/can_organizing_resuscitate_community_development/.

——. "Neighborhoods or Regions? A Trick Question." *Shelterforce,* July 17, 2013. http://www.shelterforce.org/article/3337/neighborhoods_or_regions_a_trick_question/.

Istre, G. R., M. A. McCoy, L. Osborn, J. J. Barnard, and A. Bolton. "Deaths and Injuries from House Fires." *New England Journal of Medicine* 344.25 (2001): 1911–1916.

Jackson, Kenneth T. *Crabgrass Frontier: The Suburbanization of the United States.* New York: Oxford University Press, 1987.

Jackson, Sharon, Roger Anderson, Norman Johnson, and Paul Sorlie. "The Relation of Residential Segregation to All-Cause Mortality: A Study in Black and White." *American Journal of Public Health* 90.4 (2000): 615–617.

Jargowsky, Paul. *Concentration of Poverty in the New Millennium: Changes in Prevalence, Composition and Location of High Poverty Neighborhoods.* Report by the Century Foundation and Rutgers Center for Urban Research and Education. Camden, NJ: Rutgers Center for Urban Research and Education, 2013. http://tcf.org/assets/downloads/Concentration_of_Poverty_in_the_New_Millennium.pdf.

Johnson, Jennifer, and Beata Bednarz. *Neighborhood Effects of the Low Income Housing Tax Credit Program: Final Report.* Washington, DC: U.S. Department of Housing and Urban Development, 2002.

Jolly, Kenneth S. *Black Liberation in the Midwest: The Struggle in St. Louis, Missouri, 1964–1970.* Routledge: New York, 2006.

Jones, Charles E. "The Political Repression of the Black Panther Party, 1966–1971: The Case of the Oakland Bay Area." *Journal of Black Studies* 18.4 (1988): 415–434.

Joseph, Peniel E., ed. *The Black Power Movement: Rethinking the Civil Rights–Black Power Era.* New York: Routledge, 2006.

Julian, Elizabeth K. "Recent Advocacy Related to the Low Income Housing Tax Credit and Fair Housing." *Journal of Affordable Housing* 18.2 (2009): 185–192.

Kahn, Matthew E. "Gentrification Trends in New Transit-Oriented Communities: Evidence from 14 Cities That Expanded and Built Rail Transit Systems." *Real Estate Economics* 35.2 (2007): 155–182.

Katz, Bruce, ed. *Reflections on Regionalism*. Washington, DC: Brookings Institution Press, 2000.

Kawabata, Mizuki. "Job Access and Employment among Low-Skilled Autoless Workers in US Metropolitan Areas." *Environment and Planning A* 35.9 (2003): 1651–1668.

Keating, W. Dennis. *The Suburban Racial Dilemma: Housing and Neighborhoods*. Philadelphia: Temple University Press, 1994.

Keen, Judy. "Blacks' Exodus Reshapes Cities." *USA Today*, May 19, 2011.

Kerbow, David. *Patterns of Urban Student Mobility and Local School Reform*. Technical Report No. 5. Chicago: University of Chicago Center for Research on the Education of Students Placed at Risk, 1996.

Khadduri, Jill. *Creating Balance in the Locations of LIHTC Developments: The Role of Qualified Allocation Plans*. Washington, DC: Poverty and Race Research Action Council and Abt Associates, 2013.

Khadduri, Jill, Larry Buron, and Carissa Climaco. *Are States Using the Low Income Housing Tax Credit to Enable Families with Children to Live in Low Poverty and Racially Integrated Neighborhoods?* Boston: Abt Associates, 2006. http://www.prrace.org/pdf/LIHTC_report_2006.pdf.

Khadduri, Jill, and Carissa Climaco. *LIHTC Awards in Ohio, 2006–2015: Where Are They Providing Housing for Families with Children?* Boston: Abt Associates, 2016.

King, Desmond S., and Rogers M. Smith. *Still a House Divided: Race and Politics in Obama's America*. Princeton, NJ: Princeton University Press, 2011.

King, Paul E. "Exclusionary Zoning and Open Housing: A Brief Judicial History." *Geographical Review* 1 (1978): 459–469.

Kirwan Institute. *Equity, Opportunity, and Sustainability in the Central Puget Sound Region*. Seattle, WA: Puget Sound Regional Council, 2012.

Kneebone, Elizabeth, and Alan Berube. *Confronting Suburban Poverty in America*. Washington, DC: Brookings Institution Press, 2013.

Kneebone, Elizabeth, and Emily Garr. *The Suburbanization of Poverty: Trends in Metropolitan America, 2000 to 2008*. Washington, DC: Brookings Institution, 2010. http://www.brookings.edu/~/media/research/files/papers/2010/1/20%20 poverty%20kneebone/0120_poverty_paper.pdf.

Kneebone, Elizabeth, and Natalie Holmes. *U.S. Concentrated Poverty in the Wake of the Great Recession*. Washington, DC: Brookings Institution, 2016. http://www.brookings.edu/research/reports2/2016/03/31-concentrated-poverty-recession-kneebone-holmes.

Kozol, Jonathan. *Savage Inequalities: Children in America's Schools*. New York: Broadway Books, 2012.

Krefetz, Sharon Perlman. "The Impact and Evolution of the Massachusetts Comprehensive Permit and Zoning Appeals Act: Thirty Years of Experience with a State Legislative Effort to Overcome Exclusionary Zoning." *Western New England Law Review* 22 (2000): 381.

Krivo, Lauren J., and Robert L. Kaufman. "Housing and Wealth Inequality: Racial-Ethnic Differences in Home Equity in the United States." *Demography* 41.3 (2004): 585–605.

Kruse, Kevin M. *White Flight: Atlanta and the Making of Modern Conservatism*. Princeton, NJ: Princeton University Press, 2005.

Krysan, Maria. "Prejudice, Politics, and Public Opinion: Understanding the Sources of Racial Policy Attitudes." *Annual Review of Sociology* 26 (2000): 135–168.

Krysan, Maria, and Reynolds Farley. "The Residential Preferences of Blacks: Do They Explain Persistent Segregation?" *Social Forces* 80.3 (2002): 937–980.

Lake, Robert. "Postscript: Unresolved Themes in the Evolution of Fair Housing." In Goering, *Housing Desegregation and Federal Policy*, 313–326.

Lake, Robert, and Jessica Winslow. "Integration Management: Municipal Constraints on Residential Mobility." *Urban Geography* 2.4 (1981): 311–326.

Lang, Robert E., and Jennifer B. LeFurgy. *Boomburbs: The Rise of America's Accidental Cities*. Washington, DC: Brookings Institution Press, 2007.

Laurent, Ronald. "Statement of Ronald Laurent, Senior Vice President, McElvain Reynolds Co." In *The* Gautreaux *Decision and Its Effect on Subsidized Housing: Hearing before a Subcommittee of the Committee on Government Operations, House of Representatives, Ninety-Fifth Congress, Second Session, September 22, 1978*. Washington, DC: Government Printing Office, 1978.

Lee, Chang-Moo, Dennis P. Culhane, and Susan M. Wachter. "The Differential Impacts of Federally Assisted Housing Programs on Nearby Property Values: A Philadelphia Case Study." *Housing Policy Debate* 10 (1999):75–93.

Lees, Loretta, Tim Butler, and Gary Bridge. "Introduction: Gentrification, Social Mix/ing and Mixed Communities." In *Mixed Communities: Gentrification by Stealth?*, edited by Gary Bridge, Tim Butler, and Loretta Lees, 1–17. Bristol, UK: Policy Press, 2012.

Leigh, Wilhelmina, and James D. McGhee. "A Minority Perspective on Residential Racial Integration." In Goering, *Housing Desegregation and Federal Policy*, 31–42.

Lens, Michael. "Employment Accessibility among Housing Subsidy Recipients." *Housing Policy Debate* 24.4 (2014): 671–691.

Lepore, S. J., G. W. Evans, and M. N. Palsane. "Social Hassles and Psychological Health in the Context of Chronic Crowding." *Journal of Health and Social Behavior* 32.4 (1991): 357–367.

Li, Wei. "Anatomy of a New Ethnic Settlement: The Chinese Ethnoburb in Los Angeles." *Urban Studies* 35.3 (1998): 479–501.

——. "Los Angeles' Chinese Ethnoburb: Evolution of Ethnic Community and Economy." Paper presented at the annual meeting of the Association of American Geographers, March 15, 1995.

Lichter, Daniel T., Domenico Parisi, and Michael C. Taquino. "Toward a New Macro-Segregation? Decomposing Segregation within and between Metropolitan Cities and Suburbs." *American Sociological Review* 80.4 (2015): 843–873.

Lipsitz, George, and Melvin L. Oliver. "Integration, Segregation, and the Racial Wealth Gap." In *The Integration Debate: Competing Futures for American Cities*, edited by Chester Hartman and Gregory D. Squires, 153–167. New York: Routledge, 2010.

Listokin, David. *Fair Share Housing Allocation*. New Brunswick, NJ: Center for Urban Policy Research, 1976.

Logan, John R., Brian J. Stults, and Reynolds Farley. "Segregation of Minorities in the Metropolis: Two Decades of Change." *Demography* 41.1 (2004): 1–22.

Long, James A. "Note: The Low-Income Housing Tax Credit in New Jersey: New Opportunities to Deconcentrate Poverty through the Duty to Affirmatively Further Fair Housing." *New York University Annual Survey of American Law* 66 (2010): 75–128.

Long, Larry H. "How the Racial Composition of Cities Change." *Land Economics* 51.3 (1975): 258–267.

Lucy, William H., and David L. Phillips. *Confronting Suburban Decline: Strategic Planning for Metropolitan Renewal*. Washington, DC: Island Press, 2000.

Lyons, Robert F., and Scott Loveridge. "An Hedonic Estimation of the Effect of Federally Subsidized Housing on Nearby Residential Property Values." Staff Paper P93–6. Department of Agriculture and Applied Economics, University of Minnesota, Saint Paul, 1993.

Maciag, Mike. "Gentrification in America Report." *Governing*, 2015. http://www.governing.com/gov-data/census/gentrification-in-cities-governing-report.html.

Malaby, Elizabeth G. D., and Barbara Lukermann. "Given Choice: The Effects of Portability in Section 8 Rental Housing Assistance." *CURA Reporter* 26.2 (1996): 12–15.

Manzo, Lynne C., Rachel G. Kleit, and Dawn Couch. "Moving Three Times Is Like Having Your House on Fire Once: The Experience of Place and Impending Displacement among Public Housing Residents." *Urban Studies* 45.9 (2008): 1855–1878.

Marable, Manning. *Race, Reform, and Rebellion: The Second Reconstruction in Black America, 1945–1990*. Oxford: University Press of Mississippi, 1991.

March, Elizabeth L., Stephanie E. de Cuba, Annie Gayman, John Cook, Deborah A. Frank, Alan Meyers, Johanna Flacks, Megan Sandel, and Samantha Morton. *Rx for Hunger: Affordable Housing*. Boston: Children's HealthWatch and Medical-Legal Partnership, 2009.

Marcuse, Peter. "The Enclave, the Citadel, and the Ghetto: What Has Changed in the Post-Fordist US City." *Urban Affairs Review* 33.2 (1997): 228–264.

——. "The Ghetto of Exclusion and the Fortified Enclave: New Patterns in the United States." *American Behavioral Scientist* 41.3 (1997): 311–326.

Marris, Peter. "The Social Implications of Urban Redevelopment." *Journal of the American Institute of Planners* 28.3 (1962): 180–186.

Massey, Douglas S., Len Albright, Rebecca Casciano, Elizabeth Derickson, and David N. Kinsey. *Climbing Mount Laurel: The Struggle for Affordable Housing and Social Mobility in an American Suburb*. Princeton, NJ: Princeton University Press, 2013.

Massey, Douglas S., and Nancy A. Denton. *American Apartheid: Segregation and the Making of the Underclass*. Cambridge, MA: Harvard University Press, 1993.

——. "Suburbanization and Segregation in US Metropolitan Areas." *American Journal of Sociology* 94.3 (1988): 592–626.

Massey, Douglas S., and Shawn Kanaiaupuni. "Public Housing and the Concentration of Poverty." *Social Science Quarterly* 74.1 (1993): 109–122.

Maxfield Research. *A Study of the Relationship between Affordable Family Rental Housing and Home Values in the Twin Cities*. Minneapolis: Family Housing Fund, 2000. http://www.fhfund.org/_dnld/reports/Property%20Values_Full%20Report.pdf.

McClure, Kirk. "The Low-Income Housing Tax Credit Program Goes Mainstream and Moves to the Suburbs." *Housing Policy Debate* 17 (2006): 419–446.

Medoff, Peter, and Holly Sklar. *Streets of Hope: The Fall and Rise of an Urban Neighborhood*. Boston: South End, 1994.

Meier, August, and Elliott Rudwick. *CORE: A Study in the Civil Rights Movement, 1942–1968*. New York: Oxford University Press, 1973.

Metcalf, George. *Fair Housing Comes of Age*. New York: Greenwood, 1988.

Metropolitan Council of the Twin Cities. "Response to Housing Discrimination Complaint." Saint Paul, MN, March 12, 2015.

———. *Summary Report: Determining Affordable Housing Need in the Twin Cities, 2011–2020.* Saint Paul, MN, 2006. http://www.metrocouncil.org/planning/Housing/AffHousingNeedJan06.pdf.

Meyer, Stephen Grant. *As Long as They Don't Move Next Door: Segregation and Racial Conflict in American Neighborhoods.* Lanham, MD: Rowman & Littlefield, 2000.

Meyers, Alan, Diana B. Cutts, Deborah A. Frank, Suzette Levenson, Anne Skalicky, Timothy Heeren, John Cook, Carol Berkowitz, Maureen Black, Patrick Casey, and N. Zaldivar. "Subsidized Housing and Children's Nutritional Status: Data from a Multisite Surveillance Study." *Archives of Pediatrics and Adolescent Medicine* 159 (2005): 551–556.

Meyers, Alan, D. Rubin, M. Napoleone, and K. Nichols. "Public Housing Subsidies May Improve Poor Children's Nutrition." *American Journal of Public Health* 83.1 (1993): 115.

Meyers, Michael. "Prepared Statement of Michael Meyers, Assistant Director, National Association for the Advancement of Colored People." *The* Gautreaux *Decision and Its Effect on Subsidized Housing—Hearing before a Subcommittee of the Committee on Government Operations, United States House of Representatives, 95th Congress, 2nd Session,* 94–96. Washington, DC: Government Printing Office, 1977.

Meyerson, Martin, and Edward C. Banfield. *Politics, Planning and the Public Interest: The Case of Public Housing in Chicago.* New York: Free Press, 1955.

Mikelbank, Brian A. "A Typology of U.S. Suburban Places." *Housing Policy Debate* 15.4 (2004): 935–964.

Mills, Edwin S. "Open Housing Laws as Stimulus to Central City Employment." *Journal of Urban Economics* 17 (1985): 184–188.

Mock, Brentin. "The Failures and Merits of Place-Based Initiatives." *Atlantic Citylab,* May 25, 2015. http://www.citylab.com/work/2015/05/the-failures-and-merits-of-place-based-initiatives/394025/.

Molotch, Harvey Luskin. *Managed Integration: Dilemmas of Doing Good in the City.* Berkeley: University of California Press, 1972.

National Advisory Commission on Civil Disorders. *Report of the National Advisory Commission on Civil Disorders, March 1, 1968.* New York: Bantam, 1968.

National Association of Home Builders. *The Local Economic Impact of Typical Housing Tax Credit Developments.* Washington, DC, 2010.

National Commission on Fair Housing and Equal Opportunity (NCFHEO). *The Future of Fair Housing: Report of the National Commission on Fair Housing and Equal Opportunity.* 2008.

National Fair Housing Alliance. *Expanding Opportunity: Systemic Approaches to Fair Housing.* Washington, DC, 2014.

Nettleton, Sarah, and Roger Burrows. "Mortgage Debt, Insecure Home Ownership and Health: An Exploratory Analysis." *Sociology of Health and Illness* 20.5 (1998): 731–753.

Neuwirth, Robert. "Renovation or Ruin." *Shelterforce Online* 137, September/October (2004). http://www.shelterforce.com/online/issues/137/LIHTC.html.

Nevin, Rick, and David E. Jacobs. "Windows of Opportunity: Lead Poisoning Prevention, Housing Affordability, and Energy Conservation." *Housing Policy Debate* 17.1 (2006): 185–207.

Newman, Kathe, and Edward Goetz. "Reclaiming Neighborhood from the Inside Out: Regionalism, Globalization, and Critical Community Development." *Urban Geography* 37.5 (2015): 685–699. doi:10.1080/02723638.2015.1096116.

Newman, Mark. *The Civil Rights Movement.* Westport, CT: Praeger, 2004.

Newman, Sandra J., and C. Scott Holupka. "Housing Affordability and Investments in Children." *Journal of Housing Economics* 24 (2014): 89–100.

———. "Housing Affordability and Children's Well-Being." Working paper, Center on Housing, Neighborhoods, and Communities, Institute for Health and Social Policy. Baltimore: Johns Hopkins University, 2013.

Newman, Sandra J., and Ann B. Schnare. "'. . . And a Suitable Living Environment': The Failure of Housing Programs to Deliver on Neighborhood Quality." *Housing Policy Debate* 8.4 (1997): 703–741.

Nicolaides, Becky M. *My Blue Heaven: Life and Politics in the Working-Class Suburbs of Los Angeles, 1920–1965.* Chicago: University of Chicago Press, 2002.

Oakley, Deirdre. "Locational Patterns of Low-Income Housing Tax Credit Developments: A Sociospatial Analysis of Four Metropolitan Areas." *Urban Affairs Review* 43 (2008): 599–628.

Oakley, Deirdre, and Keri Burchfeld. "Out of the Projects, Still in the Hood: The Spatial Constraints on Public Housing Residents' Relocation in Chicago." *Journal of Urban Affairs* 31.5 (2009): 589–614.

Oak Park Regional Housing Center. "Affirmatively Furthering Fair Housing and the Center for Neighborhood Technology's H+T Affordability Index." Oak Park, IL, February 2012.

O'Connor, Alice. *Poverty Knowledge: Social Science, Social Policy, and the Poor in Twentieth-Century US History.* Princeton, NJ: Princeton University Press, 2009.

Oliver, Melvin L., and Thomas Shapiro. *Black Wealth / White Wealth.* New York: Routledge, 1995.

———. "Race and Wealth." *Review of Black Political Economy* 17.4 (1989): 5–25.

Ongiri, Amy Abugo. *Spectacular Blackness: The Cultural Politics of the Black Power Movement and the Search for a Black Aesthetic.* Charlottesville: University of Virginia Press, 2010.

Orfield, Gary. "The Movement for Housing Integration: Rationale and the Nature of the Challenge." In Goering, *Housing Desegregation and Federal Policy*, 18–30.

Orfield, Myron, Will Stancil, Tom Luce, and Eric Myott. "High Costs and Segregation in Subsidized Housing Policy." *Housing Policy Debate* 25 (2015): 574–607.

Orr, Larry, Judith Feins, Robin Jacob, Erik Beecroft, Lisa Sanbonmatsu, Lawrence Katz, Jefferey Liebman, and Jeffrey Kling. *Moving to Opportunity for Fair Housing Demonstration Program: Interim Impacts Evaluation.* Washington, DC: U.S. Department of Housing and Urban Development, 2003.

Pastor, Manuel, Chris Benner, and Martha Matsuoka. *This Could Be the Start of Something Big: How Social Movements for Regional Equity Are Reshaping Metropolitan America.* Ithaca, NY: Cornell University Press, 2009.

Patillo, Mary. "The Problem of Integration." New York University, Furman Center, January 20, 2014. http://furmancenter.org/research/iri/patillo.

———. "Investing in Poor Black Neighborhoods 'As Is.'" In *Public Housing and the Legacy of Segregation*, edited by Margery Austin Turner, Susan J. Popkin, and Lynette Rawlings, 31–46. Washington, DC: Urban Institute Press, 2009.

Patterson, Orlando. *The Ordeal of Integration: Progress and Resentment in America's "Racial" Crisis.* New York: Basic Civitas, 1998.

Peach, Ceri. "Good Segregation, Bad Segregation." *Planning Perspectives* 11.4 (1996): 379–398.

Pendall, Rolf. "Why Voucher and Certificate Users Live in Distressed Neighborhoods." *Housing Policy Debate* 11.4 (2000): 881–910.

Pendall, Rolf, Christopher Hayes, Arthur George, Zach McDade, Casey Dawkins, Jae Sik Jeon, Eli Knaap, Evelyin Blumenberg, Gregory Pierce, and Michael Smart.

Driving to Opportunity: Understanding the Links among Transportation Access, Residential Outcomes, and Economic Opportunity for Housing Voucher Recipients. Washington, DC: Urban Institute, 2014.

Pendall, Rolf, and Joe Parilla. "Comment on Emily Talen and Julia Koschinsky's 'Is Subsidized Housing in Sustainable Neighborhoods? Evidence from Chicago': 'Sustainable' Urban Form and Opportunity; Frames and Expectations for Low-Income Households." *Housing Policy Debate* 21.1 (2011): 33–44.

Perez, Iris. "Workforce Housing Project Bitterly Contested in Carver." Fox 9, March 2, 2015. http://www.fox9.com/archive/1570605-story.

Pettigrew, Thomas F., and Linda R. Tropp. "A Meta-analytic Test of Intergroup Contact." *Journal of Personality and Social Psychology* 90.5 (2006):751–783.

Piven, Frances Fox, and Richard A. Cloward. "The Case against Urban Desegregation." *Social Work* 12.1 (1967): 12–21.

Pohlmann, Marcus D., ed. *African American Political Thought.* Vol. 1. New York: Taylor & Francis, 2003.

Polikoff, Alexander. "HOPE VI and the Deconcentration of Poverty." In *From Despair to Hope: HOPE VI and the New Promise of Public Housing in America's Cities,* edited by Henry Cisneros and Lora Engdahl, 65–81. Washington, DC: Brookings Institution Press, 2009.

——. *Waiting for* Gautreaux: *A Story of Segregation, Housing, and the Black Ghetto.* Evanston, IL: Northwestern University Press, 2006.

——. "Public Housing Destruction: Is It Worth It?" *For the Public Interest: The BPI Newsletter,* February 2003. http://www.bpichicago.org/wp-content/uploads/2013/12/public-housing-destruction-is-it-worth-it.pdf.

——. "Sustainable Integration or Inevitable Resegregation: The Troubling Questions." In Goering, *Housing Desegregation and Federal Policy,* 43–71.

——. "Statement of Alexander Polikoff, Executive Director, Business and Professional People in the Public Interest; Accompanied by Milton Shader, Cocounsel." *The* Gautreaux *Decision and Its Effect on Subsidized Housing—Hearing before a Subcommittee of the Committee on Government Operations, United States House of Representatives, 95th Congress, 2nd Session,* 138–140. Washington, DC: Government Printing Office, 1977.

Pollack, Craig E., and Julia Lynch. "Health Status of People Undergoing Foreclosure in the Philadelphia Region." *American Journal of Public Health* 99.10 (2009): 1833–1839.

Popkin, Susan J., George Galster, Kenneth Temkin, Carla Herbig, Diane K. Levy, and Elise Richer. *Baseline Assessment of Public Housing Desegregation Cases: Cross-Site Report.* Vol. 1. Washington, DC: U.S. Department of Housing and Urban Development, 2000.

——. *Baseline Assessment of Public Housing Desegregation Cases: Case Studies.* Vol. 2. Washington, DC: U.S. Department of Housing and Urban Development, 2000.

Popkin, Susan J., Victoria Gwiasda, Jean M. Amendolia, Andrea A. Anderson, Gordon Hanson, Wendell A. Johnson, Elise Martel, Lynn M. Olson, and Dennis P. Rosenbaum. *The Hidden War: The Battle to Control Crime in Chicago's Public Housing.* Washington, DC: Abt Associates, 1996.

Popkin, Susan J., James E. Rosenbaum, and Patricia M. Meaden. "Labor Market Experiences of Low-Income Black Women in Middle-Class Suburbs: Evidence from a Survey of Gautreaux Program Participants." *Journal of Policy Analysis and Management* 12.3 (1993): 556–573.

Population Studies Center, Institute for Social Research, University of Michigan. "Race Segregation for Largest Metro Areas." No date. http://www.psc.isr.umich.edu/dis/census/segregation2010.html.

Poverty and Race Research Action Council. *Affirmatively Furthering Fair Housing at HUD: A First Term Report Card.* Washington, DC, 2013.

powell, john. "Reflections on the Past, Looking to the Future: The Fair Housing Act at 40." *Journal of Affordable Housing and Community Development* 18.2 (2009): 145–168.

powell, john, and Jason Reece. "The Future of Fair Housing and Fair Credit: From Crisis to Opportunity." *Cleveland State Law Review* 57 (2009): 210–244.

Purnell, Brian. "'What We Need Is Brick and Mortar': Race, Gender, and Early Leadership of the Bedford-Stuyvesant Restoration Corporation." In Hill and Rabig, *Business of Black Power,* 217–244.

Quadagno, Jill S. *The Color of Welfare: How Racism Undermined the War on Poverty.* New York: Oxford University Press, 1994.

Rabiega, William A., Ta-win Lin, and Linda M. Robinson. "The Property Value Effects of Public Housing Projects in Low and Moderate Density Residential Neighborhoods." *Land Economics* 6.2 (1984):174–179.

Rabig, Julia. "'A Fight and a Question': Community Development Corporations, Machine Politics, and Corporate Philanthropy in the Long Urban Crisis." In Hill and Rabig, *Business of Black Power,* 245–273.

Raciti, Antonio, Katherine A. Lambert-Pennington, and Kenneth M. Reardon. "The Struggle for the Future of Public Housing in Memphis, Tennessee: Reflections on HUD's Choice Neighborhoods Planning Program." *Cities* 57 (2016): 6–13.

Reardon, Sean F., and Kendra Bischoff. "No Neighborhood Is an Island." *Discussion 9: Residential Income Segregation.* New York University, Furman Center, 2014. http://furmancenter.org/research/iri/reardonbischoff.

——. "Income Inequality and Income Segregation." *American Journal of Sociology* 116.4 (2011): 1092–1153.

Relman, John, Glenn Schlactus, and Shalini Goel. "Creating and Protecting Prointegration Programs under the Fair Housing Act." In *The Integration Debate: Competing Futures for American Cities,* edited by Chester Hartman and Gregory D. Squires, 39–52. New York: Routledge, 2010.

Reynolds, Arthur J., Chin-Chih Chen, and Janette E. Herbers. "School Mobility and Education Success: A Research Synthesis and Evidence on Prevention." Paper prepared for the Workshop on the Impact of Mobility and Change on the Lives of Young Children, Schools, and Neighborhoods, National Academies, Washington, DC, June 29–30, 2009.

Roisman, Florence. "Constitutional and Statutory Mandates for Residential Racial Integration and the Validity of Race-Conscious, Affirmative Action to Achieve It." In *The Integration Debate: Competing Futures for American Cities,* edited by Chester Hartman and Gregory D. Squires, 67–84. New York: Routledge, 2010.

——. "Affirmatively Furthering Fair Housing in Regional Housing Markets: The Baltimore Public Housing Desegregation Litigation." *Wake Forest Law Review* 42.2 (2007): 333–392.

——. "Mandates Unsatisfied: The Low Income Housing Tax Credit Program and Civil Rights Laws." *University of Miami Law Review* 52 (1998): 1011–1049.

Ross, Stephen L., and Margery Austin Turner. "Housing Discrimination in Metropolitan America: Explaining Changes between 1989 and 2000." *Social Problems* 52.2 (2005): 152–180.

Rubinowitz, Leonard S., and James E. Rosenbaum. *Crossing the Class and Color Lines: From Public Housing to White Suburbia.* Chicago: University of Chicago Press, 2000.

Rubinowitz, Leonard S., and Elizabeth Trosman. "Affirmative Action and the American Dream: Implementing Fair Housing Policies in Federal Homeownership Programs." *Northwestern University Law Review* 74 (1979): 491–616.

Rusk, David. *Inside Game, Outside Game: Winning Strategies for Saving Urban America.* Washington, DC: Brookings Institution Press, 1999.

Sadler, Bill, Elizabeth Wampler, Jeff Wood, Matt Barry, and Jordan Wirfs-Brock. *The Denver Regional Equity Atlas: Mapping Access to Opportunity at a Regional Scale.* Denver: Mile High Connects, 2012. http://www.reconnectingamerica.org/resource-center/books-and-reports/2012/the-denver-regional-equity-atlas-mapping-opportunity-at-the-regional-scale/.

Saltman, Juliet. *Open Housing: Dynamics of a Social Movement.* New York: Praeger, 1978.

———. *Open Housing as a Social Movement: Challenge, Conflict and Change.* Lexington, MA: Heath Lexington Books, 1971.

Sampson, Robert J. *Great American City: Chicago and the Enduring Neighborhood Effect.* Chicago: University of Chicago Press, 2012.

Sampson, Robert J., and Jeffrey D. Morenoff. "Durable Inequality." In *Poverty Traps,* edited by Samuel Bowles, Steven N. Durlauf, and Karla Hoff, 176–203. Princeton, NJ: Princeton University Press, 2006.

Sanchez, Thomas W., and Marc Brenman, with Jacinta S. Ma and Richard H. Stolz. *The Right to Transportation: Moving to Equity.* Chicago: Planners Press, APA, 2007.

Savitch, Hank V., and Ronald K. Vogel. "Suburbs without a City: Power and City-County Consolidation." *Urban Affairs Review* 39.6 (2004): 758–790.

Scanlon, Edward, and Kevin Devine. "Residential Mobility and Youth Well-Being: Research, Policy, and Practice Issues." *Journal of Sociology and Social Welfare* 28.1 (2001): 119–138.

Schelling, Thomas C. "A Process of Residential Segregation: Neighborhood Tipping." In *Racial Discrimination in Economic Life,* edited by Anthony H. Pascal, 157–174. Lexington, MA: Lexington Books, 1972.

Schill, Michael H. "Deconcentrating the Inner City Poor." *Chicago-Kent Law Review* 67 (1991): 795–853.

Schill, Michael H., and Susan M. Wachter. "The Spatial Bias of Federal Housing Law and Policy: Concentrated Poverty in Urban America." *University of Pennsylvania Law Review* 143 (1995): 1285–1342.

Schwartz, Alex E. "The Low-Income Housing Tax Credit, Community Development, and Fair Housing: A Response to Orfield et al." *Housing Policy Debate* 26.2 (2016): 276–283.

Schwartz, Alex E., Ingrid G. Ellen, Ionu Voicu, and Michael H. Schill. "The External Effects of Place-Based Subsidized Housing." *Regional Science and Urban Economics* 36.6 (2006): 679–707.

Schwartz, Alex E., Scott Susin, and Ionu Voicu. "Has Falling Crime Driven New York City's Real Estate Boom?" *Journal of Housing Research* 14.1 (2003): 101–135.

Schwemm, Robert G. "Overcoming Structural Barriers to Integrated Housing: A Back-to-the-Future Reflection on the Fair Housing Act's 'Affirmatively Further' Mandate." *Kentucky Law Journal* 100 (2011): 125–176.

Segal, Jerome M. *Graceful Simplicity: The Philosophy and Politics of the Alternative American Dream.* Berkeley: University of California Press, 2003.

Seicshnaydre, Stacey. "The Fair Housing Choice Myth." *Cardozo Law Review* 33.3 (2012): 967–1019.

———. "How Government Housing Perpetuates Racial Segregation: Lessons from Post-Katrina New Orleans." *Catholic University Law Review* 60 (2010): 661–718.

Self, Robert O. *American Babylon: Race and the Struggle for Postwar Oakland*. Princeton, NJ: Princeton University Press, 2006.

Seng, Michael P., and F. Willis Caruso. "Achieving Integration through Private Litigation." In *The Integration Debate: Competing Futures for American Cities*, edited by Chester Hartman and Gregory D. Squires, 53–66. New York: Routledge, 2009.

Sharkey, Patrick. *Stuck in Place: Urban Neighborhoods and the End of Progress toward Racial Equality*. Chicago: University of Chicago Press, 2013.

Shelby, Tommie. *Dark Ghettos: Injustice, Dissent, and Reform*. Cambridge, MA: Belknap Press of Harvard University Press, 2016.

"Shelterforce Exclusive: Interview with HUD Secretary Julian Castro." February 4, 2016. http://www.shelterforce.org/article/4245/ishelterforce_i_exclusive_ interview_with_hud_secretary_julian_castro/.

Shen, Qing. "A Spatial Analysis of Job Openings and Access in a U.S. Metropolitan Area." *Journal of the American Planning Association* 67 (2001): 53–68.

——. "Location Characteristics of Inner-City Neighborhoods and Employment Accessibility of Low-Wage Workers." *Environment and Planning B: Planning and Design* 25 (1998): 345–365.

Sidney, Mara S. "Fair Housing and Affordable Housing Advocacy: Reconciling the Dual Agenda." In *The Geography of Opportunity: Race and Housing Choice in Metropolitan America*, edited by Xavier de Souza Briggs, 266–286. Washington, DC: Brookings Institution Press, 2005.

——. *Unfair Housing: How National Policy Shapes Community Action*. Lawrence: University Press of Kansas, 2003.

Siegel, Frederick. *Troubled Journey: From Pearl Harbor to Ronald Reagan*. New York: Hill & Wang, 1984.

Sigelman, Lee, and Susan Welch. "The Contact Hypothesis Revisited: Black-White Interaction and Positive Racial Attitudes." *Social Forces* 71.3 (1993): 781–795.

Simons, Robert A., A. J. Magner, and Esmail Baku. "Do Housing Rehabs Pay Their Way? A National Case Study." *Journal of Real Estate Research* 25.4 (2003): 431–461.

Singer, Audrey. *New Geography of United States Immigration*. Washington, DC: Brookings Institution, 2009.

Skobba, Kimberly, and Edward G. Goetz. "Mobility Decisions of Very Low-Income Households." *Cityscape* 15.2 (2013): 155–171.

Smith, Janet L. "Integration: Solving the Wrong Problem." In *The Integration Debate: Competing Futures for American Cities*, edited by Chester Hartman and Gregory D. Squires, 229–246. New York: Routledge, 2010.

Smith, Preston H., III. *Racial Democracy and the Black Metropolis: Housing Policy in Postwar Chicago*. Minneapolis: University of Minnesota Press, 2012.

Smith, Susan J., Donna Easterlow, Moira Munro, and Katrina M. Turner. "Housing as Health Capital: How Health Trajectories and Housing Paths Are Linked." *Journal of Social Issues* 59.3 (2003): 501–525.

Sniderman, Paul, and Edward G. Carmines. "Reaching beyond Race." *PS: Political Science & Politics* 30.3 (1997): 466–471.

Spinner-Halev, Jeff. "The Trouble with Diversity." In *Critical Urban Studies: New Directions*, edited by Jonathan S. Davies and David L. Imbroscio, 107–120. Albany: SUNY Press, 2010.

Squires, Gregory, and Charles E. Kubrin. *Privileged Places: Race, Residence, and the Structure of Opportunity*. Boulder, CO: Lynne Rienner, 2006.

Stack, Carole. *All Our Kin: Strategies for Survival in a Black Community*. New York: Harper & Row, 1975.

Steffan, Barry, George R. Carter, Marge Martin, Danilo Pelletiere, David A. Vandenbroucke, and Yunn-Gann David Yao. *Worst Case Housing Needs: A 2015 Report to Congress*. Washington, DC: U.S. Department of Housing and Urban Development, 2015.

Stein, Perry. "Is Pricey Shaw a Model for Retaining Affordability amid Regentrification?" *Washington Post*, May 21, 2015. https://www.washingtonpost. com/local/dc-politics/is-pricey-shaw-a-model-for-retaining-affordability-amidst-regentrification/2015/05/21/912f3504-ffde-11e4-805c-c3f407e5a9e9_ story.html.

Steinberg, Stephen. "The Myth of Concentrated Poverty." In *The Integration Debate: Competing Futures for American Cities*, edited by Chester Hartman and Gregory Squires, 213–228. New York: Routledge, 2010.

Stroub, Kori J., and Meredith P. Richards. "From Resegregation to Reintegration: Trends in the Racial/Ethnic Segregation of Metropolitan Public School." *American Educational Research Journal* 3 (2013): 497–531.

Sugrue, Thomas J. *Sweet Land of Liberty: The Forgotten Struggle for Civil Rights in the North*. New York: Random House, 2009.

Suro, Robert, Jill Wilson, and Audrey Singer. "Immigration and Poverty in America's Suburbs." Brookings Institution, Paper No. 20, Metropolitan Opportunity Series, 2011. http://www.brookings.edu/research/papers/2011/08/04-immigration-suro-wilson-singer.

Tach, Laura. "More Than Bricks and Mortar: Neighborhood Frames, Social Processes, and the Mixed-Income Redevelopment of a Public Housing Project." *City & Community* 8 (2009): 269–299.

Taeuber, Karl E. "Residential Segregation." *Scientific American* 213.2 (1965): 12–19.

Talen, Emily, and Julia Koschinsky. "Is Subsidized Housing in Sustainable Neighborhoods? Evidence from Chicago." *Housing Policy Debate* 21.1 (2011): 1–28.

Tegeler, Philip. "In Pursuit of a 'Both/and' Housing Policy—the Case of Housing Choice Vouchers." *Rooflines*, April 7, 2014. http://www.rooflines.org/3680/in_ pursuit_of_a_both_and_housing_policythe_case_of_housing_choice_vouchers.

Tegeler, Philip, and Hanna Chouest. "The 'Housing + Transportation Index' and Fair Housing." Poverty and Race Research Action Council, Policy Brief, 2011. http:// www.prrac.org/pdf/fair_housing_and_the_H+T_Index.pdf.

Tein, Michael R. "The Devaluation of Nonwhite Community in Remedies for Subsidized Housing Discrimination." *University of Pennsylvania Law Review* 140.4 (1992): 1463–1503.

Thompson, Heather Ann. "Rethinking the Politics of White Flight in the Postwar City: Detroit, 1945–1980." *Journal of Urban History* 25 (1999): 163–198.

Thompson, J. Philip. "Review of *Place Matters*." *Urban Affairs Review* 37.3 (2002): 446–448.

Tighe, J. Rosie. "Public Opinion and Affordable Housing: A Review of the Literature." *Journal of Planning Literature* 25.1 (2010): 3–17.

Tracy, James. *Dispatches against Displacement: Field Notes from San Francisco's Housing Wars*. Oakland, CA: AK, 2014.

Treuhaft, Sarah. *Community Mapping for Health Equity Advocacy*. New York: Opportunity Agenda, 2009. http://opportunityagenda.org/files/field_file/ Community%20Mapping%20for%20Health%20Equity%20-%20Treuhaft.pdf.

Trudeau, Daniel. "The Persistence of Segregation in Buffalo, New York: *Comer vs. Cisneros* and Geographies of Relocation Decisions among Low-Income Black Households." *Urban Geography* 27.1 (2006): 20–44.

Turner, Margery A., Stephen Ross, George C. Galster, and John Yinger. *Discrimination in Metropolitan Housing Markets: National Results from Phase 1 of the Housing Discrimination Study (HDS)*. Washington, DC: Urban Institute, 2002.

Tyner, James. *The Geography of Malcolm X: Black Radicalism and the Remaking of American Space*. New York: Routledge, 2006.

Umoja, Akinyele O. "1964: The Beginning of the End of Nonviolence in the Mississippi Freedom Movement." *Radical History Review* 85 (2003): 201–226.

U.S. Commission on Civil Rights. *Housing: 1961 Commission on Civil Rights Report*. Washington, DC: Government Printing Office, 1961.

U.S. Department of Housing and Urban Development. "Rootedness." May 17, 2016. http://portal.hud.gov/hudportal/HUD?src=%2Fstates%2Foregon%2Fstories%2F2016-05-17.

Vale, Lawrence. *From the Puritans to the Projects: Public Housing and Public Neighbors*. Cambridge, MA: Harvard University Press, 2009.

Van Berkel, Jessie. "Minneapolis and St. Paul Settle Federal Housing Complaints, Agree to Further Review." *Minneapolis Star-Tribune*, May 17, 2016. http://www.startribune.com/minneapolis-and-st-paul-settle-federal-housing-complaints-agree-to-further-review/379885031/.

Van DeBurg, William L. *New Day in Babylon: The Black Power Movement and American Culture, 1965–1975*. Chicago: University of Chicago Press, 1992.

Van Zandt, Shannon, and Pratik C. Mhatre. "Growing Pains: Perpetuating Inequality through the Production of Low-Income Housing in the Dallas / Fort Worth Metroplex." *Urban Geography* 30.5 (2009): 490–513.

Venkatesh, Sudhir. *Off the Books: The Underground Economy of the Urban Poor*. Cambridge, MA: Harvard University Press, 2006.

——. *American Project: The Rise and Fall of a Modern Ghetto*. Cambridge, MA: Harvard University Press, 2000.

Vernarelli, Michael J. "Where Should HUD Locate Assisted Housing? The Evolution of Fair Housing Policy." In Goering, *Housing Desegregation and Federal Policy*, 214–234.

Von Hoffman, Alexander. "Like Fleas on a Tiger? A Brief History of the Open Housing Movement." Harvard University, Joint Center for Housing Studies, 1998.

Walker, Chris. *Affordable Housing for Families and Neighborhoods: The Value of Low-Income Housing Tax Credits in New York City*. Columbia, MD, and Washington, DC: Enterprise Community Partners Inc. and Local Initiatives Support Corporation, 2010.

Walker, Renee E., Christopher R. Keane, and Jessica G. Burke. "Disparities and Access to Healthy Food in the United States: A Review of the Food Deserts Literature." *Health and Place* 16.5 (2010): 876–884.

Wardrip, Keith, Laura Williams, and Suzanne Hague. *The Role of Affordable Housing in Creating Jobs and Stimulating Local Economic Development: A Review of the Literature*. Washington, DC: Center for Housing Policy, 2011.

Weich, Scott, and Glyn Lewis. "Poverty, Unemployment, and Common Mental Disorders: Population Based Cohort Study." *British Medical Journal* 317 (1998): 115–119.

Weisbrot, Robert, and G. Calvin Mackenzie. *The Liberal Hour: Washington and the Politics of Change in the 1960s*. New York: Penguin, 2009.

Wiese, Andrew. *Places of Their Own: African American Suburbanization in the Twentieth Century*. Chicago: University of Chicago Press, 2004.

Wilen, William P., and Wendy Stasell. "*Gautreaux* and Chicago's Public Housing Crisis: The Conflict between Achieving Integration and Providing Decent Housing for Very Low-Income African Americans." *Clearinghouse Review* 34.3–4 (2000): 117–145.

Wilkes, Rima, and John Iceland. "Hypersegregation in the Twenty-First Century." *Demography* 41.1 (2004): 23–36.

Williams, Rhonda. *The Politics of Public Housing: Black Women's Struggles against Urban Inequality.* New York: Oxford University Press, 2004.

Williams, Stockton, and Maya Brennan. "A New Landscape of Housing Access and Opportunity." *Urban Land: The Magazine of the Urban Land Institute,* November 30, 2015. http://urbanland.uli.org/economy-markets-trends/new-landscape-housing-access-opportunity/.

Wilson, James Q. *Negro Politics: The Search for Leadership.* Glencoe, IL: Free Press, 1960.

Wilson, William J., and Richard Taub. *There Goes the Neighborhood: Racial, Ethnic and Class Tensions in Four Chicago Neighborhoods and Their Meaning for America.* Knopf Doubleday, 2011.

Wish, Naomi Bailin, and Stephen Eisdorfer. "The Impact of Mount Laurel Initiatives: An Analysis of the Characteristics of Applicants and Occupants." *Seton Hall Law Review* 27 (1997): 1268–1337.

Wood, David L., R. Burciaga Valdez, Toshi Hayashi, and Albert Shen. "Health of Homeless Children and Housed, Poor Children." *Pediatrics* 86.6 (1990): 858–866.

Wright, Patricia. "Community Resistance to CHA Transformation: The History, Evolution, Struggles, and Accomplishments of the Coalition to Protect Public Housing." In *Where Are Poor People to Live? Transforming Public Housing Communities,* edited by Larry Bennett, Janet Smith, and Patricia Wright, 125–167. Armonk, NY: M. E. Sharpe, 2006.

Wyly, Elvin, and Daniel Hammel. "Islands of Decay in Seas of Renewal: Housing Policy and the Resurgence of Gentrification." *Housing Policy Debate* 10.4 (1999): 711–771.

Yentel, Diane, Andrew Aurand, Dan Emmanuel, Ellen Errico, Gar Meng Leong, and Kate Rodrigues. *Out of Reach, 2016.* Washington, DC: National Low Income Housing Coalition, 2016. http://nlihc.org/sites/default/files/oor/OOR_2016.pdf.

Young, Iris Marion. *Inclusion and Democracy.* New York: Oxford University Press, 2002.

——. *Justice and the Politics of Difference.* Princeton, NJ: Princeton University Press, 1990.

Youngblood, Mtamanik, and Harold Barnette. "Community Development Corporations at a Crossroads." *Shelterforce,* July 17, 2013. http://www.shelterforce.org/article/3333/community_development_corporations_at_a_crossroads/.

Zielenbach, Sean, Richard Voith, and Michael Mariano. "Estimating the Local Economic Impacts of HOPE VI." *Housing Policy Debate* 20.3 (2010): 485–522.

Zima, Bonnie T., K. B. Wells, and H. E. Freeman. "Emotional Behavioral Problems and Severe Academic Delays among Sheltered Homeless Children in Los Angeles County." *American Journal of Public Health* 84.2 (1994): 260–264.

Index

9 781501 748479